DATE DUE

JAN 2 9 2011		
1/27/14		
FEB 1 3 2014		
1/30/15		
FEB 1 6 2016		
1/23/17		
1/27/17		
2/6/18		

MAESTRO REPRINTS

WILLIAM HAZLITT

CHARACTERS OF SHAKESPEARE'S PLAYS

ISBN: 1453737472

WILLIAM HAZLITT

Characters of Shakespeare's Plays ISBN: 1453737472

Characters of Shakespeare's Plays

By

William Hazlitt

Contents

INTRODUCTION

William Hazlitt (1778-1830) came of an Irish Protestant stock, and of a branch of it transplanted in the reign of George I from the county of Antrim to Tipperary. His father migrated, at nineteen, to the University of Glasgow (where he was contemporary with Adam Smith), graduated in 1761 or thereabouts, embraced the principles of the Unitarians, joined their ministry, and crossed over to England; being successively pastor at Wisbech in Cambridgeshire, at Marshfield in Gloucestershire, and at Maidstone. At Wisbech he married Grace Loftus, the daughter of a neighbouring farmer. Of the many children granted to them but three survived infancy. William, the youngest of these, was born in Mitre Lane, Maidstone, on April 10, 1778. From Maidstone the family moved in 1780 to Bandon, Co. Cork; and from Bandon in 1783 to America, where Mr. Hazlitt preached before the new Assembly of the States-General of New Jersey, lectured at Philadelphia on the Evidences of Christianity, founded the First Unitarian Church at Boston, and declined a proffered diploma of D.D. In 1786-7 he returned to England and took up his abode at Wem, in Shropshire. His elder son, John, was now old enough to choose a vocation, and chose that of a miniature-painter. The second child, Peggy, had begun to paint also, amateurishly in oils. William, aged eight—a child out of whose recollection all memories of Bandon and of America (save the taste of barberries) soon faded— took his education at home and at a local school. His father designed him for the Unitarian ministry.

The above dry recital contains a number of facts not to be overlooked as predisposing causes in young Hazlitt's later career; as that he was Irish by blood, intellectual by geniture, born into dissent, and a minority of dissent, taught at home to value the things of the mind, in early childhood a nomad, in later childhood 'privately educated'—a process which (whatever its merits) is apt to develop the freak as against the citizen, the eccentric and lop-sided as against what is proportionate and disciplined. Young Hazlitt's cleverness and his passion for individual liberty were alike precocious. In 1791, at the age of thirteen, he composed and published in The Shrewsbury Chronicle a letter of protest against the calumniators of Dr. Priestley: a performance which, for the gravity of its thought as for the balance of its expression, would do credit to ninety-nine grown men in a hundred. At fifteen, his father designing that he should enter the ministry, he proceeded to the Unitarian College, Hackney; where his master, a Mr. Corrie, found him 'rather backward in many of the ordinary points of learning and, in general, of a dry, intractable understanding', the truth being that the lad had set his heart against the ministry, aspiring rather to be a philosopher—in particular a political philosopher. At fourteen he had conceived ('in consequence of a dispute one day, after coming out of Meeting, between my father and an old lady of the congregation, respecting the repeal of the Corporation and Test Acts and the limits of religious toleration') the germ of his Project for a New Theory of Civil and Criminal Legislation, published in his maturer years (1828), but drafted and scribbled upon constantly in these days, to the neglect of his theological studies. His father, hearing of the project, forbade him to pursue it.

Thus four or five years at the Unitarian College were wasted, or, at least, had been spent without apparent profit; and in 1798 young Hazlitt, aged close upon twenty, unsettled in his plans as in his prospects, was at home again and (as the saying is) at a loose end; when of a sudden his life found its spiritual apocalypse. It came with the descent of Samuel Taylor Coleridge upon Shrewsbury, to take over the charge of a Unitarian Congregation there.

He did not come till late on the Saturday afternoon before he was to preach; and Mr. Rowe [the abdicating minister], who himself went down to the coach in a state of anxiety and expectation to look for the arrival of his successor, could find no one at all answering the description, but a round-faced man, in a short black coat (like a shooting-jacket) which hardly seemed to have been made for him, but who seemed to be talking at a great rate to his fellow-passengers. Mr. Rowe had scarce returned to give an account of his disappointment when the round-faced man in black entered, and dissipated all doubts on the subject by beginning to talk. He did not cease while he stayed; nor has he since.

Of his meeting with Coleridge, and of the soul's awakening that followed, Hazlitt has left an account (My First Acquaintance with Poets) that will fascinate so long as English prose is read. 'Somehow that period [the time just after the French Revolution] was not a time when NOTHING WAS GIVEN FOR NOTHING. The mind opened, and a softness might be perceived coming over the heart of individuals beneath "the scales that fence" our self-interest.' As Wordsworth wrote:

Bliss was it in that dawn to be alive,   But to be young was very Heaven.

It was in January, 1798, that I was one morning before daylight, to walk ten miles in the mud, to hear this celebrated person preach. Never, the longest day I have to live, shall I have such another walk as this cold, raw, comfortless one in the winter of 1798. Il-y- a des impressions que ni le tems ni les circonstances peuvent effacer. Dusse-je vivre des siecles entiers, le doux tems de ma jeunesse ne peut renaitre pour moi, ni s'effacer jamais dans ma memoire. When I got there the organ was playing the 100th Psalm, and when it was done Mr. Coleridge rose and gave out his text, 'And he went up into the mountain to pray, HIMSELF, ALONE.' As he gave out this text, his voice 'rose like a stream of distilled perfumes', and when he came to the two last words, which he pronounced loud, deep, and distinct, it seemed to me, who was then young, as if the sounds had echoed from the bottom of the human heart, and as if that prayer might have floated in solemn silence through the universe ... The preacher then launched into his subject, like an eagle dallying with the wind.

Coleridge visited Wem, walked and talked with young Hazlitt, and wound up by inviting the disciple to visit him at Nether Stowey in the Quantocks. Hazlitt went, made acquaintance with William and Dorothy Wordsworth, and was drawn more deeply under the spell. In later years as the younger man grew cantankerous and the elder declined, through opium, into a 'battered seraph', there was an estrangement. But Hazlitt never forgot his obligation.

My soul has indeed remained in its original bondage, dark, obscure, with longings infinite and unsatisfed; my heart, shut up in the prison-house of this rude clay, has never found, nor will it ever find, a heart to speak to; but that my understanding also did not remain dumb and brutish, or at length found a language that expresses itself, I owe to Coleridge.

Coleridge, sympathizing with the young man's taste for philosophy and abetting it, encouraged him to work. upon a treatise which saw the light in 1805, An Essay on the Principles of Human Action: Being an Argu-ment in favour of the Natural Disinterestedness of the Human Mind. Meantime, however,—the ministry having been renounced—the question of a vocation became more and more urgent, and after long indecision Hazlitt packed his portmanteau for London, resolved to learn painting under his brother John, who had begun to do prosperously. John taught him some rudiments, and packed him off to Paris, where he studied for some four months in the Louvre and learned to idolize Bonaparte. This sojourn in Paris—writes his grandson and biographer—'was one long beau jour to him'. His allusions to it are constant. He returned to England in 1803, with formed tastes and predilections, very few of which he afterwards modified, much less forsook.

We next find him making a tour as a portrait-painter through the north of England, where (as was to be expected) he attempted a portrait of Wordsworth, among others. 'At his desire', says Wordsworth, 'I sat to him, but as he did not satisfy himself or my friends, the unfinished work was destroyed.' He was more successful with Charles Lamb, whom he painted (for a whim) in the dress of a Venetian Senator. As a friend of Coleridge and Wordsworth he had inevitably made acquaintance with the Lambs. He first met Lamb at one of the Godwins' strange evening parties and the two became intimate friends and fellow theatre-goers.

Hazlitt's touchy and difficult temper suspended this inintimacy in later years, though to the last Lamb regarded him as 'one of the finest and wisest spirits breathing'; but for a while it was unclouded. At the Lambs', moreover, Hazlitt made acquaintance with a Dr. Stoddart, owner of some property at Winterslow near Salisbury, and his sister Sarah, a lady wearing past her first youth but yet addicted to keeping a number of beaux to her string. Hazlitt, attracted to her from the first,—he made a gloomy lover and his subsequent performances in that part were unedifying—for some years played walking gentleman behind the leading suitors with whom Miss Stoddart from time to time diversified her comedy. But Mary Lamb was on his side; the rivals on one excuse or another went their ways or were dismissed; and on May 1, 1808, the marriage took place at St. Andrew's Church, Holborn. Lamb attended, foreboding little happiness to the couple from his knowledge of their temperaments. Seven years after (August 9, 1815), he wrote to Southey. 'I was at Hazlitt's marriage, and had like to have been turned out several times during the ceremony. Anything awful makes me laugh.' The marriage was not a happy one.

Portrait-painting had been abandoned long before this. The Essay on the Principles of Human Action (1805) had fallen, as the saying is, stillborn from the press: Free Thoughts on Public Affairs (1806) had earned for the author many enemies but few readers: and a treatise attacking Malthus's theory of population (1807) had allured the public as little. A piece of hack-work, The Eloquence of the British Senate, also belongs to 1807: A New and Improved Grammar of the English Tongue for the use of Schools to 1810. The nutriment to be derived from these works, again, was not of the sort that replenishes the family table, and in 1812 Hazlitt left Winterslow (where he had been quarrelling with his brother-in-law), settled in London in 19 York Street, Westminster—once the home of John Milton- -and applied himself strenuously to lecturing and journalism. His lectures, on the English Philosophers, were delivered at the Russell Institution: his most notable journalistic work, on politics and the drama, was done for The Morning Chronicle, then edited by Mr. Perry. From an obituary notice of Hazlitt contributed many years later (October 1830) to an old magazine I cull the following:

He obtained an introduction, about 1809 or 1810, to the late Mr. Perry, of The Morning Chronicle, by whom he was engaged to report Parliamentary debates, write original articles, etc. He also furnished a number of theatrical articles on the acting of Kean. As a political writer he was apt to be too violent; though in general he was not a man of violent temper. He was also apt to conceive strong and rooted prejudices against individuals on very slight grounds. But he was a good-hearted man ... Private circumstances, it is said, contributed to sour his temper and to produce a peculiar excitement which too frequently held its sway over him. Mr. Hazlitt and Mr. Perry did not agree. Upon one occasion, to the great annoyance of some of his colleagues, he preferred his wine with a few friends to taking his share in reporting an important discussion in the House of Commons. Added to this, he either did not understand the art of reporting, or would not take the trouble to master it.... His original articles required to be carefully looked after, to weed them of strong expressions.

Hazlitt's reputation grew, notwithstanding. In 1814 Jeffrey enlisted him to write for The Edinburgh Review, and in 1815 he began to contribute to Leigh Hunt's paper The Examiner. In February 1816 he reviewed Schlegel's 'Lectures on Dramatic Literature' for the Edinburgh, and this would seem to have started him on his Characters of Shakespeare's Plays. Throughout 1816 he wrote at it sedulously.

The MS., when completed, was accepted by Mr. C. H. Reynell, of 21, Piccadilly, the head of a printing establishment of old and high standing; and it was agreed that 100 pounds should be paid to the author for the entire copyright ... The volume was published by Mr. Hunter of St. Paul's Churchyard; and the author was gratified by the prompt insertion of a complimentary notice in the Edinburgh Review. The whole edition went off in six weeks; and yet it was a half-guinea book.' [Footnote: Memoirs of William Hazlitt, by W. Carew Hazlitt, 1887. Vol. i, p. 228.]

The reader, who comes to it through this Introduction, will note two points to qualify his appreciation of the book as a specimen of Hazlitt's critical writing, and a third that helps to account for its fortune in 1817. It was the work of a man in his thirty-eighth year, and to that extent has maturity. But it was also his first serious essay, after many false starts, in an art and in a style which, later on, he brilliantly mastered. The subject is most pleasantly handled, and with an infectious enthusiasm: the reader feels all the while that his sympathy with Shakespeare is being stimulated and his understanding promoted: but it scarcely yields either the light or the music which Hazlitt communicates in his later and more famous essays.

For the third point, Hazlitt had made enemies nor had ever been cautious of making them: and these enemies were now the 'upper dog'. Indeed, they always had been: but the fall of Napoleon, which almost broke his heart, had set them in full cry, and they were not clement in their triumph. It is not easy, even on the evidence before us, to realize that a number of the finest spirits in this country, nursed in the hopes of the French Revolution, kept their admiration of Napoleon, the hammer of old bad monarchies, down to the end and beyond it: that Napier, for example, historian of the war in the Peninsula and as gallant a soldier as ever fought under Wellington, when—late in life, as he lay on his sofa tortured by an old wound— news was brought him of Napoleon's death, burst into a storm of weeping that would not be controlled. On Hazlitt, bound up heart and soul in what he regarded as the cause of French and European liberty and enlightenment, Waterloo, the fall of the Emperor, the restoration of the Bourbons, fell as blows almost stupefying, and his indignant temper charged Heaven with them as wrongs not only public but personal to himself.

In the writing of the Characters he had found a partial drug for despair. But his enemies, as soon as might be, took hold of the anodyne. Like the Bourbons, they had learnt nothing and forgotten nothing.

The Quarterly Review moved—for a quarterly—with something like agility. A second edition of the book had been prepared, and was selling briskly, when this Review launched one of its diatribes against the work and its author.

Taylor and Hessey [the booksellers] told him subsequently that they had sold nearly two editions in about three months, but after the Quarterly review of them came out they never sold another copy. 'My book,' he said, 'sold well—the first edition had gone off in six weeks—till that review came out. I had just prepared a second edition—such was called for—but then the Quarterly told the public that I was a fool and a dunce, and more, that I was an evil disposed person: and the public, supposing Gifford to know best, confessed that it had been a great ass to be pleased where it ought not to be, and the sale completely stopped.

The review, when examined, is seen to be a smart essay in detraction with its arguments ad invidiam very deftly inserted. But as a piece of criticism it misses even such points as might fairly have been made against the book; as, for example, that it harps too monotonously upon the tense string of enthusiasm. Hazlitt could not have applied to this work the motto—'For I am nothing if not critical'—which he chose for his View of the English Stage in 1818; the Characters being anything but 'critical' in the sense there connoted. Jeffrey noted this in the forefront of a sympathetic article in the Edinburgh.

It is, in truth, rather an encomium on Shakespeare than a commentary or a critique on him—and it is written more to show extraordinary love than extraordinary knowledge of his productions ... The author is not merely an admirer of our great dramatist, but an Idolater of him; and openly professes his idolatry. We have ourselves too great a leaning to the same superstition to blame him very much for his error: and though we think, of course, that our own admiration is, on the whole, more discriminating and judicious, there are not many points on which, especially after reading his eloquent exposition of them, we should be much inclined to disagree with him.

The book, as we have already intimated, is written less to tell the reader what Mr. H. KNOWS about Shakespeare or his writings than what he FEELS about them—and WHY he feels so—and thinks that all who profess to love poetry should feel so likewise.... He seems pretty generally, indeed, in a state of happy intoxication—and has borrowed from his great original, not indeed the force or brilliancy of his fancy, but something of its playfulness, and a large share of his apparent joyousness and self-indulgence in its exercise. It is evidently a great pleasure to him to be fully possessed with the beauties of his author, and to follow the impulse of his unrestrained eagerness to impress them upon his readers.

Upon this, Hazlitt, no doubt, would have commented, 'Well, and why not? I choose to understand drama through my FEELINGS.' To surrender to great art was, for him, and defnitely, a part of the critic's function—' A genuine criticism should, as I take it, repeat the colours, the light and shade, the soul and body of a work.' This contention, for which Hazlitt fought all his life and fought brilliantly, is familiar to us by this time as the gage flung to didactic criticism by the 'impressionist', and in our day, in the generation just closed or closing, with a Walter Pater or a

Jules Lemaitre for challenger, the betting has run on the impressionist. But in 1817 Hazlitt had all the odds against him when he stood up and accused the great Dr. Johnson of having made criticism 'a kind of Procrustes' bed of genius, where he might cut down imagination to matter-of-fact, regulate the passions according to reason, and translate the whole into logical diagrams and rhetorical declamation'.

Thus he says of Shakespeare's characters, in contradiction to what Pope had observed, and to what every one else feels, that each character is a species, instead of being an individual. He in fact found the general species or DIDACTIC form in Shakespeare's characters, which was all he sought or cared for; he did not find the individual traits, or the DRAMATIC distinctions which Shakespeare has engrafted on this general nature, because he felt no interest in them.

Nothing is easier to prove than that in this world nobody ever invented anything. So it may be proved that, Johnson having written 'Great thoughts are always general', Blake had countered him by affirming (long before Hazlitt) that 'To generalize is to be an idiot. To particularize is the great distinction of merit': even as it may be demonstrable that Charles Lamb, in his charming personal chat about the Elizabethan dramatists and his predilections among them, was already putting into practice what he did not trouble to theorize. But when it comes to setting out the theory, grasping the worth of the principle, stating it and fighting for it, I think Hazlitt may fairly claim first share in the credit.

He did not, when he wrote the following pages, know very much, even about his subject. As his biographer says:

My grandfather came to town with very little book-knowledge ... He had a fair stock of ideas ... But of the volumes which form the furniture of a gentleman's library he was egregiously ignorant ... Mr. Hazlitt's resources were emphatically internal; from his own mind he drew sufficient for himself.

Now while it may be argued with plausibility, and even with truth, that the first qualification of a critic—at any rate of a critic of poetry—is, as Jeffrey puts the antithesis, to FEEL rather than to KNOW; while to be delicately sensitive and sympathetic counts more than to be well-informed; nevertheless learning remains respectable. He who can assimilate it without pedantry (which is another word for intellectual indigestion) actually improves and refines his feelings while enlarging their scope and at the same time enlarging his resources of comparison and illustration. Hazlitt, who had something like a genius for felicitous, apposite quotation, and steadily bettered it as he grew older, would certainly have said 'Yes' to this. At all events learning impresses; it carries weight: and therefore it has always seemed to me that he showed small tact, if some modesty, by heaping whole pages of Schlegel into his own preface.

For Schlegel [Footnote: Whose work, by the way, cries aloud for a new and better English translation.] was not only a learned critic but a great one: and this mass of him—cast with seeming carelessness, just here, into the scales—does give the reader, as with a jerk, the sensation that Hazlitt has, of his rashness, invited that which suddenly throws him up in the air to kick the beam: that he has provoked a comparison which exhibits his own performance as clever but flimsy.

Nor is this impression removed by his admirer the late Mr. Ireland, who claims for the Characters that, 'although it professes to be dramatic criticism, it is in reality a discourse on the philosophy of life and human nature, more suggestive than many approved treatises expressly devoted to that subject'. Well, for the second half of this pronouncement—constat. 'You see, my friend,' writes Goldsmith's Citizen of the World ,'there is nothing so ridiculous that it has not at some time been said by some philosopher.' But for the first part, while a priori Mr. Ireland ought to be right—since Hazlitt, as we have seen, came to literary criticism by the road of philosophical writing—I confess to finding very little philosophy in this book.

Over and above the gusto of the writing, which is infectious enough, and the music of certain passages in which we foretaste the masterly prose of Hazlitt's later Essays, I find in the book three merits which, as I study it, more and more efface that first impression of flimsiness.

(1) To begin with, Hazlitt had hold of the right end of the stick. He really understood that Shakespeare was a dramatic craftsman, studied him as such, worshipped him for his incomparable skill in doing what he tried, all his life and all the time, to do. In these days much merit must be allowed to a Shakespearian critic who takes his author steadily as a dramatist and not as a philosopher, or a propagandist, or a lawyer's clerk, or a disappointed lover, or for his acquaintance with botany, politics, cyphers, Christian Science, any of the thousand and one things that with their rival degrees of intrinsic importance agree in being, for Shakespeare, nihil ad rem.

(2) Secondly, Hazlitt always treats Shakespeare as, in my opinion, he deserves to be treated; that is, absolutely and as 'patrone and not compare' among the Elizabethans. I harbour an ungracious doubt that he may have done so in 1816-17 for the simple and sufficient reason that he had less than a bowing acquaintance with the other Elizabethan dramatists. But he made their acquaintance in due course, and discussed them, yet never (so far as I recall) committed the error of ranking them alongside Shakespeare. With all love for the memory of Lamb, and with all respect for the memory of Swinburne, I hold that these two in their generations, both soaked in enjoyment of the Elizabethan style—an enjoyment derivative from Shakespeare—did some disservice to criticism by classing them with him in the light they borrow; whenas truly he differs from them in kind and beyond any reach of degrees. One can no more estimate Shakespeare's genius in comparison with this, that, or the other man's of the sixteenth century, than Milton's in comparison with any one's of the seventeenth. Some few men are absolute and can only be judged absolutely.

(3) For the third merit—if the Characters be considered historically—what seems flimsy in them is often a promise of what has since been substantiated; what seems light and almost juvenile in the composition of this man, aged thirty-nine, gives the scent on which nowadays the main pack of students is pursuing. No one not a fool can read Johnson's notes on Shakespeare without respect or fail to turn to them again with an increased trust in his common-sense, as no one not a fool can read Hazlitt without an equal sense that he has the root of the matter, or of the spirit which is the matter.

PREFACE

It is observed by Mr. Pope, that 'If ever any author deserved the name of an ORIGINAL, it was Shakespeare. Homer himself drew not his art so immediately from the fountains of nature; it proceeded through AEgyptian strainers and channels, and came to him not without some tincture of the learning, or some cast of the models, of those before him. The poetry of Shakespeare was inspiration: indeed, he is not so much an imitator, as an instrument of nature; and it is not so just to say that he speaks from her, as that she speaks through him.

His CHARACTERS are so much nature herself, that it is a sort of injury to call them by so distant a name as copies of her. Those of other poets have a constant resemblance, which shows that they received them from one another, and were but multipliers of the same image: each picture, like a mock-rainbow, is but the reflection of a reflection. But every single character in Shakespeare, is as much an individual, as those in life itself; it is as impossible to find any two alike; and such, as from their relation or affinity in any respect appear most to be twins, will, upon comparison, be found remarkably distinct. To this life and variety of character, we must add the wonderful preservation of it; which is such throughout his plays, that had all the speeches been printed without the very names of the persons, I believe one might have applied them with certainty to every speaker.'

The object of the volume here offered to the public, is to illustrate these remarks in a more particular manner by a reference to each play. A gentleman of the name of Mason, [Footnote: Hazlitt is here mistaken. The work to which he alludes, 'Remarks on some of the Characters of Shakespeare, by the Author of Observations on Modern Gardening', was by Thomas Whately, Under-Secretary of State under Lord North. Whately died in 1772, and the Essay was published posthumously in 1785 [2nd edition, 1808; 3rd edition, with a preface by Archbishop Whately, the author's nephew, 1839]. Hazlitt confused T. Whately's Observations on Modern Gardening with George Mason's Essay on Design in Gardening, and the one error led to the other.] the author of a Treatise on Ornamental Gardening (not Mason the poet), began a work of a similar kind about forty years ago, but he only lived to finish a parallel between the characters of Macbeth and Richard III which is an exceedingly ingenious piece of analytical criticism. Richardson's Essays include but a few of Shakespeare's principal characters. The only work which seemed to supersede the necessity of an attempt like the present was Schlegel's very admirable Lectures on the Drama, which give by far the best account of the plays of Shakespeare that has hitherto appeared. The only circumstances in which it was thought not impossible to improve on the manner in which the German critic has executed this part of his design, were in avoiding an appearance of mysticism in his style, not very attractive to the English reader, and in bringing illustrations from particular passages of the plays themselves, of which Schlegel's work, from the extensiveness of his plan, did not admit. We will at the same time confess, that some little jealousy of the character of the national understanding was not without its share in producing the following undertaking, for 'we were piqued' that it should be reserved for a foreign critic to give 'reasons for the faith which we English have in Shakespeare'. Certainly, no writer among ourselves has shown either the same enthusiastic admiration of his genius, or the same philosophical acuteness in pointing out his characteristic excellences. As we have pretty well exhausted all we had to say upon this subject in the body of the work, we shall here transcribe Schlegel's general account of Shakespeare, which is in the following words:

'Never, perhaps, was there so comprehensive a talent for the delineation of character as Shakespeare's. It not only grasps the diversities of rank, sex, and age, down to the dawnings of infancy; not only do the king and the beggar, the hero and the pickpocket, the sage and the idiot, speak and act with equal truth; not only does he transport himself to distant ages and foreign nations, and pourtray in the most accurate manner, with only a few apparent violations of costume, the spirit of the ancient Romans, of the French in their wars with the English, of the English themselves during a great part of their history, of the Southern Europeans (in the serious part of many comedies) the cultivated society of that time, and the former rude and barbarous state of the North; his human characters have not only such depth and precision that they cannot be arranged under classes, and are inexhaustible, even in conception:—no—this Prometheus not merely forms men, he opens the gates of the magical world of spirits; calls up the midnight ghost; exhibits before us his witches amidst their unhallowed mysteries; peoples the air with sportive fairies and sylphs:—and these beings, existing only in imagination, possess such truth and consistency, that even when deformed monsters like Caliban, he extorts the conviction, that if there should be such beings, they would so conduct themselves. In a word, as he carries with him the most fruitful and daring fancy into the kingdom of nature,—on the other hand, he carries nature into the regions of fancy, lying beyond the confines of reality. We are lost in astonishment at seeing the extraordinary, the wonderful, and the unheard of, in such intimate nearness.

'If Shakespeare deserves our admiration for his characters, he is equally deserving of it for his exhibition of passion, taking this word in its widest signification, as including every mental condition, every tone from indifference or familiar mirth to the wildest rage and despair. He gives us the history of minds; he lays open to us, in a single word, a whole series of preceding conditions. His passions do not at first stand displayed to us in all their height, as is the case with so many tragic poets, who, in the language of Lessing, are thorough masters of the legal style of love. He paints, in a most inimitable manner, the gradual progress from the first origin. "He gives", as Lessing says, "a living picture of all the most minute and secret artifices by which a feeling steals into our souls; of all the imperceptible advantages which it there gains; of all the stratagems by which every other passion is made subservient to it, till it becomes the sole tyrant of our desires and our aversions." Of all poets, perhaps, he alone has pourtrayed the mental diseases,—melancholy, delirium, lunacy,— with such inexpressible, and, in every respect, definite truth, that the physician may enrich his observations from them in the same manner as from real cases.

'And yet Johnson has objected to Shakespeare, that his pathos is not always natural and free from affectation. There are, it is true, passages, though, comparatively speaking, very few, where his poetry exceeds the bounds of true dialogue, where a too soaring imagination, a too luxuriant wit, rendered the complete dramatic forgetfulness of himself impossible. With this exception, the censure originates only in a fanciless way of thinking, to which everything appears unnatural that does not suit its own tame insipidity. Hence, an idea has been formed of simple and natural pathos, which consists in exclamations destitute of imagery, and nowise elevated above every-day life. But energetical passions electrify the whole of the mental powers, and will, consequently, in highly favoured natures, express themselves in an ingenious and figurative manner. It has been often remarked, that indignation gives wit; and, as despair occasionally breaks out into laughter, it may sometimes also give vent to itself in antithetical comparisons.

10

'Besides, the rights of the poetical form have not been duly weighed. Shakespeare, who was always sure of his object, to move in a sufficiently powerful manner when he wished to do so, has occasionally, by indulging in a freer play, purposely moderated the impressions when too painful, and immediately introduced a musical alleviation of our sympathy. He had not those rude ideas of his art which many moderns seem to have, as if the poet, like the clown in the proverb, must strike twice on the same place. An ancient rhetorician delivered a caution against dwelling too long on the excitation of pity; for nothing, he said, dries so soon as tears; and Shakespeare acted conformably to this ingenious maxim, without knowing it.

"The objection, that Shakespeare wounds our feelings by the open display of the most disgusting moral odiousness, harrows up the mind unmercifully, and tortures even our senses by the exhibition of the most insupportable and hateful spectacles, is one of much greater importance. He has never, in fact, varnished over wild and blood- thirsty passions with a pleasing exterior,— never clothed crime and want of principle with a false show of greatness of soul; and in that respect he is every way deserving of praise. Twice he has pourtrayed downright villains; and the masterly way in which he has contrived to elude impressions of too painful a nature, may be seen in Iago and Richard the Third. The constant reference to a petty and puny race must cripple the boldness of the poet. Fortunately for his art, Shakespeare lived in an age extremely susceptible of noble and tender impressions, but which had still enough of the firmness inherited from a vigorous olden time not to shrink back with dismay from every strong and violent picture. We have lived to see tragedies of which the catastrophe consists in the swoon of an enamoured princess. If Shakespeare falls occasionally into the opposite extreme, it is a noble error, originating in the fulness of a gigantic strength: and yet this tragical Titan, who storms the heavens, and threatens to tear the world from off its hinges; who, more terrible than AEschylus, makes our hair stand on end, and congeals our blood with horror, possessed, at the same time, the insinuating loveliness of the sweetest poetry. He plays with love like a child; and his songs are breathed out like melting sighs. He unites in his genius the utmost elevation and the utmost depth; and the most foreign, and even apparently irreconcilable properties subsist in him peaceably together. The world of spirits and nature have laid all their treasures at his feet. In strength a demi-god, in profundity of view a prophet, in all-seeing wisdom a protecting spirit of a higher order, he lowers himself to mortals, as if unconscious of his superiority: and is as open and unassuming as a child.

'Shakespeare's comic talent is equally wonderful with that which he has shown in the pathetic and tragic: it stands on an equal elevation, and possesses equal extent and profundity. All that I before wished was, not to admit that the former preponderated. He is highly inventive in comic situations and motives. It will be hardly possible to show whence he has taken any of them; whereas, in the serious part of his drama, he has generally laid hold of something already known. His comic characters are equally true, various, and profound, with his serious. So little is he disposed to caricature, that we may rather say many of his traits are almost too nice and delicate for the stage, that they can only be properly seized by a great actor, and fully understood by a very acute audience. Not only has he delineated many kinds of folly; he has also contrived to exhibit mere stupidity in a most diverting and entertaining manner.' Vol. ii, p. 145.

We have the rather availed ourselves of this testimony of a foreign critic in behalf of Shakespeare, because our own countryman, Dr. Johnson, has not been so favourable to him. It may be said of Shakespeare, that 'those who are not for him are against him': for indifference is here the height of injustice. We may sometimes, in order 'to do a great right, do a little wrong'. An over-strained enthusiasm is more pardonable with respect to Shakespeare than the want of it; for our admiration cannot easily surpass his genius. We have a high respect for Dr. Johnson's character and understanding, mixed with something like personal attachment: but he was neither a poet nor a judge of poetry. He might in one sense be a judge of poetry as it falls within the limits and rules of prose, but not as it is poetry. Least of all was he qualified to be a judge of Shakespeare, who 'alone is high fantastical'. Let those who have a prejudice against Johnson read Boswell's Life of him: as those whom he has prejudiced against Shakespeare should read his Irene. We do not say that a man to be a critic must necessarily be a poet: but to be a good critic, he ought not to be a bad poet. Such poetry as a man deliberately writes, such, and such only will he like. Dr. Johnson's Preface to his edition of Shakespeare looks like a laborious attempt to bury the characteristic merits of his author under a load of cumbrous phraseology, and to weigh his excellences and defects in equal scales, stuffed full of 'swelling figures and sonorous epithets'. Nor could it well be otherwise; Dr. Johnson's general powers of reasoning overlaid his critical susceptibility. All his ideas were cast in a given mould, in a set form: they were made out by rule and system, by climax, inference, and antithesis:— Shakespeare's were the reverse. Johnson's understanding dealt only in round numbers: the fractions were lost upon him. He reduced everything to the common standard of conventional propriety; and the most exquisite refinement or sublimity produced an effect on his mind, only as they could be translated into the language of measured prose. To him an excess of beauty was a fault; for it appeared to him like an excrescence; and his imagination was dazzled by the blaze of light. His writings neither shone with the beams of native genius, nor reflected them. The shifting shapes of fancy, the rainbow hues of things, made no impression on him: he seized only on the permanent and tangible. He had no idea of natural objects but 'such as he could measure with a two-fool rule, or tell upon ten fingers': he judged of human nature in the same way, by mood and figure: he saw only the definite, the positive, and the practical, the average forms of things, not their striking differences—their classes, not their degrees. He was a man of strong common sense and practical wisdom, rather than of genius or feeling. He retained the regular, habitual impressions of actual objects, but he could not follow the rapid flights of fancy, or the strong movements of passion. That is, he was to the poet what the painter of still life is to the painter of history. Common sense sympathizes with the impressions of things on ordinary minds in ordinary circumstances: genius catches the glancing combinations presented to the eye of fancy, under the influence of passion. It is the province of the didactic reasoner to take cognizance of those results of human nature which are constantly repeated and always the same, which follow one another in regular succession, which are acted upon by large classes of men, and embodied in received customs, laws, language, and institutions; and it was in arranging, comparing, and arguing on these kind of general results, that Johnson's excellence lay. But he could not quit his hold of the commonplace and mechanical, and apply the general rule to the particular exception, or show how the nature of man was modified by the workings of passion, or the infinite fluctuations of thought and accident. Hence he could judge neither of the heights nor depths of poetry. Nor is this all; for being conscious of great powers in himself, and those powers of an adverse tendency to those of his author, he would be for setting up a foreign jurisdiction over poetry, and making criticism a kind of Procrustes' bed of genius, where he might cut down imagination to matter-of-fact, regulate the passions according to reason, and translate the whole into logical diagrams and rhetorical declamation. Thus he says of Shakespeare's characters, in contradiction to what Pope had observed, and to what every one else feels, that each character is a species, instead of being an individual. He in fact found the general species or DIDACTIC form in Shakespeare's characters, which was all he sought or cared for; he did not find the individual traits, or the DRAMATIC distinctions which Shakespeare has engrafted on this general nature, because he felt no interest in them. Shakespeare's bold and happy flights of imagination were equally thrown away upon our author. He was not only without any particular fineness of organic sensibility, alive to all the 'mighty world of ear and eye', which is necessary to the painter or musician, but without that intenseness of passion, which, seeking to exaggerate whatever excites the feelings of pleasure or power in the mind, and moulding the impressions of natural objects according to the impulses of imagination, produces a genius and a taste for poetry. According to Dr. Johnson, a mountain is sublime, or a rose is beautiful; for that their name and definition imply. But he would no more be able to give the description of Dover cliff in Lear, or the description of flowers in The Winter's Tale, than to describe the objects of a sixth sense; nor do we think he would have any very profound feeling of the beauty of the passages here referred to. A stately common-place, such as Congreve's description of a ruin in The Mourning Bride, would have answered Johnson's purpose just as well, or better than the first; and an indiscriminate profusion of scents and hues would have interfered less with the ordinary routine of his imagination than Perdita's lines, which seem enamoured of their own sweetness—

Daffodils That come before the swallow dares, and take

The winds of March with beauty; violets dim,

But sweeter than the lids of Juno's eyes, Or Cytherea's breath.—

No one who does not feel the passion which these objects inspire can go along with the imagination which seeks to express that passion and the uneasy sense of delight accompanying it by something still more beautiful, and no one can feel this passionate love of nature without quick natural sensibility. To a mere literal and formal apprehension, the inimitably characteristic epithet, 'violets DIM', must seem to imply a defect, rather than a beauty; and to any one, not feeling the full force of that epithet, which suggests an image like 'the sleepy eye of love', the allusion to 'the lids of Juno's eyes' must appear extravagant and unmeaning. Shakespeare's fancy lent words and images to the most refined sensibility to nature, struggling for expression: his descriptions are identical with the things themselves, seen through the fine medium of passion: strip them of that connexion, and try them by ordinary conceptions and ordinary rules, and they are as grotesque and barbarous as you please!—By thus lowering Shakespeare's genius to the standard of common-place invention, it was easy to show that his faults were as great as his beauties; for the excellence, which consists merely in a conformity to rules, is counterbalanced by the technical violation of them. Another circumstance which led to Dr. Johnson's indiscriminate praise or censure of Shakespeare, is the very structure of his style. Johnson wrote a kind of rhyming prose, in which he was as much compelled to finish the different clauses of his sentences, and to balance one period against another, as the writer of heroic verse is to keep to lines of ten syllables with similar terminations. He no sooner acknowledges the merits of his author in one line than the periodical revolution in his style carries the weight of his opinion completely over to the side of objection, thus keeping up a perpetual alternation of perfections and absurdities.

We do not otherwise know how to account for such assertions as the following: 'In his tragic scenes, there is always something wanting, but his comedy often surpasses expectation or desire. His comedy pleases by the thoughts and the language, and his tragedy, for the greater part, by incident and action. His tragedy seems to be skill, his comedy to be instinct.' Yet after saying that 'his tragedy was skill', he affirms in the next page, 'His declamations or set speeches are commonly cold and weak, for his power was the power of nature: when he endeavoured, like other tragic writers, to catch opportunities of amplification, and instead of inquiring what the occasion demanded, to show how much his stores of knowledge could supply, he seldom escapes without the pity or resentment of his reader.' Poor Shakespeare! Between the charges here brought against him, of want of nature in the first instance, and of want of skill in the second, he could hardly escape being condemned. And again, 'But the admirers of this great poet have most reason to complain when he approaches nearest to his highest excellence, and seems fully resolved to sink them in dejection, or mollify them with tender emotions by the fall of greatness, the danger of innocence, or the crosses of love. What he does best, he soon ceases to do. He no sooner begins to move than he counteracts himself; and terror and pity, as they are rising in the mind, are checked and blasted by sudden frigidity.' In all this, our critic seems more bent on maintaining the equilibrium of his style than the consistency or truth of his opinions.—If Dr. Johnson's opinion was right, the following observations on Shakespeare's plays must be greatly exaggerated, if not ridiculous. If he was wrong, what has been said may perhaps account for his being so, without detracting from his ability and judgement in other things.

It is proper to add, that the account of the MIDSUMMER NIGHT'S DREAM has appeared in another work.

April 15, 1817

14

CYMBELINE

CYMBELINE is one of the most delightful of Shakespeare's historical plays. It may be considered as a dramatic romance, in which the most striking parts of the story are thrown into the form of a dialogue, and the intermediate circumstances are explained by the different speakers, as occasion renders it necessary. The action is less concentrated in consequence; but the interest becomes more aerial and refined from the principle of perspective introduced into the subject by the imaginary changes of scene as well as by the length of time it occupies. The reading of this play is like going [on?] a journey with some uncertain object at the end of it, and in which the suspense is kept up and heightened by the long intervals between each action. Though the events are scattered over such an extent of surface, and relate to such a variety of characters, yet the links which bind the different interests of the story together are never entirely broken. The most straggling and seemingly casual incidents are contrived in such a manner as to lead at last to the most complete development of the catastrophe. The ease and conscious unconcern with which this is effected only makes the skill more wonderful. The business of the plot evidently thickens in the last act; the story moves forward with increasing rapidity at every step; its various ramifications are drawn from the most distant points to the same centre; the principal characters are brought together, and placed in very critical situations; and the fate of almost every person in the drama is made to depend on the solution of a single circumstance—the answer of Iachimo to the question of Imogen respecting the obtaining of the ring from Posthumus. Dr. Johnson is of opinion that Shakespeare was generally inattentive to the winding up of his plots. We think the contrary is true; and we might cite in proof of this remark not only the present play, but the conclusion of LEAR, of ROMEO AND JULIET, of MACBETH, of OTHELLO, even of HAMLET, and of other plays of less moment, in which the last act is crowded with decisive events brought about by natural and striking means.

The pathos in CYMBELINE is not violent or tragical, but of the most pleasing and amiable kind. A certain tender gloom o'erspreads the whole. Posthumus is the ostensible hero of the piece, but its greatest charm is the character of Imogen. Posthumus is only interesting from the interest she takes in him, and she is only interesting herself from her tenderness and constancy to her husband. It is the peculiar characteristic of Shakespeare's heroines, that they seem to exist only in their attachment to others. They are pure abstractions of the affections. We think as little of their persons as they do themselves, because we are let into the secrets of their hearts, which are more important. We are too much interested in their affairs to stop to look at their faces, except by stealth and at intervals. No one ever hit the true perfection of the female character, the sense of weakness leaning on the strength of its affections for support, so well as Shakespeare— no one ever so well painted natural tenderness free from affectation and disguise—no one else ever so well showed how delicacy and timidity, when driven to extremity, grow romantic and extravagant; for the romance of his heroines (in which they abound) is only an excess of the habitual prejudices of their sex, scrupulous of being false to their vows, truant to their affections, and taught by the force of feeling when to forgo the forms of propriety for the essence of it. His women were in this respect exquisite logicians; for there is nothing so logical as passion. They knew their own minds exactly; and only followed up a favourite idea, which they had sworn to with their tongues, and which was engraven on their hearts, into its untoward consequences. They were the prettiest little set of martyrs and confessors on record. Cibber, in speaking of the early English stage, accounts for the want of prominence and theatrical display in Shakespeare's female characters from the circumstance, that women in those days were not allowed to play the parts of women, which made it necessary to keep them a good deal in the background. Does not this state of manners itself, which prevented their exhibiting themselves in public, and confined them to the relations and charities of domestic life, afford a truer explanation of the matter? His women are certainly very unlike stage-heroines; the reverse of tragedy-queens.

We have almost as great an affection for Imogen as she had for Posthumus; and she deserves it better. Of all Shakespeare's women she is perhaps the most tender and the most artless. Her incredulity in the opening scene with Iachimo, as to her husband's infidelity, is much the same as Desdemona's backwardness to believe Othello's jealousy. Her answer to the most distressing part of the picture is only, 'My lord, I fear, has forgot Britain.' Her readiness to pardon Iachimo's false imputations and his designs against herself, is a good lesson to prudes; and may show that where there is a real attachment to virtue, it has no need to bolster itself up with an outrageous or affected antipathy to vice. The scene in which Pisanio gives Imogen his master's letter, accusing her of incontinency on the treacherous suggestions of Iachimo, is as touch-ing as it is possible for any thing to be:

Pisanio. What cheer, Madam? Imogen. False to his bed! What is it to be false? To lie in watch there, and to think on him? To weep 'twixt clock and clock? If sleep charge nature, To break it with a fearful dream of him, And cry myself awake? That's false to's bed, is it? Pisanio. Alas, good lady! Imogen. I false? thy conscience witness, Iachimo, Thou didst accuse him of incontinency, Thou then look'dst like a villain: now methinks, Thy favour's good enough. Some jay of Italy, Whose mother was her painting, hath betrayed him: Poor I am stale, a garment out of fashion, And for I am richer than to hang by th' walls, I must be ript; to pieces with me. Oh, Men's vows are women's traitors. All good seeming, By thy revolt, oh husband, shall be thought Put on for villany: not born where't grows, But worn a bait for ladies. Pisanio. Good madam, hear me— Imogen. Talk thy tongue weary, speak: I have heard I am a strumpet, and mine ear, Therein false struck, can take no greater wound, Nor tent to bottom that.—

When Pisanio, who had been charged to kill his mistress, puts her in a way to live, she says:

Why, good fellow,   What shall I do the while? Where bide? How live?

Or in my life what comfort, when I am

Dead to my husband?

Yet when he advises her to disguise herself in boy's clothes, and suggests 'a course pretty and full in view', by which she may 'happily be near the residence of Posthumus', she exclaims:

Oh, for such means,

Though peril to my modesty, not death on't,

I would adventure.

And when Pisanio, enlarging on the consequences, tells her she must change

16

                    —Fear and niceness,
The handmaids of all women, or more truly,
Woman its pretty self, into a waggish courage,
Ready in gibes, quick answer'd, saucy, and
As quarrellous as the weasel—

she interrupts him hastily;

        Nay, be brief;
I see into thy end, and am almost
A man already.

In her journey thus disguised to Milford Haven, she loses her guide and her way; and unbosoming her complaints, says beautifully:

        —My dear Lord,
Thou art one of the false ones; now I think on thee,
My hunger's gone; but even before, I was
At point to sink for food.

She afterwards finds, as she thinks, the dead body of Posthumus, and engages herself as a foot-boy to serve a Roman officer, when she has done all due obsequies to him whom she calls her former master:

        —And when
With wild wood-leaves and weeds I ha' strew'd his grave,
And on it said a century of pray'rs,
Such as I can, twice o'er, I'll weep and sigh,
And leaving so his service, follow you,
So please you entertain me.

Now this is the very religion of love. She all along relies little on her personal charms, which she fears may have been eclipsed by some painted jay of Italy; she relies on her merit, and her merit is in the depth of her love, her truth and constancy. Our admiration of her beauty is excited with as little consciousness as possible on her part. There are two delicious descriptions given of her, one when she is asleep, and one when she is supposed dead. Arviragus thus addresses her:

        —With fairest flowers,
While summer lasts, and I live here, Fidele,
I'll sweeten thy sad grave; thou shalt not lack
The flow'r that's like thy face, pale primrose, nor
The azur'd hare-bell, like thy veins, no, nor
The leaf of eglantine, which not to slander,
Out-sweeten'd not thy breath.

The yellow Iachimo gives another thus, when he steals into her bed- chamber:

>   —Cytherea,
> How bravely thou becom'st thy bed! Fresh lily,
> And whiter than the sheets I That I might touch—
> But kiss, one kiss—Tis her breathing that
> Perfumes the chamber thus: the flame o' th' taper
> Bows toward her, and would under-peep her lids,
> To see th' enclosed lights now canopied
> Under the windows, white and azure, laced
> With blue of Heav'ns own tinct—on her left breast
> A mole cinque-spotted, like the crimson drops
> I' the bottom of a cowslip.

There is a moral sense in the proud beauty of this last image, a rich surfeit of the fancy,—as that well—known passage beginning, 'Me of my lawful pleasure she restrained, and prayed me oft forbearance,' sets a keener edge upon it by the inimitable picture of modesty and self-denial.

The character of Cloten, the conceited, booby lord, and rejected lover of Imogen, though not very agreeable in itself, and at present obsolete, is drawn with great humour and knowledge of character. The description which Imogen gives of his unwelcome addresses to her— 'Whose love-suit hath been to me as fearful as a siege'—is enough to cure the most ridiculous lover of his folly. It is remarkable that though Cloten makes so poor a figure in love, he is described as assuming an air of consequence as the Queen's son in a council of state, and with all the absurdity of his person and manners, is not without shrewdness in his observations. So true is it that folly is as often owing to a want of proper sentiments as to a want of under- standing! The exclamation of the ancient critic, 'O Menander and Nature, which of you copied from the other?' would not be misapplied to Shakespeare.

The other characters in this play are represented with great truth and accuracy, and as it happens in most of the author's works, there is not only the utmost keeping in each separate character; but in the casting of the different parts, and their relation to one another, there is an affinity and harmony, like what we may observe in the gradations of colour in a picture. The striking and powerful contrasts in which Shakespeare abounds could not escape observation; but the use he makes of the principle of analogy to reconcile the greatest diversities of character and to maintain a continuity of feeling throughout, has not been sufficiently attended to. In Cymbeline, for instance, the principal interest arises out of the unalterable fidelity of Imogen to her husband under the most trying circumstances. Now the other parts of the picture are filled up with subordinate examples of the same feeling, variously modified by different situations, and applied to the purposes of virtue or vice. The plot is aided by the amorous importunities of Cloten, by the tragical determination of Iachimo to conceal the defeat of his project by a daring imposture: the faithful attachment of Pisanio to his mistress is an affecting accompaniment to the whole; the obstinate adherence to his purpose in Bellarius, who keeps the fate of the young princes so long a secret in resentment for the ungrateful return to his former services, the incorrigible wickedness of the Queen, and even the blind uxorious confidence of Cymbeline, are all so many lines of the same story, tending to the same point. The effect of this coincidence is rather felt than observed; and as the impression exists unconsciously in the mind of the reader, so it probably arose in the same manner in the mind of the author, not from design, but from the force of natural association, a particular train of feeling suggesting different inflections of the same predominant principle, melting into, and strengthening one another, like chords in music.

The characters of Bellarius, Guiderius, and Arviragus, and the romantic scenes in which they appear, are a fine relief to the intrigues and artificial refinements of the court from which they are banished. Nothing can surpass the wildness and simplicity of the descriptions of the mountain life they lead. They follow the business of huntsmen, not of shepherds; and this is in keeping with the spirit of adventure and uncertainty in the rest of the story, and with the scenes in which they are afterwards called on to act. How admirably the youthful fire and impatience to emerge from their obscurity in the young princes is opposed to the cooler calculations and prudent resignation of their more experienced counsellor! How well the disadvantages of knowledge and of ignorance, of solitude and society, are placed against each other!

> Guiderius. Out of your proof you speak: we poor unfledg'd
>   Have never wing'd from view o' th' nest; nor know not
>   What air's from home. Haply this life is best,
>   If quiet life is best; sweeter to you
>   That have a sharper known; well corresponding
>   With your stiff age: but unto us it is
>   A cell of ignorance; travelling a-bed,
>   A prison for a debtor, that not dares
>   To stride a limit.
>
> Arviragus. What should we speak of
>   When we are old as you? When we shall hear
>   The rain and wind beat dark December! How,
>   In this our pinching cave, shall we discourse
>   The freezing hours away? We have seen nothing.
>   We are beastly; subtle as the fox for prey,
>   Like warlike as the wolf for what we eat:
>   Our valour is to chase what flies; our cage
>   We make a quire, as doth the prison'd bird,
>   And sing our bondage freely.

The answer of Bellarius to this expostulation is hardly satisfactory; for nothing can be an answer to hope, or the passion of the mind for unknown good, but experience.—The forest of Arden in As You Like It can alone compare with the mountain scenes in Cymbeline: yet how different the contemplative quiet of the one from the enterprising boldness and precarious mode of subsistence in the other! Shakespeare not only lets us into the minds of his characters, but gives a tone and colour to the scenes he describes from the feelings of their imaginary inhabitants. He at the same time preserves the utmost propriety of action and passion, and gives all their local accompaniments. If he was equal to the greatest things, he was not above an attention to the smallest. Thus the gallant sportsmen in Cymbeline have to encounter the abrupt declivities of hill and valley: Touchstone and Audrey jog along a level path. The deer in Cymbeline are only regarded as objects of prey, 'The game's a-foot', &c.—with Jaques they are fine subjects to moralize upon at leisure, 'under the shade of melancholy boughs'.

We cannot take leave of this play, which is a favourite with us, without noticing some occasional touches of natural piety and morality. We may allude here to the opening of the scene in which Bellarius instructs the young princes to pay their orisons to heaven:

> —See, Boys! this gate
> Instructs you how t' adore the Heav'ns; and bows you
> To morning's holy office.

Guiderius. Hail, Heav'n!

Arviragus. Hail, Heav'n!

Bellarius. Now for our mountain-sport, up to yon hill.

What a grace and unaffected spirit of piety breathes in this passage! In like manner, one of the brothers says to the other, when about to perform the funeral rites to Fidele:

> Nay, Cadwall, we must lay his head to the east;
> My Father hath a reason for't.

Shakespeare's morality is introduced in the same simple, unobtrusive manner. Imogen will not let her companions stay away from the chase to attend her when sick, and gives her reason for it:

> Stick to your journal course; THE BREACH OF CUSTOM
> IS BREACH OF ALL!

When the Queen attempts to disguise her motives for procuring the poison from Cornelius, by saying she means to try its effects on 'creatures not worth the hanging', his answer conveys at once a tacit reproof of her hypocrisy, and a useful lesson of humanity:

> —Your Highness
> Shall from this practice but make hard your heart.

MACBETH

> The poet's eye in a fine frenzy rolling
> Doth glance from heaven to earth, from earth to heaven;
> And as imagination bodies forth
> The forms of things unknown, the poet's pen
> Turns them to shape, and gives to airy nothing
> A local habitation and a name.

MACBETH and Lear, Othello and Hamlet, are usually reckoned Shakespeare's four principal tragedies. Lear stands first for the profound intensity of the passion; Macbeth for the wildness of the imagination and the rapidity of the action; Othello for the progressive interest and powerful alternations of feeling; Hamlet for the refined development of thought and sentiment. If the force of genius shown in each of these works is astonishing, their variety is not less so. They are like different creations of the same mind, not one of which has the slightest reference to the rest. This distinctness and originality is indeed the necessary consequence of truth and nature. Shakespeare's genius alone appeared to possess the resources of nature. He is 'your only tragedy-maker'. His plays have the force of things upon the mind. What he represents is brought home to the bosom as a part of our experience, implanted in the memory as if we had known the places, persons, and things of which he treats. Macbeth is like a record of a preternatural and tragical event. It has the rugged severity of an old chronicle with all that the imagination of the poet can engraft upon traditional belief. The castle of Macbeth, round which 'the air smells wooingly', and where 'the temple-haunting martlet builds', has a real subsistence in the mind; the Weird Sisters meet us in person on 'the blasted heath'; the 'air-drawn dagger' moves slowly before our eyes; the 'gracious Duncan', the 'blood-boltered Banquo' stand before us; all that passed through the mind of Macbeth passes, without the loss of a tittle, through ours. All that could actually take place, and all that is only pos-sible to be conceived, what was said and what was done, the workings of passion, the spells of magic, are brought before us with the same absolute truth and vividness.-Shakespeare excelled in the openings of his plays: that of Macbeth is the most striking of any. The wildness of the scenery, the sudden shifting of the situations and characters, the bustle, the expectations excited, are equally extraordinary. From the first entrance of the Witches and the description of them when they meet Macbeth:

> —What are these
> So wither'd and so wild in their attire,
> That look not like the inhabitants of th' earth
> And yet are on't?

the mind is prepared for all that follows.

This tragedy is alike distinguished for the lofty imagination it displays, and for the tumultuous vehemence of the action; and the one is made the moving principle of the other. The overwhelming pressure of preternatural agency urges on the tide of human passion with redoubled force. Macbeth himself appears driven along by the violence of his fate like a vessel drifting before a storm: he reels to and fro like a drunken man; he staggers under the weight of his own purposes and the suggestions of others; he stands at bay with his situation; and from the superstitious awe and breathless suspense into which the communications of the Weird Sisters throw him, is hurried on with daring impatience to verify their predictions, and with impious and bloody hand to tear aside the veil which hides the uncertainty of the future. He is not equal to the struggle with fate and conscience. He now 'bends up each corporal instrument to the terrible feat'; at other times his heart misgives him, and he is cowed and abashed by his success. 'The deed, no less than the attempt, confounds him.' His mind is assailed by the stings of remorse, and full of 'preternatural solicitings'. His speeches and soliloquies are dark riddles on human life, baffling solution, and entangling him in their labyrinths. In thought he is absent and perplexed, sudden and desperate in act, from a distrust of his own resolution. His energy springs from the anxiety and agitation of his mind. His blindly rushing forward on the objects of his ambition and revenge, or his recoiling from them, equally betrays the harassed state of his feelings.—This part of his character is admirably set off by being brought in connexion with that of Lady Macbeth, whose obdurate strength of will and masculine firmness give her the ascendancy over her husband's faltering virtue. She at once seizes on the opportunity that offers for the accomplishment of all their wished-for greatness, and never flinches from her object till all is over. The magnitude of her resolution almost covers the magnitude of her guilt. She is a great bad woman, whom we hate, but whom we fear more than we hate. She does not excite our loathing and abhorrence like Regan and Goneril. She is only wicked to gain a great end; and is perhaps more distinguished by her commanding presence of mind and inexorable self-will, which do not suffer her to be diverted from a bad purpose, when once formed, by weak and womanly regrets, than by the hardness of her heart or want of natural affections. The impression which her lofty determination of character makes on the mind of Macbeth is well described where he exclaims:

    —Bring forth men children only;
For thy undaunted mettle should compose
Nothing but males!

Nor do the pains she is at to 'screw his courage to the sticking- place', the reproach to him, not to be 'lost so poorly in himself', the assurance that 'a little water clears them of this deed', show anything but her greater consistency in depravity. Her strong-nerved ambition furnishes ribs of steel to 'the sides of his intent'; and she is herself wound up to the execution of her baneful project with the same unshrinking fortitude in crime, that in other circumstances she would probably have shown patience in suffering. The deliberate sacrifice of all other considerations to the gaining 'for their future days and nights sole sovereign sway and masterdom', by the murder of Duncan, is gorgeously expressed in her invocation on hearing of 'his fatal entrance under her battlements':

    —Come all you spirits
That tend on mortal thoughts, unsex me here:
And fill me, from the crown to th' toe, top-full
Of direst cruelty; make thick my blood,
Stop up the access and passage of remorse,
That no compunctious visitings of nature
Shake my fell purpose, nor keep peace between
The effect and it. Come to my woman's breasts,

And take my milk for gall, you murthering ministers,
Wherever in your sightless substances
You wait on nature's mischief. Come, thick night!
And pall thee in the dunnest smoke of hell,
That my keen knife see not the wound it makes,
Nor heav'n peep through the blanket of the dark,
To cry, hold, hold!—

When she first hears that 'Duncan comes there to sleep' she is so overcome by the news, which is beyond her utmost expectations, that she answers the messenger, 'Thou'rt mad to say it': and on receiving her husband's account of the predictions of the Witches, conscious of his instability of purpose, and that her presence is necessary to goad him on to the consummation of his promised greatness, she exclaims:

—Hie thee hither,
That I may pour my spirits in thine ear,
And chastise with me valour of my tongue
All that impedes thee from the golden round,
Which fate and metaphysical aid doth seem
To have thee crowned withal.

This swelling exultation and keen spirit of triumph, this uncontrollable eagerness of anticipation, which seems to dilate her form and take possession of all her faculties, this solid, substantial flesh-and-blood display of passion, exhibit a striking contrast to the cold, abstracted, gratuitous, servile malignity of the Witches, who are equally instrumental in urging Macbeth to his fate for the mere love of mischief, and from a disinterested delight in deformity and cruelty. They are hags of mischief, obscene panders to iniquity, malicious from their impotence of enjoyment, enamoured of destruction, because they are themselves unreal, abortive, half-existences, and who become sublime from their exemption from all human sympathies and contempt for all human affairs, as Lady Macbeth does by the force of passion! Her fault seems to have been an excess of that strong principle of self-interest and family aggrandizement, not amenable to the common feelings of compassion and justice, which is so marked a feature in barbarous nations and times. A passing reflection of this kind, on the resemblance of the sleeping king to her father, alone prevents her from slaying Duncan with her own hand.

In speaking of the character of Lady Macbeth, we ought not to pass over Mrs. Siddons's manner of acting that part. We can conceive of nothing grander. It was something above nature. It seemed almost as if a being of a superior order had dropped from a higher sphere to awe the world with the majesty of her appearance. Power was seated on her brow, passion emanated from her breast as from a shrine; she was tragedy personified. In coming on in the sleeping-scene, her eyes were open, but their sense was shut. She was like a person bewildered and unconscious of what she did. Her lips moved involuntarily—all her gestures were involuntary and mechanical. She glided on and off the stage like an apparition. To have seen her in that character was an event in every one's life, not to be forgotten.

The dramatic beauty of the character of Duncan, which excites the respect and pity even of his murderers, has been often pointed out. It forms a picture of itself. An instance of the author's power of giving a striking effect to a common reflection, by the manner of introducing it, occurs in a speech of Duncan, complaining of his having been deceived in his opinion of the Thane of Cawdor, at the very moment that he is expressing the most unbounded confidence in the loyalty and services of Macbeth.

> There is no art
> To find the mind's construction in the face:
> He was a gentleman, on whom I built
> An absolute trust.
> O worthiest cousin, [addressing himself to Macbeth]
> The sin of my ingratitude e'en now
> Was great upon me, &c.

Another passage to show that Shakespeare lost sight of nothing that could in anyway give relief or heightening to his subject, is the conversation which takes place between Banquo and Fleance immediately before the murder-scene of Duncan.

Banquo. How goes the night, boy?

Fleance. The moon is down: I have not heard the clock.

Banquo. And she goes down at twelve.

Fleance. I take't, tis later, Sir.

> Banquo. Hold, take my sword. There's husbandry in heav'n,
> Their candles are all out.—
> A heavy summons lies like lead upon me,
> And yet I would not sleep: Merciful Powers,
> Restrain in me the cursed thoughts that nature
> Gives way to in repose.

In like manner, a fine idea is given of the gloomy coming on of evening, just as Banquo is going to be assassinated.

> Light thickens and the crow
> Makes wing to the rooky wood.
>   . . . . .
> Now spurs the lated traveller apace
> To gain the timely inn.

Macbeth (generally speaking) is done upon a stronger and more systematic principle of contrast than any other of Shakespeare's plays. It moves upon the verge of an abyss, and is a constant struggle between life and death. The action is desperate and the reaction is dreadful. It is a huddling together of fierce extremes, a war of opposite natures which of them shall destroy the

24

other. There is nothing but what has a violent end or violent beginnings. The lights and shades are laid on with a determined hand; the transitions from triumph to despair, from the height of terror to the repose of death, are sudden and startling; every passion brings in its fellow-contrary, and the thoughts pitch and jostle against each other as in the dark. The whole play is an unruly chaos of strange and forbidden things, where the ground rocks under our feet. Shakespeare's genius here took its full swing, and trod upon the furthest bounds of nature and passion. This circumstance will account tor the abruptness and violent antitheses of the style, the throes and labour which run through the expression, and from defects will turn them into beauties. 'So fair and foul a day I have not seen,' &c. 'Such welcome and unwelcome news together.' 'Men's lives are like the flowers in their caps, dying or ere they sicken.' 'Look like the innocent flower, but be the serpent under it.' The scene before the castle-gate follows the appearance of the Witches on the heath, and is followed by a midnight murder. Duncan is cut off betimes by treason leagued with witchcraft, and Macduff is ripped untimely from his mother's womb to avenge his death. Macbeth, after the death of Banquo, wishes for his presence in extravagant terms, 'To him and all we thirst,' and when his ghost appears, cries out, 'Avaunt and quit my sight,' and being gone, he is 'himself again'. Macbeth resolves to get rid of Macduff, that 'he may sleep in spite of thunder'; and cheers his wife on the doubtful intelligence of Banquo's taking-off with the encouragement—'Then be thou jocund: ere the bat has flown his cloistered flight; ere to black Hecate's summons the shard-born beetle has rung night's yawning peal, there shall be done—a deed of dreadful note.' In Lady Macbeth's speech, 'Had he not resembled my father as he slept, I had done't,' there is murder and filial piety together, and in urging him to fulfil his vengeance against the defenceless king, her thoughts spare the blood neither of infants nor old age. The description of the Witches is full of the same contradictory principle; they 'rejoice when good kings bleed'; they are neither of the earth nor the air, but both; 'they should be women, but their beards forbid it'; they take all the pains possible to lead Macbeth on to the height of his ambition, only to betray him in deeper consequence, and after showing him all the pomp of their art, discover their malignant delight in his disappointed hopes, by that bitter taunt, 'Why stands Macbeth thus amazedly?' We might multiply such instances everywhere.

The leading features in the character of Macbeth are striking enough, and they form what may be thought at first only a bold, rude, Gothic outline. By comparing it with other characters of the same author we shall perceive the absolute truth and identity which is observed in the midst of the giddy whirl and rapid career of events. Macbeth in Shakespeare no more loses his identity of character in the fluctuations of fortune or the storm of passion, than Macbeth in himself would have lost the identity of his person. Thus he is as distinct a being from Richard III as it is possible to imagine, though these two characters in common hands, and indeed in the hands of any other poet, would have been a repetition of the same general idea, more or less exaggerated. For both are tyrants, usurpers, murderers, both aspiring and ambitious, both courageous, cruel, treacherous. But Richard is cruel from nature and constitution. Macbeth becomes so from accidental circumstances. Richard is from his birth deformed in body and mind, and naturally incapable of good. Macbeth is full of 'the milk of human kindness, is frank, sociable, generous. He is tempted to the commission of guilt by golden opportunities, by the instigations of his wife, and by prophetic warnings. Fate and metaphysical aid conspire against his virtue and his loyalty. Richard, on the contrary, needs no prompter, but wades through a series of crimes to the height of his ambition from the ungovernable violence of his temper and a reckless love of mischief. He is never gay but in the prospect or in the success of his villanies; Macbeth is full of horror at the thoughts of the murder of Duncan, which he is with difficulty prevailed on to commit, and of remorse after its perpetration. Richard has no mixture of common humanity in his composition, no regard to kindred or posterity, he owns no fellowship with others, he is 'himself alone'. Macbeth is not destitute of feelings of sympathy, is accessible to pity, is even made in some measure the dupe of his uxoriousness, ranks the loss of friends, of the cordial love of his followers, and of his good name, among the causes which have made him weary of life, and regrets that he has ever seized the crown by unjust means, since he cannot transmit it to his own posterity:

> For Banquo's issue have I 'fil'd my mind—
> For them the gracious Duncan have I murther'd,
> To make them kings, the seed of Banquo kings.

In the agitation of his thoughts, he envies those whom he has sent to peace. 'Duncan is in his grave; after life's fitful fever he sleeps well.' It is true, he becomes more callous as he plunges deeper in guilt, 'direness is thus rendered familiar to his slaughterous thoughts', and he in the end anticipates his wife in the boldness and bloodiness of his enterprises, while she, for want of the same stimulus of action, is 'troubled with thick-coming fancies that rob her of her rest', goes mad and dies.

Macbeth endeavours to escape from reflection on his crimes by repelling their consequences, and banishes remorse for the past by the meditation of future mischief. This is not the principle of Richard's cruelty, which resembles the wanton malice of a fiend as much as the frailty of human passion. Macbeth is goaded on to acts of violence and retaliation by necessity; to Richard, blood is a pastime.—There are other decisive differences inherent in the two characters. Richard may be regarded as a man of the world, a plotting, hardened knave, wholly regardless of everything but his own ends, and the means to secure them.—Not so Macbeth. The superstitions of the age, the rude state of society, the local scenery and customs, all give a wildness and imaginary grandeur to his character. From the strangeness of the events that surround him, he is full of amazement and fear; and stands in doubt between the world of reality and the world of fancy. He sees sights not shown to mortal eye, and hears unearthly music. All is tumult and disorder within and without his mind; his purposes recoil upon himself, are broken and disjointed; he is the double thrall of his passions and his evil destiny. Richard is not a character either of imagination or pathos, but of pure self-will. There is no conflict of opposite feelings in his breast. The apparitions which he sees only haunt him in his sleep; nor does he live like Macbeth in a waking dream. Macbeth has considerable energy and manliness of character; but then he is 'subject to all the skyey influences'. He is sure of nothing but the present moment. Richard in the busy turbulence of his projects never loses his self-possession, and makes use of every circumstance that happens as an instrument of his long-reaching designs. In his last extremity we can only regard him as a wild beast taken in the toils: we never entirely lose our concern for Macbeth; and he calls back all our sympathy by that fine close of thoughtful melancholy:

> My way of life is fallen into the sear,
> The yellow leaf; and that which should accompany old age,

As honour, troops of friends, I must not look to have;
But in their stead, curses not loud but deep,
Mouth-honour, breath, which the poor heart
Would fain deny and dare not.

We can conceive a common actor to play Richard tolerably well; we can conceive no one to play Macbeth properly, or to look like a man that had encountered the Weird Sisters. All the actors that we have ever seen, appear as if they had encountered them on the boards of Covent Garden or Drury Lane, but not on the heath at Fores, and as if they did not believe what they had seen. The Witches of Macbeth indeed are ridiculous on the modern stage, and we doubt if the furies of Aeschylus would be more respected. The progress of manners and knowledge has an influence on the stage, and will in time perhaps destroy both tragedy and comedy. Filch's picking pockets, in the Beggars' Opera, is not so good a jest as it used to be: by the force of the police and of philosophy, Lillo's murders and the ghosts in Shakespeare will become obsolete. At last there will be nothing left, good nor bad, to be desired or dreaded, on the theatre or in real life. A question has been started with respect to the originality of Shakespeare's Witches, which has been well answered by Mr. Lamb in his notes to the Specimens of Early Dramatic Poetry:

"Though some resemblance may be traced between the charms in Macbeth and the incantations in this play (the Witch of Middleton), which is supposed to have preceded it, this coincidence will not detract much from the originality of Shakespeare. His Witches are distinguished from the Witches of Middleton by essential differences. These are creatures to whom man or woman plotting some dire mischief might resort for occasional consultation. Those originate deeds of blood, and begin bad impulses to men. From the moment that their eyes first meet with Macbeth's, he is spellbound. That meeting sways his destiny. He can never break the fascination. These Witches can hurt the body; those have power over the soul.—Hecate in Middleton has a son, a low buffoon: the hags of Shakespeare have neither child of their own, nor seem to be descended from any parent. They are foul anomalies, of whom we know not whence they are sprung, nor whether they have beginning or ending. As they are without human passions, so they seem to be without human relations. They come with thunder and lightning, and vanish to airy music. This is all we know of them.—Except Hecate, they have no names, which heightens their mysteriousness. The names, and some of the properties which Middleton has given to his hags, excite smiles. The Weird Sisters are serious things. Their presence cannot co-exist with mirth. But, in a lesser degree, the Witches of Middleton are fine creations. Their power too is, in some measure, over the mind. They raise jars, jealousies, strifes, 'LIKE A THICK SCURF O'ER LIFE.'

JULIUS CAESAR

JULIUS CAESAR was one of three principal plays by different authors, pitched upon by the celebrated Earl of Halifax to be brought out in a splendid manner by subscription, in the year 1707. The other two were the King and No King of Fletcher, and Dryden's Maiden Queen. There perhaps might be political reasons for this selection, as far as regards our author. Otherwise, Shakespeare's Julius Caesar is not equal, as a whole, to either of his other plays taken from the Roman history. It is inferior in interest to Coriolanus, and both in interest and power to Antony and Cleopatra. It, however, abounds in admirable and affecting passages, and is remarkable for the profound knowledge of character, in which Shakespeare could scarcely fail. If there is any exception to this remark, it is in the hero of the piece himself. We do not much admire the representation here given of Julius Caesar, nor do we think it answers to the portrait given of him in his Commentaries. He makes several vapouring and rather pedantic speeches, and does nothing. Indeed, he has nothing to do. So far, the fault of the character might be the fault of the plot.

The spirit with which the poet has entered at once into the manners of the common people, and the jealousies and heartburnings of the different factions, is shown in the first scene, when Flavius and Marullus, tribunes of the people, and some citizens of Rome, appear upon the stage.

Flavius. Thou art a cobbler, art thou?

> Cobbler. Truly, Sir, ALL that I live by, is the AWL: I meddle with no tradesman's
> matters, nor woman's matters, but with-al, I am indeed, Sir, a surgeon to old shoes;
> when they are in great danger, I recover them.

> Flavius. But wherefore art not in thy shop to-day? Why dost thou lead these men
> about the streets?

> Cobbler. Truly, Sir, to wear out their shoes, to get myself
> into more work. But indeed. Sir, we make holiday to see
> Caesar, and rejoice in his triumph.

To this specimen of quaint low humour immediately follows that unexpected and animated burst of indignant eloquence, put into the mouth of one of the angry tribunes.

Marullus. Wherefore rejoice!—What conquest brings he home?
  What tributaries follow him to Rome,
  To grace in captive-bonds his chariot-wheels?
  Oh you hard hearts, you cruel men of Rome!
  Knew you not Pompey? Many a time and oft
  Have you climb'd up to walls and battlements,
  To towers and windows, yea, to chimney-tops,
  Your infants in your arms, and there have sat
  The live-long day with patient expectation,
  To see great Pompey pass the streets of Rome:
  And when you saw his chariot but appear,

Have you not made an universal shout,
That Tiber trembled underneath his banks
To hear the replication of your sounds,
Made in his concave shores?
And do you now put on your best attire?
And do you now cull out an holiday?
And do you now strew flowers in his way
That comes in triumph over Pompey's blood?
Begone—
Run to your houses, fall upon your knees,
Pray to the Gods to intermit the plague,
That needs must light on this ingratitude.

The well-known dialogue between Brutus and Cassius, in which the latter breaks the design of the conspiracy to the former, and partly gains him over to it, is a noble piece of high-minded declamation. Cassius's insisting on the pretended effeminacy of Caesar's character, and his description of their swimming across the Tiber together, 'once upon a raw and gusty day', are among the finest strokes in it. But perhaps the whole is not equal to the short scene which follows when Caesar enters with his train.

Brutus. The games are done, and Caesar is returning.

  Cassius. As they pass by, pluck Casca by the sleeve,
  And he will, after his sour fashion, tell you
  What has proceeded worthy note to-day.

  Brutus. I will do so; but look you, Cassius—
  The angry spot doth glow on Caesar's brow,
  And all the rest look like a chidden train.
  Calphurnia's cheek is pale; and Cicero
  Looks with such ferret and such fiery eyes,
  As we have seen him in the Capitol,
  Being crost in conference by some senators.

Cassius. Casca will tell us what the matter is.

Caesar. Antonius—

Antony. Caesar?

  Caesar. Let me have men about me that are fat,
  Sleek-headed men, and such as sleep a-nights:
  Yond Cassius has a lean and hungry look,
  He thinks too much; such men are dangerous.

  Antony. Fear him not, Caesar, he's not dangerous;
  He is a noble Roman, and well given.

Caesar. Would he were fatter; but I fear him not:
  Yet if my name were liable to fear,
  I do not know the man I should avoid
  So soon as that spare Cassius. He reads much;
  He is a great observer; and he looks
  Quite through the deeds of men. He loves no plays,
  As thou dost, Antony; he hears no music;
  Seldom he smiles, and smiles in such a sort,
  As if he mock'd himself, and scorn'd his spirit,
  That could be mov'd to smile at any thing.
  Such men as he be never at heart's ease,
  Whilst they behold a greater than themselves;
  And therefore are they very dangerous.
  I rather tell thee what is to be fear'd
  Than what I fear; for always I am Caesar.
  Come on my right hand, for this ear is deaf,
  And tell me truly what thou think'st of him.

We know hardly any passage more expressive of the genius of Shakespeare than this. It is as if he had been actually present, had known the different characters and what they thought of one another, and had taken down what he heard and saw, their looks, words, and gestures, just as they happened.

The character of Mark Antony is further speculated upon where the conspirators deliberate whether he shall fall with Caesar. Brutus is against it:

  And for Mark Antony, think not of him:
  For "he can do no more than Caesar's arm,
  When Caesar's head is off."

  Cassius. Yet do I fear him:
  For in th' ingrafted love he bears to Caesar—

  Brutus. Alas, good Cassius, do not think of him:
  If he love Caesar, all that he can do
  Is to himself, take thought, and die for Caesar:
  And that were much, he should; for he is giv'n
  To sports, to wildness, and much company.

  Trebonius. There is no fear in him; let him not die.
  For he will live, and laugh at this hereafter.

They were in the wrong; and Cassius was right.

The honest manliness of Brutus is, however, sufficient to find out the unfitness of Cicero to be included in their enterprise, from his affected egotism and literary vanity.

O, name him not: let us not break with him;
For he will never follow any thing,
That other men begin.

His scepticism as to prodigies and his moralizing on the weather— "This disturbed sky is not to walk in"—are in the same spirit of refined imbecility.

Shakespeare has in this play and elsewhere shown the same penetration into political character and the springs of public events as into those of everyday life. For instance, the whole design to liberate their country fails from the generous temper and overweening confidence of Brutus in the goodness of their cause and the assistance of others. Thus it has always been. Those who mean well themselves think well of others, and fall a prey to their security. That humanity and sincerity which dispose men to resist injustice and tyranny render them unfit to cope with the cunning and power of those who are opposed to them. The friends of liberty trust to the professions of others because they are themselves sincere, and endeavour to secure the public good with the least possible hurt to its enemies, who have no regard to anything but their own unprincipled ends, and stick at nothing to accomplish them. Cassius was better cut out for a conspirator. His heart prompted his head. His habitual jealousy made him fear the worst that might happen, and his irritability of temper added to his inveteracy of purpose, and sharpened his patriotism. The mixed nature of his motives made him fitter to contend with bad men. The vices are never so well employed as in combating one another. Tyranny and servility are to be dealt with after their own fashion: otherwise, they will triumph over those who spare them, and finally pronounce their funeral panegyric, as Antony did that of Brutus. All the conspirators, save only he,

Did that they did in envy of great Caesar:
He only in a general honest thought
And common good to all, made one of them.

The quarrel between Brutus and Cassius is managed in a masterly way. The dramatic fluctuation of passion, the calmness of Brutus, the heat of Cassius, are admirably described; and the exclamation of Cassius on hearing of the death of Portia, which he does not learn till after the reconciliation, 'How 'scap'd I killing when I crost you so?' gives double force to all that has gone before. The scene between Brutus and Portia, where she endeavours to extort the secret of the conspiracy from him, is conceived in the most heroical spirit, and the burst of tenderness in Brutus:

You are my true and honourable wife;
As dear to me as are the ruddy drops
That visit my sad heart—

is justified by her whole behaviour. Portia's breathless impatience to learn the event of the conspiracy, in the dialogue with Lucius, is full of passion. The interest which Portia takes in Brutus and that which Calphurnia takes in the fate of Caesar are discriminated with the nicest precision. Mark Antony's speech over the dead body of Caesar has been justly admired for the mixture of pathos and artifice in it: that of Brutus certainly is not so good.

31

The entrance of the conspirators to the house of Brutus at midnight is rendered very impressive. In the midst of this scene we meet with one of those careless and natural digressions which occur so frequently and beautifully in Shakespeare. After Cassius has introduced his friends one by one, Brutus says:

They are all welcome.
What watchful cares do interpose themselves
Betwixt your eyes and night?

Cassius. Shall I entreat a word? [They whisper.]

Decius. Here lies the east: doth not the day break here?

Casca. No.

Cinna. O pardon, Sir, it doth; and yon grey lines,
  That fret the clouds, are messengers of day.

Casca. You shall confess, that you are both deceiv'd:
  Here, as I point my sword, the sun arises,
  Which is a great way growing on the south,
  Weighing the youthful, season of the year.
  Some two months hence, up higher toward the north
  He first presents his fire, and the high east
  Stands as the Capitol, directly here.

We cannot help thinking this graceful familiarity better than all the formality in the world. The truth of history in Julius Caesar is very ably worked up with dramatic effect. The councils of generals, the doubtful turns of battles, are represented to the life. The death of Brutus is worthy of him—it has the dignity of the Roman senator with the firmness of the Stoic philosopher. But what is perhaps better than either, is the little incident of his boy, Lucius, falling asleep over his instrument, as he is playing to his master in his tent, the night before the battle. Nature had played him the same forgetful trick once before on the night of the conspiracy. The humanity of Brutus is the same on both occasions.

  —It is no matter;
Enjoy the honey-heavy dew of slumber.
Thou hast no figures nor no fantasies,
Which busy care draws in the brains of men.
Therefore thou sleep'st so sound.

OTHELLO

It has been said that tragedy purifies the affections by terror and pity. That is, it substitutes imaginary sympathy for mere selfishness. It gives us a high and permanent interest, beyond ourselves, in humanity as such. It raises the great, the remote, and the possible to an equality with the real, the little and the near. It makes man a partaker with his kind. It subdues and softens the stubbornness of his will. It teaches him that there are and have been others like himself, by showing him as in a glass what they have felt, thought, and done. It opens the chambers of the human heart. It leaves nothing indifferent to us that can affect our common nature. It excites our sensibility by exhibiting the passions wound up to the utmost pitch by the power of imagination or the temptation of circumstances; and corrects their fatal excesses in ourselves by pointing to the greater extent of sufferings and of crimes to which they have led others. Tragedy creates a balance of the affections. It makes us thoughtful spectators in the lists of life. It is the refiner of the species; a discipline of humanity. The habitual study of poetry and works of imagination is one chief part of a well-grounded education. A taste for liberal art is necessary to complete the character of a gentleman, Science alone is hard and mechanical. It exercises the understanding upon things out of ourselves, while it leaves the affections unemployed, or engrossed with our own immediate, narrow interests.—OTHELLO furnishes an illustration of these remarks. It excites our sympathy in an extraordinary degree. The moral it conveys has a closer application to the concerns of human life than that of any other of Shakespeare's plays. 'It comes directly home to the bosoms and business of men.' The pathos in LEAR is indeed more dreadful and overpowering: but it is less natural, and less of every day's occurrence. We have not the same degree of sympathy with the passions described in MACBETH. The interest in HAMLET is more remote and reflex. That of OTHELLO is at once equally profound and affecting.

The picturesque contrasts of character in this play are almost as remarkable as the depth of the passion. The Moor Othello, the gentle Desdemona, the villain Iago, the good-natured Cassio, the fool Roderigo, present a range and variety of character as striking and palpable as that produced by the opposition of costume in a picture. Their distinguishing qualities stand out to the mind's eye, so that even when we are not thinking of their actions or sentiments, the idea of their persons is still as present to us as ever. These characters and the images they stamp upon the mind are the farthest asunder possible, the distance between them is immense: yet the compass of knowledge and invention which the poet has shown in embodying these extreme creations of his genius is only greater than the truth and felicity with which he has identified each character with itself, or blended their different qualities together in the same story. What a contrast the character of Othello forms to that of Iago: at the same time, the force of conception with which these two figures are opposed to each other is rendered still more intense by the complete consistency with which the traits of each character are brought out in a state of the highest finishing. The making one black and the other white, the one unprincipled, the other unfortunate in the extreme, would have answered the common purposes of effect, and satisfied the ambition of an ordinary painter of character. Shakespeare has laboured the finer shades of difference in both with as much care and skill as if he had had to depend on the execution alone for the success of his design. On the other hand, Desdemona and Aemilia are not meant to be opposed with anything like strong contrast to each other. Both are, to outward appearance, characters of common life, not more distinguished than women usually are, by difference of rank and situation. The difference of their thoughts and sentiments is, however, laid as open, their minds are separated from each other by signs as plain and as little to be mistaken as the complexions of their husbands.

The movement of the passion in OTHELLO is exceedingly different from that of MACBETH. In MACBETH there is a violent struggle between opposite feelings, between ambition and the stings of conscience, almost from first to last: in Othello, the doubtful conflict between contrary passions, though dreadful, continues only for a short time, and the chief interest is excited by the alternate ascendancy of different passions, the entire and unforeseen change from the fondest love and most unbounded confidence to the tortures of jealousy and the madness of hatred. The revenge of Othello, after it has once taken thorough possession of his mind, never quits it, but grows stronger and stronger at every moment of its delay. The nature of the Moor is noble, confiding, tender, and generous; but his blood is of the most inflammable kind; and being once roused by a sense of his wrongs, he is stopped by no considerations of remorse or pity till he has given a loose to all the dictates of his rage and his despair. It is in working his noble nature up to this extremity through rapid but gradual transitions, in raising passion to its height from the smallest beginnings and in spite of all obstacles, in painting the expiring conflict between love and hatred, tenderness and resentment, jealousy and remorse, in unfolding the strength and the weaknesses of our nature, in uniting sublimity of thought with the anguish of the keenest woe, in putting in motion the various impulses that agitate this our mortal being, and at last blending them in that noble tide of deep and sustained passion, impetuous but majestic, that 'flows on to the Propontic, and knows no ebb', that Shakespeare has shown the mastery of his genius and of his power over the human heart. The third act of Othello is his masterpiece, not of knowledge or passion separately, but of the two combined, of the knowledge of character with the expression of passion, of consummate art in the keeping up of appearances with the profound workings of nature, and the convulsive movements of uncontrollable agony, of the power of inflicting torture and of suffering it. Not only is the tumult of passion heaved up from the very bottom of the soul, but every the slightest undulation of feeling is seen on the surface, as it arises from the impulses of imagination or the different probabilities maliciously suggested by Iago. The progressive preparation for the catastrophe is wonderfully managed from the Moor's first gallant recital of the story of his love, of 'the spells and witchcraft he had used', from his unlooked- for and romantic success, the fond satisfaction with which he dotes on his own happiness, the unreserved tenderness of Desdemona and her innocent importunities in favour of Cassio, irritating the suspicions instilled into her husband's mind by the perfidy of Iago, and rankling there to poison, till he loses all command of himself, and his rage can only be appeased by blood. She is introduced, just before Iago begins to put his scheme in practice, pleading for Cassio with all the thoughtless gaiety of friendship and winning confidence in the love of Othello.

> What! Michael Cassio?
> That came a wooing with you, and so many a time,
> When I have spoke of you dispraisingly,
> Hath ta'en your part, to have so much to do
> To bring him in?—Why this is not a boon:
> 'Tis as I should entreat you wear your gloves,
> Or feed on nourishing meats, or keep you warm;
> Or sue to you to do a peculiar profit

> To your person. Nay, when I have a suit,
> Wherein I mean to touch your love indeed,
> It shall be full of poise, and fearful to be granted.

Othello's confidence, at first only staggered by broken hints and insinuations, recovers itself at sight of Desdemona; and he exclaims

> If she be false, O then Heav'n mocks itself:
> I'll not believe it.

But presently after, on brooding over his suspicions by himself, and yielding to his apprehensions of the worst, his smothered jealousy breaks out into open fury, and he returns to demand satisfaction of Iago like a wild beast stung with the envenomed shaft of the hunters. 'Look where he comes', &c. In this state of exasperation and violence, after the first paroxysms of his grief and tenderness have had their vent in that passionate apostrophe, 'I felt not Cassio's kisses on her lips,' Iago by false aspersions, and by presenting the most revolting images to his mind, [Footnote: See the passage beginning, 'It is impossible you should see this, Were they as prime as goats,' &c.] easily turns the storm of Passion from himself against Desdemona, and works him up into a trembling agony of doubt and fear, in which he abandons all his love and hopes in a breath.

> Now do I see'tis true. Look here, Iago,
> All my fond love thus do I blow to Heav'n. Tis gone.
> Arise, black vengeance, from the hollow hell;
> Yield up, O love, thy crown and hearted throne
> To tyrannous hate! Swell, bosom, with thy fraught;
> For'tis of aspicks' tongues.

From this time, his raging thoughts 'never look back, ne'er ebb to humble love' till his revenge is sure of its object, the painful regrets and involuntary recollections of past circumstances which cross his mind amidst the dim trances of passion, aggravating the sense of his wrongs, but not shaking his purpose. Once indeed, where Iago shows him Cassio with the handkerchief in his hand, and making sport (as he thinks) of his misfortunes, the intolerable bitterness of his feelings, the extreme sense of shame, makes him fall to praising her accomplishments and relapse into a momentary fit of weakness, 'Yet, oh, the pity of it, Iago, the pity of it!' This returning fondness, however, only serves, as it is managed by Iago, to whet his revenge, and set his heart more against her. In his conversations with Desdemona, the persuasion of her guilt and the immediate proofs of her duplicity seem to irritate his resentment and aversion to her; but in the scene immediately preceding her death, the recollection of his love returns upon him in all its tenderness and force; and after her death, he all at once forgets his wrongs in the sudden and irreparable sense of his loss:

> My wife! My wife! What wife? I have no wife.
> Oh insupportable! Oh heavy hour!

This happens before he is assured of her innocence; but afterwards his remorse is as dreadful as his revenge has been, and yields only to fixed and death like despair. His farewell speech, before he kills himself, in which he conveys his reasons to the senate for the murder of his wife, is equal to the first speech in which he gave them an account of his courtship of her, and 'his whole course of love'. Such an ending was alone worthy of such a commencement.

If anything could add to the force of our sympathy with Othello, or compassion for his fate, it would be the frankness and generosity of his nature, which so little deserve it. When Iago first begins to practise upon his unsuspecting friendship, he answers:

> —Tis not to make me jealous,
> To say my wife is fair, feeds well, loves company,
> Is free of speech, sings, plays, and dances well;
> Where virtue is, these are most virtuous.
> Nor from my own weak merits will I draw
> The smallest fear or doubt of her revolt,
> For she had eyes and chose me.

This character is beautifully (and with affecting simplicity) confirmed by what Desdemona herself says of him to Aemilia after she has lost the handkerchief, the first pledge of his love to her:

> Believe me, I had rather have lost my purse
> Full of cruzadoes. And but my noble Moor
> Is true of mind, and made of no such baseness,
> As jealous creatures are, it were enough
> To put him to ill thinking.

Aemilia. Is he not jealous?

> Desdemona. Who he? I think the sun where he was born drew all such humours from him.

In a short speech of Aemilia's there occurs one of those side- intimations of the fluctuations of passion which we seldom meet with but in Shakespeare. After Othello has resolved upon the death of his wife, and bids her dismiss her attendant for the night, she answers:

I will, my Lord.

Aemilia. How goes it now? HE LOOKS GENTLER THAN HE DID.

Shakespeare has here put into half a line what some authors would have spun out into ten set speeches.

The character of Desdemona herself is inimitable both in itself, and as it contrasts with Othello's groundless jealousy, and with the foul conspiracy of which she is the innocent victim. Her beauty and external graces are only indirectly glanced at; we see 'her visage in her mind'; her character everywhere predominates over her person:

36

A maiden never bold:
Of spirit so still and quiet, that her motion
Blushed at itself.

There is one fine compliment paid to her by Cassio, who exclaims triumphantly when she comes ashore at Cyprus after the storm:

Tempests themselves, high seas, and howling winds,
As having sense of beauty, do omit
Their mortal natures, letting safe go by
The divine Desdemona.

In general, as is the case with most of Shakespeare's females, we lose sight of her personal charms in her attachment and devotedness to her husband. 'She is subdued even to the very quality of her lord'; and to Othello's 'honours and his valiant parts her soul and fortunes consecrates'. The lady protests so much herself, and she is as good as her word. The truth of conception, with which timidity and boldness are united in the same character, is marvellous. The extravagance of her resolutions, the pertinacity of her affections, may be said to arise out of the gentleness of her nature. They imply an unreserved reliance on the purity of her own intentions, an entire surrender of her fears to her love, a knitting of herself (heart and soul) to the fate of another. Bating the commencement of her passion, which is a little fantastical and headstrong (though even that may perhaps be consistently accounted for from her inability to resist a rising inclination [Footnote: Iago. Ay, too gentle. Othello. Nay, that's certain.]) her whole character consists in having no will of her own, no prompter but her obedience. Her romantic turn is only a consequence of the domestic and practical part of her disposition; and instead of following Othello to the wars, she would gladly have 'remained at home a moth of peace', if her husband could have stayed with her. Her resignation and angelic sweetness of temper do not desert her at the last. The scenes in which she laments and tries to account for Othello's estrangement from her are exquisitely beautiful. After he has struck her, and called her names, she says:

—Alas, Iago,
What shall I do to win my lord again?
Good friend, go to him; for by this light of heaven,
I know not how I lost him. Here I kneel;
If e'er my will did trespass 'gainst his love,
Either in discourse, or thought, or actual deed,
Or that mine eyes, mine ears, or any sense
Delighted them on any other form-
Or that I do not, and ever did
And ever will, though he do shake me off
To beggarly divorcement, love him dearly,
Comfort forswear me. Unkindness may do much,
And his unkindness may defeat my life,
But never taint my love.

Iago. I pray you be content:'tis but his humour.
The business of the state does him offence.

Desdemona. If'twere no other!—

The scene which follows with Aemilia and the song of the Willow are equally beautiful, and show the author's extreme power of varying the expression of passion, in all its moods and in all circumstances;

Aemilia. Would you had never seen him.

Desdemona. So would not I: my love doth so approve him,
That even his stubbornness, his checks, his frowns,
Have grace and favour in them, &c.

Not the unjust suspicions of Othello, not Iago's treachery, place Desdemona in a more amiable or interesting light than the casual conversation (half earnest, half jest) between her and Aemilia on the common behaviour of women to their husbands. This dialogue takes place just before the last fatal scene. If Othello had overheard it, it would have prevented the whole catastrophe; but then it would have spoiled the play.

The character of Iago is one of the supererogations of Shakespeare's genius. Some persons, more nice than wise, have thought this whole character unnatural, because his villainy is WITHOUT A SUFFICIENT MOTIVE. Shakespeare, who was as good a philosopher as he was a poet, thought otherwise. He knew that the love of power, which is another name for the love of mischief, is natural to man. He would know this as well or better than if it had been demonstrated to him by a logical diagram, merely from seeing children paddle in the dirt or kill flies for sport. Iago in fact belongs to a class of characters common to Shakespeare and at the same time peculiar to him; whose heads are as acute and active as their hearts are hard and callous. Iago is, to be sure, an extreme instance of the kind; that is to say, of diseased intellectual activity, with an almost perfect indifference to moral good or evil, or rather with a decided preference of the latter, because it falls more readily in with his favourite propensity, gives greater zest to his thoughts and scope to his actions. He is quite or nearly as indifferent to his own fate as to that of others; he runs all risks for a trifling and doubtful advantage; and is himself the dupe and victim of his ruling passion- -an insatiable craving after action of the most difficult and dangerous kind. 'Our ancient' is a philosopher, who fancies that a lie that kills has more point in it than an alliteration or an antithesis; who thinks a fatal experiment on the peace of a family a better thing than watching the palpitations in the heart of a flea in a microscope; who plots the ruin of his friends as an exercise for his ingenuity, and stabs men in the dark to prevent ennui. His gaiety, such as it is, arises from the success of his treachery; his ease from the torture he has inflicted on others. He is an amateur of tragedy in real life; and instead of employing his invention on imaginary characters, or long-forgotten incidents, he takes the bolder and more desperate course of getting up his plot at home, casts the principal parts among his nearest friends and connexions, and rehearses it in downright earnest, with steady nerves and unabated resolution. We will just give an illustration or two.

One of his most characteristic speeches is that immediately after the marriage of Othello.

Roderigo. What a full fortune does the thick lips owe,
   If he can carry her thus!

Iago. Call up her father:
   Rouse him [Othello], make after him, poison his delight,
   Proclaim him in the streets, incense her kinsmen,
   And tho' he in a fertile climate dwell,
   Plague him with flies: Tho' that his joy be joy,
   Yet throw such changes of vexation on it,
   As it may lose some colour.

In the next passage, his imagination runs riot in the mischief he is plotting, and breaks out into the wildness and impetuosity of real enthusiasm.

Roderigo. Here is her father's house: I'll call aloud.

Iago. Do, with like timorous accent and dire yell,
   As when, by night and negligence, the fire
   Is spied in populous cities.

One of his most favourite topics, on which he is rich indeed, and in descanting on which his spleen serves him for a Muse, is the disproportionate match between Desdemona and the Moor. This is a clue to the character of the lady which he is by no means ready to part with. It is brought forward in the first scene, and he recurs to it, when in answer to his insinuations against Desdemona, Roderigo says:

   I cannot believe that in her—she's full of most blest conditions.

   Iago. Bless'd fig's end. The wine she drinks is made of grapes. If she had been blest,
   she would never have married the Moor.

And again with still more spirit and fatal effect afterwards, when he turns this very suggestion arising in Othello's own breast to her prejudice.

Othello. And yet how nature erring from itself—

   Iago. Aye, there's the point;—as to be bold with you,
   Not to affect many proposed matches
   Of her own clime, complexion, and degree, &c.

This is probing to the quick. Iago here turns the character of poor Desdemona, as it were, inside out. It is certain that nothing but the genius of Shakespeare could have preserved the entire interest and delicacy of the part, and have even drawn an additional elegance and dignity from the peculiar circumstances in which she is placed. The habitual licentiousness of Iago's conversation is not to be traced to the pleasure he takes in gross or lascivious images, but to his desire of finding out the worst side of everything, and of proving himself an over-match for appearances. He has none of 'the milk of human kindness' in his composition. His imagination rejects everything that has not a strong infusion of the most unpalatable ingredients; his mind digests only poisons. Virtue or goodness or whatever has the least 'relish of salvation in it' is, to his depraved appetite, sickly and insipid: and he even resents the good opinion entertained of his own integrity, as if it were an affront cast on the masculine sense and spirit of his character. Thus at the meeting between Othello and Desdemona, he exclaims, 'Oh, you are well tuned now: but I'll set down the pegs that make this music, AS HONEST AS I AM—his character of bonhommie not sitting at all easily upon him. In the scenes where he tries to work Othello to his purpose, he is proportionally guarded, insidious, dark, and deliberate. We believe nothing ever came up to the profound dissimulation and dexterous artifice of the well-known dialogue in the third act, where he first enters upon the execution of his design.

Iago. My noble lord.

Othello. What dost thou say, Iago?

  Iago. Did Michael Cassio,
    When you woo'd my lady, know of your love?

  Othello. He did from first to last.
    Why dost thou ask?

  Iago. But for a satisfaction of my thought,
    No further harm.

Othello. Why of thy thought, Iago?

Iago. I did not think he had been acquainted with it.

Othello. O yes, and went between us very oft—

Iago. Indeed!

Othello. Indeed? Ay, indeed. Discern'st thou aught of that? Is he not honest?

Iago. Honest, my lord?

Othello. Honest? Ay, honest.

Iago. My lord, for aught I know.

Othello. What do'st thou think?

Iago. Think, my lord!

 Othello. Think, my lord! Alas, thou echo'st me, As if there was some monster in thy thought Too hideous to be shown.

The stops and breaks, the deep workings of treachery under the mask of love and honesty, the anxious watchfulness, the cool earnestness, and if we may so say, the PASSION of hypocrisy marked in every line, receive their last finishing in that inconceivable burst of pretended indignation at Othello's doubts of his sincerity.

> O grace! O Heaven forgive me!
> Are you a man? Have you a soul or sense?
> God be wi' you; take mine office. O wretched fool,
> That lov'st to make thine honesty a vice!
> Oh monstrous world! take note, take note, O world!
> To be direct and honest, is not safe.
> I thank you for this profit, and from hence
> I'll love no friend, since love breeds such offence.

If Iago is detestable enough when he has business on his hands and all his engines at work, he is still worse when he has nothing to do, and we only see into the hollowness of his heart. His indifference when Othello falls into a swoon, is perfectly diabolical.

Iago. How is it. General? Have you not hurt your head?

Othello. Dost thou mock me?

Iago. I mock you not, by Heaven, &c.

The part indeed would hardly be tolerated, even as a foil to The virtue and generosity of the other characters in the play, But for its indefatigable industry and inexhaustible resources, Which divert the attention of the spectator (as well as his own) from the end he has in view to the means by which it must be accomplished.—Edmund the Bastard in Lear is something of the same character, placed in less prominent circumstances. Zanga is a vulgar caricature of it.

TIMON OF ATHENS

TIMON OF ATHENS always appeared to us to be written with as intense a feeling of his subject as any one play of Shakespeare. It is one of the few in which he seems to be in earnest throughout, never to trifle nor go out of his way. He does not relax in his efforts, nor lose sight of the unity of his design. It is the only play of our author in which spleen is the predominant feeling of the mind. It is as much a satire as a play: and contains some of the finest pieces of invective possible to be conceived, both in the snarling, captious answers of the cynic Apemantus, and in the impassioned and more terrible imprecations of Timon. The latter remind the classical reader of the force and swelling impetuosity of the moral declamations in Juvenal, while the former have all the keenness and caustic severity of the old Stoic philosophers. The soul of Diogenes appears to have been seated on the lips of Apemantus. The churlish profession of misanthropy in the cynic is contrasted with the profound feeling of it in Timon, and also with the soldierlike and determined resentment of Alcibiades against his countrymen, who have banished him, though this forms only an incidental episode in the tragedy.

The fable consists of a single event—of the transition from the highest pomp and profusion of artificial refinement to the most abject state of savage life, and privation of all social intercourse. The change is as rapid as it is complete; nor is the description of the rich and generous Timon, banqueting in gilded palaces, pampered by every luxury, prodigal of his hospitality, courted by crowds of flatterers, poets, painters, lords, ladies, who:

> Follow his strides, his lobbies fill with tendance,
> Rain sacrificial whisperings in his ear;
> And through him drink the free air—

more striking than that of the sudden falling off of his friends and fortune, and his naked exposure in a wild forest digging roots from the earth for his sustenance, with a lofty spirit of self-denial, and bitter scorn of the world, which raise him higher in our esteem than the dazzling gloss of prosperity could do. He grudges himself the means of life, and is only busy in preparing his grave. How forcibly is the difference between what he was and what he is described in Apemantus's taunting questions, when he comes to reproach him with the change in his way of life!

> —What, think'st thou,
> That the bleak air, thy boisterous chamberlain,
> Will put thy shirt on warm? will these moist trees
> That have out-liv'd the eagle, page thy heels,
> And skip when thou point'st out? will the cold brook,
> Candied with ice, caudle thy morning taste
> To cure thy o'er-night's surfeit? Call the creatures,
> Whose naked natures live in all the spight
> Of wreakful heav'n, whose bare unhoused trunks,
> To the conflicting elements expos'd,
> Answer mere nature, bid them flatter thee.

42

The manners are everywhere preserved with distinct truth. The poet and painter are very skilfully played off against one another, both affecting great attention to the other, and each taken up with his own vanity, and the superiority of his own art. Shakespeare has put into the mouth of the former a very lively description of the genius of poetry and of his own in particular.

> —A thing slipt idly from me.
> Our poesy is as a gum, which issues
> From whence 'tis nourish'd. The fire i' th' flint
> Shows not till it be struck: our gentle flame
> Provokes itself—and like the current flies
> Each bound it chafes.

The hollow friendship and shuffling evasions of the Athenian lords, their smooth professions and pitiful ingratitude, are very satisfactorily exposed, as well as the different disguises to which the meanness of self-love resorts in such cases to hide a want of generosity and good faith. The lurking selfishness of Apemantus does not pass undetected amidst the grossness of his sarcasms and his contempt for the pretensions of others. Even the two courtezans who accompany Alcibiades to the cave of Timon are very characteristically sketched; and the thieves who come to visit him are also 'true men' in their way.—An exception to this general picture of selfish depravity is found in the old and honest steward, Flavius, to whom Timon pays a full tribute of tenderness. Shakespeare was unwilling to draw a picture 'all over ugly with hypocrisy'. He owed this character to the good-natured solicitations of his Muse. His mind was well said by Ben Jonson to be the 'sphere of humanity'.

The moral sententiousness of this play equals that of Lord Bacon's Treatise on the Wisdom of the Ancients, and is indeed seasoned with greater variety. Every topic of contempt or indignation is here exhausted; but while the sordid licentiousness of Apemantus, which turns everything to gall and bitterness, shows only the natural virulence of his temper and antipathy to good or evil alike, Timon does not utter an imprecation without betraying the extravagant workings of disappointed passion, of love altered to hate. Apemantus sees nothing good in any object, and exaggerates whatever is disgusting: Timon is tormented with the perpetual contrast between things and appearances, between the fresh, tempting outside and the rottenness within, and invokes mischiefs on the heads of mankind proportioned to the sense of his wrongs and of their treacheries. He impatiently cries out, when he finds the gold,

> This yellow slave
> Will knit and break religions; bless the accurs'd;
> Make the hoar leprosy ador'd; place thieves,
> And give them title, knee, and approbation,
> With senators on the bench; this is it,
> That makes the wappen'd widow wed again;
> She, whom the spital-house
> Would cast the gorge at, THIS EMBALMS AND SPICES
> TO TH' APRIL DAY AGAIN.

One of his most dreadful imprecations is that which occurs immediately on his leaving Athens.

Let me look back upon thee, O thou wall,
That girdlest in those wolves! Dive in the earth,
And fence not Athens! Matrons, turn incontinent;
Obedience fail in children; slaves and fools
Pluck the grave wrinkled senate from the bench,
And minister in their steads. To general filths
Convert o' th' instant green virginity!
Do't in your parents' eyes. Bankrupts, hold fast;
Rather than render back, out with your knives,
And cut your trusters' throats! Bound servants, steal:
Large-handed robbers your grave masters are,
And pill by law. Maid, to thy master's bed:
Thy mistress is o' th' brothel. Son of sixteen,
Pluck the lin'd crutch from thy old limping sire,
And with it beat his brains out! Fear and piety,
Religion to the Gods, peace, justice, truth,
Domestic awe, night-rest, and neighbourhood,
Instructions, manners, mysteries and trades,
Degrees, observances, customs and laws,
Decline to your confounding contraries;
And let confusion live!—Plagues, incident to men,
Your potent and infectious fevers heap
On Athens, ripe for stroke! Thou cold sciatica,
Cripple our senators, that their limbs may halt
As lamely as their manners! Lust and liberty
Creep in the minds and manners of our youth,
That 'gainst the stream of virtue they may strive,
And drown themselves in riot! Itches, blains,
Sow all th' Athenian bosoms; and their crop
Be general leprosy: breath infect breath,
That their society (as their friendship) may
Be merely poison!

Timon is here just as ideal in his passion for ill as he had before been in his belief of good. Apemantus was satisfied with the mischief existing in the world, and with his own ill-nature. One of the most decisive intimations of Timon's morbid jealousy of appearances is in his answer to Apemantus, who asks him:

What things in the world can'st thou nearest compare with thy flatterers?

Timon. Women nearest: but men, men are the things themselves.

Apemantus, it is said, 'loved few things better than to abhor himself'. This is not the case with Timon, who neither loves to abhor himself nor others. All his vehement misanthropy is forced, up-hill work. From the slippery turns of fortune, from the turmoils of passion and adversity, he wishes to sink into the quiet of the grave. On that subject his thoughts are intent, on that he finds time and place to grow romantic. He digs his own grave by the sea- shore; contrives his funeral ceremonies amidst the pomp of desolation, and builds his mausoleum of the elements.

> Come not to me again; but say to Athens,
> Timon hath made his everlasting mansion
> Upon the beached verge of the salt flood;
> Which once a-day with his embossed froth
> The turbulent surge shall cover.—Thither come,
> And let my grave-stone be your oracle.

And again, Alcibiades, after reading his epitaph, says of him:

> These well express in thee thy latter spirits:
> Though thou abhorred'st in us our human griefs,
> Scorn'd'st our brain's flow, and those our droplets, which
> From niggard nature fall; yet rich conceit
> Taught thee to make vast Neptune weep for aye
> On thy low grave—

thus making the winds his funeral dirge, his mourner the murmuring ocean; and seeking in the everlasting solemnities of nature oblivion of the transitory splendour of his lifetime.

CORIOLANUS

Shakespeare has in this play shown himself well versed in history and state affairs. CORIOLANUS is a storehouse of political commonplaces. Any one who studies it may save himself the trouble of reading Burke's Reflections, or Paine's Rights of Man, or the Debates in both Houses of Parliament since the French Revolution or our own. The arguments for and against aristocracy or democracy, on the privileges of the few and the claims of the many, on liberty and slavery, power and the abuse of it, peace and war, are here very ably handled, with the spirit of a poet and the acuteness of a philosopher. Shakespeare himself seems to have had a leaning to the arbitrary side of the question, perhaps from some feeling of contempt for his own origin; and to have spared no occasion of baiting the rabble. What he says of them is very true: what he says of their betters is also very true, though he dwells less upon it.— The cause of the people is indeed but little calculated as a subject for poetry: it admits of rhetoric, which goes into argument and explanation, but it presents no immediate or distinct images to the mind, 'no jutting frieze, buttress, or coigne of vantage' for poetry 'to make its pendant bed and procreant cradle in'. The language of poetry naturally falls in with the language of power. The imagination is an exaggerating and exclusive faculty: it takes from one thing to add to another: it accumulates circumstances together to give the greatest possible effect to a favourite object. The understanding is a dividing and measuring faculty: it judges of things, not according to their immediate impression on the mind, but according to their relations to one another. The one is a monopolizing faculty, which seeks the greatest quantity of present excitement by inequality and disproportion; the other is a distributive faculty, which seeks the greatest quantity of ultimate good, by justice and proportion. The one is an aristocratical, the other a republican faculty. The principle of poetry is a very anti- levelling principle. It aims at effect, it exists by contrast. It admits of no medium. It is everything by excess. It rises above the ordinary standard of sufferings and crimes. It presents a dazzling appearance. It shows its head turretted, crowned, and crested. Its front is gilt and blood-stained. Before it 'it carries noise, and behind it tears'. It has its altars and its victims, sacrifices, human sacrifices. Kings, priests, nobles, are its train-bearers, tyrants and slaves its executioners.—'Carnage is its daughter.' Poetry is right-royal. It puts the individual for the species, the one above the infinite many, might before right. A lion hunting a flock of sheep or a herd of wild asses is a more poetical object than they; and we even take part with the lordly beast, because our vanity or some other feeling makes us disposed to place ourselves in the situation of the strongest party. So we feel some concern for the poor citizens of Rome when they meet together to compare their wants and grievances, till Coriolanus comes in and with blows and big words drives this set of 'poor rats', this rascal scum, to their homes and beggary before him. There is nothing heroical in a multitude of miserable rogues not wishing to be starved, or complaining that they are like to be so: but when a single man comes forward to brave their cries and to make them submit to the last indignities, from mere pride and self-will, our admiration of his prowess is immediately converted into contempt for their pusillanimity. The insolence of power is stronger than the plea of necessity. The tame submission to usurped authority or even the natural resistance to it has nothing to excite or flatter the imagination: it is the assumption of a right to insult or oppress others that carries an imposing air of superiority with it. We had rather be the oppressor than the oppressed. The love of power in ourselves and the admiration of it in others are both natural to man: the one makes him a tyrant, the other a slave. Wrong dressed out in pride, pomp, and circumstance has more attraction than abstract right.—Coriolanus complains of the fickleness of the people: yet the instant he cannot gratify his pride and obstinacy at their expense, he turns his arms against his country. If his country was not worth defending, why did he build his pride on its defence? He is a conqueror and a hero; he conquers other countries, and makes this a plea for enslaving his own; and when he is prevented from doing so, he leagues with its enemies to destroy his country. He rates the people 'as if he were a God to punish, and not a man of their infirmity'. He scoffs at one of their tribunes for maintaining their rights and franchises: 'Mark you his absolute SHALL?' not marking his own absolute WILL to take everything from them, his impatience of the slightest opposition to his own pretensions being in proportion to their arrogance and absurdity. If the great and powerful had the beneficence and wisdom of Gods, then all this would have been well: if with a greater knowledge of what is good for the people, they had as great a care for their interest as they have themselves, if they were seated above the world, sympathizing with the welfare, but not feeling the passions of men, receiving neither good nor hurt from them, but bestowing their benefits as free gifts on them, they might then rule over them like another Providence. But this is not the case. Coriolanus is unwilling that the senate should show their 'cares' for the people, lest their 'cares' should be construed into 'fears', to the subversion of all due authority; and he is no sooner disappointed in his schemes to deprive the people not only of the cares of the state, but of all power to redress themselves, than Volumnia is made madly to exclaim:

> Now the red pestilence strike all trades in Rome,
> And occupations perish.

This is but natural: it is but natural for a mother to have more regard for her son than for a whole city; but then the city should be left to take some care of itself. The care of the state cannot, we here see, be safely entrusted to maternal affection, or to the domestic charities of high life. The great have private feelings of their own, to which the interests of humanity and justice must curtsy. Their interests are so far from being the same as those of the community, that they are in direct and necessary opposition to them; their power is at the expense of OUR weakness; their riches of OUR poverty; their pride of OUR degradation; their splendour of OUR wretchedness; their tyranny of OUR servitude. If they had the superior knowledge ascribed to them (which they have not) it would only render them so much more formidable; and from Gods would convert them into Devils. The whole dramatic moral of Coriolanus is that those who have little shall have less, and that those who have much shall take all that others have left. The people are poor; therefore they ought to be starved. They are slaves; therefore they ought to be beaten. They work hard; therefore they ought to be treated like beasts of burden. They are ignorant; therefore they ought not to be allowed to feel that they want food, or clothing, or rest, that they are enslaved, oppressed, and miserable. This is the logic of the imagination and the passions; which seek to aggrandize what excites admiration and to heap contempt on misery, to raise power into tyranny, and to make tyranny absolute; to thrust down that which is low still lower, and to make wretches desperate: to exalt magistrates into kings, kings into gods; to degrade subjects to the rank of slaves, and slaves to the condition of brutes. The history of mankind is a romance, a mask, a tragedy, constructed upon the principles of POETICAL JUSTICE; it is a noble or royal hunt, in which what is sport to the few is death to the many, and in which the spectators halloo and encourage the strong to set upon the weak, and cry havoc in the chase, though they do not share in the spoil. We may depend upon it that what men delight to read in books, they will put in practice in reality.

One of the most natural traits in this play is the difference of the interest taken in the success of Coriolanus by his wife and mother. The one is only anxious for his honour; the other is fearful for his life.

> Volumnia. Methinks I hither hear your husband's drum:
> I see him pluck Aufidius down by th' hair:
> Methinks I see him stamp thus—and call thus—
> Come on, ye cowards; ye were got in fear
> Though you were born in Rome; his bloody brow
> With his mail'd hand then wiping, forth he goes
> Like to a harvest man, that's task'd to mow
> Or all, or lose his hire.

Virgila. His bloody brow! Oh Jupiter, no blood.

> Volumnia. Away, you fool; it more becomes a man
> Than gilt his trophy. The breast of Hecuba,
> When she did suckle Hector, look'd not lovelier
> Than Hector's forehead, when it spit forth blood
> At Grecian swords contending.

When she hears the trumpets that proclaim her son's return, she says in the true spirit of a Roman matron:

> These are the ushers of Martius: before him
> He carries noise, and behind him he leaves tears.
> Death, that dark spirit, in's nervy arm doth lie,
> Which being advanc'd, declines, and then men die.

Coriolanus himself is a complete character: his love of reputation, his contempt of popular opinion, his pride and modesty, are consequences of each other. His pride consists in the inflexible sternness of his will; his love of glory is a determined desire to bear down all opposition, and to extort the admiration both of friends and foes. His contempt for popular favour, his unwillingness to hear his own praises, spring from the same source. He cannot contradict the praises that are bestowed upon him; therefore he is impatient at hearing them. He would enforce the good opinion of others by his actions, but does not want their acknowledgements in words.

> Pray now, no more: my mother,
> Who has a charter to extol her blood,
> When she does praise me, grieves me.

His magnanimity is of the same kind. He admires in an enemy that courage which he honours in himself: he places himself on the hearth of Aufidius with the same confidence that he would have met him in the field, and feels that by putting himself in his power, he takes from him all temptation for using it against him.

In the title-page of Coriolanus it is said at the bottom of the Dramatis Personae, 'The whole history exactly followed, and many of the principal speeches copied, from the life of Coriolanus in Plutarch.' It will be interesting to our readers to see how far this is the case. Two of the principal scenes, those between Coriolanus and Aufidius and between Coriolanus and his mother, are thus given in Sir Thomas North's translation of Plutarch, dedicated to Queen Elizabeth, 1579. The first is as follows:

It was even twilight when he entered the city of Antium, and many people met him in the streets, but no man knew him. So he went directly to Tullus Aufidius' house, and when he came thither, he got him up straight to the chimney-hearth, and sat him down, and spake not a word to any man, his face all muffled over. They of the house spying him, wondered what he should be, and yet they durst not bid him rise. For ill-favouredly muffled and disguised as he was, yet there appeared a certain majesty in his countenance and in his silence: whereupon they went to Tullus, who was at supper, to tell him of the strange disguising of this man. Tullus rose presently from the board, and coming towards him, asked him what he was, and wherefore he came. Then Martius unmuffled himself, and after he had paused awhile, making no answer, he said unto himself, If thou knowest me not yet, Tullus, and seeing me, dost not perhaps believe me to be the man I am indeed, I must of necessity discover myself to be that I am. 'I am Caius Martius, who hath done to thyself particularly, and to all the Volsces generally, great hurt and mischief, which I cannot deny for my surname of Coriolanus that I bear. For I never had other benefit nor recompence of the true and painful service I have done, and the extreme dangers I have been in, but this only surname; a good memory and witness of the malice and displeasure thou shouldest bear me. Indeed the name only remaineth with me; for the rest, the envy and cruelty of the people of Rome have taken from me, by the sufferance of the dastardly nobility and magistrates, who have forsaken me, and let me be banished by the people. This extremity hath now driven me to come as a poor suitor, to take thy chimney-hearth, not of any hope I have to save my life thereby. For if I had feared death, I would not have come hither to put myself in hazard; but pricked forward with desire to be revenged of them that thus have banished me, which now I do begin, in putting my person into the hands of their enemies. Wherefore if thou hast any heart to be wrecked of the injuries thy enemies have done thee, speed thee now, and let my misery serve thy turn, and so use it as my service may be a benefit to the Volsces: promising thee, that I will fight with better good will for all you, than I did when I was against you. Knowing that they fight more valiantly who know the force of the enemy, than such as have never proved it. And if it be so that thou dare not, and that thou art weary to prove fortune any more, then am I also weary to live any longer. And it were no wisdom in thee to save the life of him who hath been heretofore thy mortal enemy, and whose service now can nothing help, nor. pleasure thee.' Tullus hearing what he said, was a marvellous glad man, and taking him by the hand, he said unto him: 'Stand up, O Martius, and be of good cheer, for in proffering thyself unto us, thou doest us great honour: and by this means thou mayest hope also of greater things at all the Volsces' hands.' So he feasted him for that time, and entertained him in the honourablest manner he could, talking with him of no other matter at that present: but within few days after, they fell to consultation together in what sort they should begin their wars.

The meeting between Coriolanus and his mother is also nearly the same as in the play.

Now was Martius set then in the chair of state, with all the honours of a general, and when he had spied the women coming afar off, he marvelled what the matter meant: but afterwards knowing his wife which came foremost, he determined at the first to persist in his obstinate and inflexible rancour. But overcome in the end with natural affection, and being altogether altered to see them, his heart would not serve him to tarry their coining to his chair, but coming down in haste, he went to meet them, and first he kissed his mother, and embraced her a pretty while, then his wife and little children. And nature so wrought with him, that the tears fell from his eyes, and he could not keep himself from making much of them, but yielded to the affection of his blood, as if he had been violently carried with the fury of a most swift-running stream. After he had thus lovingly received them, and perceiving that his mother Volumnia would begin to speak to him, he called the chiefest of the council of the Volsces to hear what she would say. Then she spake in this sort: 'If we held our peace, my son, and determined not to speak, the state of our poor bodies, and present sight of our raiment, would easily betray to thee what life we have led at home, since thy exile and abode abroad; but think now with thyself, how much more unfortunate than all the women living, we are come hither, considering that the sight which should be most pleasant to all others to behold, spiteful fortune had made most fearful to us: making myself to see my son, and my daughter here her husband, besieging the walls of his native country: so as that which is the only comfort to all others in their adversity and misery, to pray unto the Gods, and to call to them for aid, is the only thing which plungeth us into most deep perplexity. For we cannot, alas, together pray, both for victory to our country, and for safety of thy life also: but a world of grievous curses, yea more than any mortal enemy can heap upon us, are forcibly wrapped up in our prayers. For the bitter sop of most hard choice is offered thy wife and children, to forgo one of the two; either to lose the person of thyself, or the nurse of their native country. For myself, my son, I am determined not to tarry till fortune in my lifetime do make an end of this war. For if I cannot persuade the rather to do good unto both parties, than to overthrow and destroy the one, preferring love and nature before the malice and calamity of wars, thou shalt see, my son, and trust unto it, thou shalt no sooner march forward to assault thy country, but thy foot shall tread upon thy mother's womb, that brought thee first into this world. And I may not defer to see the day, either that my son be led prisoner in triumph by his natural countrymen, or that he himself do triumph of them, and of his natural country. For if it were so, that my request tended to save thy country, in destroying the Volsces, I must confess, thou wouldest hardly and doubtfully resolve on that. For as to destroy thy natural country, it is altogether unmeet and unlawful, so were it not just and less honourable to betray those that put their trust in thee. But my only demand consisteth, to make a gaol delivery of all evils, which delivereth equal benefit and safety, both to the one and the other, but most honourable for the Volsces. For it shall appear, that having victory in their hands, they have of special favour granted us singular graces, peace and amity, albeit themselves have no less part of both than we. Of which good, if so it came to pass, thyself is the only author, and so hast thou the only honour. But if it fail, and fall out contrary, thyself alone deservedly shalt carry the shameful reproach and burthen of either party. So, though the end of war be uncertain, yet this notwithstanding is most certain, that if it be thy chance to conquer, this benefit shalt thou reap of thy goodly conquest, to be chronicled the plague and destroyer of thy country. And if fortune overthrow thee, then the world will say, that through desire to, revenge thy private injuries, thou hast for ever undone thy

50

good friends, who did most lovingly and courteously receive thee.' Martius gave good ear unto his mother's words, without interrupting her speech at all, and after she had said what she would, he held his peace a pretty while, and answered not a word. Hereupon she began again to speak unto him, and said; 'My son, why dost thou not answer me? Dost thou think it good altogether to give place unto thy choler and desire of revenge, and thinkest thou it not honesty for thee to grant thy mother's request in so weighty a cause? Dost thou take it honourable for a nobleman, to remember the wrongs and injuries done him, and dost not in like case think it an honest nobleman's part to be thankful for the goodness that parents do show to their children, acknowledging the duty and reverence they ought to bear unto them? No man living is more bound to show himself thankful in all parts and respects than thyself; who so universally showest all ingratitude. Moreover, my son, thou hast sorely taken of thy country, exacting grievous payments upon them, in revenge of the injuries offered thee; besides, thou hast not hitherto showed thy poor mother any courtesy. And therefore it is not only honest, but due unto me, that without compulsion I should obtain my so just and reasonable request of thee. But since by reason I cannot persuade thee to it, to what purpose do I defer my last hope?' And with these words herself, his wife and children, fell down upon their knees before him: Martius seeing that, could refrain no longer, but went straight and lifted her up, crying out, 'Oh mother, what have you done to me?' And holding her hard by the right hand, 'Oh mother,' said he, 'you have won a happy victory for your country, but mortal and unhappy for your son: for I see myself vanquished by you alone.' These words being spoken openly, he spake a little apart with his mother and wife, and then let them return again to Rome, for so they did request him; and so remaining in the camp that night, the next morning he dis-lodged, and marched homeward unto the Volsces' country again.

Shakespeare has, in giving a dramatic form to this passage, adhered very closely and properly to the text. He did not think it necessary to improve upon the truth of nature. Several of the scenes in JULIUS CAESAR, particularly Portia's appeal to the confidence of her husband by showing him the wound she had given herself, and the appearance of the ghost of Caesar to Brutus, are, in like manner, taken from the history.

TROILUS AND CRESSIDA

This is one of the most loose and desultory of our author's plays: it rambles on just as it happens, but it overtakes, together with some indifferent matter, a prodigious number of fine things in its way. Troilus himself is no character: he is merely a common lover; but Cressida and her uncle Pandarus are hit off with proverbial truth. By the speeches given to the leaders of the Grecian host, Nestor, Ulysses, Agamemnon, Achilles, Shakespeare seems to have known them as well as if he had been a spy sent by the Trojans into the enemy's camp—to say nothing of their being very lofty examples of didactic eloquence. The following is a very stately and spirited declamation:

Ulysses. Troy, yet upon her basis, had been down,
  And the great Hector's sword had lack'd a master,
  But for these instances.
  The specialty of rule hath been neglected.

  The heavens themselves, the planets, and this centre,
  Observe degree, priority, and place,
  Insisture, course, proportion, season, form,
  Office, and custom, in all line of order:
  And therefore is the glorious planet, Sol,
  In noble eminence, enthron'd and spher'd
  Amidst the other, whose med'cinable eye
  Corrects the ill aspects of planets evil,
  And posts, like the commandment of a king,
  Sans check, to good and bad. But, when the planets,
  In evil mixture to disorder wander,
  What plagues and what portents? what mutinies?
  What raging of the sea? shaking of earth?
  Commotion in the winds? frights, changes, horrors,
  Divert and crack, rend and deracinate
  The unity and married calm of states
  Quite from their fixture! O, when degree is shaken,
  (Which is the ladder to all high designs)
  The enterprise is sick! How could communities,
  Degrees in schools, and brotherhoods in cities,
  Peaceful commerce from dividable shores,
  The primogenitive and due of birth,
  Prerogative of age, crowns, sceptres, laurels,
  (But by degree) stand in authentic place?
  Take but degree away, untune that string,
  And hark what discord follows! each thing meets
  In mere oppugnancy. The bounded waters
  Would lift their bosoms higher than the shores,
  And make a sop of all this solid globe:
  Strength would be lord of imbecility,

And the rude son would strike his father dead:
Force would be right; or rather, right and wrong
(Between whose endless jar Justice resides)
Would lose their names, and so would Justice too.
Then everything includes itself in power,
Power into will, will into appetite;
And appetite (an universal wolf,
So doubly seconded with will and power)
Must make perforce an universal prey,
And last, eat up himself. Great Agamemnon,
This chaos, when degree is suffocate,
Follows the choking:
And this neglection of degree it is,
That by a pace goes backward, in a purpose
It hath to climb. The general's disdained
By him one step below; he, by the next;
That next, by him beneath: so every step,
Exampled by the first pace that is sick
Of his superior, grows to an envious fever
Of pale and bloodless emulation;
And 'tis this fever that keeps Troy on foot,
Not her own sinews. To end a tale of length,
Troy in our weakness lives, not in her strength.

It cannot be said of Shakespeare, as was said of some one, that he was 'without o'erflowing full'. He was full, even to o'erflowing. He gave heaped measure, running over. This was his greatest fault. He was only in danger 'of losing distinction in his thoughts' (to borrow his own expression)

As doth a battle when they charge on heaps
The enemy flying.

There is another passage, the speech of Ulysses to Achilles, showing him the thankless nature of popularity, which has a still greater depth of moral observation and richness of illustration than the former. It is long, but worth the quoting. The sometimes giving an entire extract from the unacted plays of our author may with one class of readers have almost the use of restoring a lost passage; and may serve to convince another class of critics, that the poet's genius was not confined to the production of stage effect by preternatural means.—

Ulysses. Time hath, my lord, a wallet at his back,
Wherein he puts alms for Oblivion;
A great-siz'd monster of ingratitudes:
Those scraps are good deeds past,
Which are devour'd as fast as they are made,
Forgot as soon as done: Persev'rance, dear my lord,
Keeps Honour bright: to have done, is to hang

Quite out of fashion, like a rusty mail
In monumental mockery. Take the instant way;
For Honour travels in a strait so narrow,
Where one but goes abreast; keep then the path,
For Emulation hath a thousand sons,
That one by one pursue; if you give way,
Or hedge aside from the direct forth-right,
Like to an entered tide, they all rush by,
And leave you hindmost;—
Or, like a gallant horse fall'n in first rank,
O'er-run and trampled on: then what they do in present,
Tho' less than yours in past, must o'ertop yours:
For Time is like a fashionable host,
That slightly shakes his parting guest by th' hand,
And with his arms out-stretch'd, as he would fly,
Grasps in the comer: the Welcome ever smiles,
And Farewell goes out sighing. O, let not virtue seek
Remuneration for the thing it was; for beauty, wit,
High birth, vigour of bone, desert in service,
Love, friendship, charity, are subjects all
To envious and calumniating time:
One touch of nature makes the whole world kin,
That all, with one consent, praise new-born gauds,
Tho' they are made and moulded of things past.
The present eye praises the present object.
Then marvel not, thou great and complete man,
That all the Greeks begin to worship Ajax;
Since things in motion sooner catch the eye,
Than what not stirs. The cry went out on thee,
And still it might, and yet it may again,
If thou would'st not entomb thyself alive,
And case thy reputation in thy tent.—

The throng of images in the above lines is prodigious; and though they sometimes jostle against one another, they everywhere raise and carry on the feeling, which is metaphysically true and profound. The debates beween the Trojan chiefs on the restoring of Helen are full of knowledge of human motives and character. Troilus enters well into the philosophy of war, when he says in answer to something that falls from Hector:

Why there you touch'd the life of our design:
Were it not glory that we more affected,
Than the performance of our heaving spleens,
I would not wish a drop of Trojan blood
Spent more in her defence. But, worthy Hector,
She is a theme of honour and renown,
A spur to valiant and magnanimous deeds.

The character of Hector, in the few slight indications which appear of it, is made very amiable. His death is sublime, and shows in a striking light the mixture of barbarity and heroism of the age. The threats of Achilles are fatal; they carry their own means of execution with them.

> Come here about me, you my Myrmidons,
> Mark what I say.—Attend me where I wheel:
> Strike not a stroke, but keep yourselves in breath;
> And when I have the bloody Hector found,
> Empale him with your weapons round about:
> In fellest manner execute your arms.
> Follow me, sirs, and my proceeding eye.

He then finds Hector and slays him, as if he had been hunting down a wild beast. There is something revolting as well as terrific in the ferocious coolness with which he singles out his prey: nor does the splendour of the achievement reconcile us to the cruelty of the means.

The characters of Cressida and Pandarus are very amusing and instructive. The disinterested willingness of Pandarus to serve his friend in an affair which lies next his heart is immediately brought forward. 'Go thy way, Troilus, go thy way; had I a sister were a grace, or a daughter were a goddess, he should take his choice. O admirable man! Paris, Paris is dirt to him, and I warrant Helen, to change, would give money to boot.' This is the language he addresses to his niece; nor is she much behindhand in coming into the plot. Her head is as light and fluttering as her heart. It is the prettiest villain, she fetches her breath so short as a new-ta'en sparrow.' Both characters are originals, and quite different from what they are in Chaucer. In Chaucer, Cressida is represented as a grave, sober, considerate personage (a widow—he cannot tell her age, nor whether she has children or no) who has an alternate eye to her character, her interest, and her pleasure: Shakespeare's Cressida is a giddy girl, an unpractised jilt, who falls in love with Troilus, as she afterwards deserts him, from mere levity and thoughtlessness of temper. She may be wooed and won to anything and from anything, at a moment's warning: the other knows very well what she would be at, and sticks to it, and is more governed by substantial reasons than by caprice or vanity. Pandarus again, in Chaucer's story, is a friendly sort of go-between, tolerably busy, officious, and forward in bringing matters to bear: but in Shakespeare he has 'a stamp exclusive and professional': he wears the badge of his trade; he is a regular knight of the game. The difference of the manner in which the subject is treated arises perhaps less from intention, than from the different genius of the two poets. There is no double entendre in the characters of Chaucer: they are either quite serious or quite comic. In Shakespeare the ludicrous and ironical are constantly blended with the stately and the impassioned. We see Chaucer's characters as they saw themselves, not as they appeared to others or might have appeared to the poet. He is as deeply implicated in the affairs of his personages as they could be themselves. He had to go a long journey with each of them, and became a kind of necessary confidant. There is little relief, or light and shade in his pictures. The conscious smile is not seen lurking under the brow of grief or impatience. Everything with him is intense and continuous—a working out of what went before.— Shakespeare never committed himself to his characters. He trifled, laughed, or wept with them as he chose. He has no prejudices for or against them; and it seems a matter of perfect indifference whether he shall be in jest or earnest. According to him, 'the web of our lives is of a mingled yam, good and ill together'. His genius was dramatic, as Chaucer's was historical. He saw both sides of a question, the different views taken of it according to the different interests of the parties concerned, and he was at once an actor and spectator in the scene. If anything, he is too various and flexible; too full of transitions, of glancing lights, of salient points. If Chaucer followed up his subject too doggedly, perhaps Shakespeare was too volatile and heedless. The Muse's wing too often lifted him off his feet. He made infinite excursions to the right and the left.

—He hath done
Mad and fantastic execution,
Engaging and redeeming of himself
With such a careless force and forceless care,
As if that luck in very spite of cunning
Bade him win all.

Chaucer attended chiefly to the real and natural, that is, to the involuntary and inevitable impressions on the mind in given circumstances: Shakespeare exhibited also the possible and the fantastical,—not only what things are in themselves, but whatever they might seem to be, their different reflections, their endless combinations. He lent his fancy, wit, invention, to others, and borrowed their feelings in return. Chaucer excelled in the force of habitual sentiment; Shakespeare added to it every variety of passion, every suggestion of thought or accident. Chaucer described external objects with the eye of a painter, or he might be said to have embodied them with the hand of a sculptor, every part is so thoroughly made out, and tangible: Shakespeare's imagination threw over them a lustre

—Prouder than when blue Iris bends.

Everything in Chaucer has a downright reality. A simile or a sentiment is as if it were given in upon evidence. In Shakespeare the commonest matter-of-fact has a romantic grace about it; or seems to float with the breath of imagination in a freer element. No one could have more depth of feeling or observation than Chaucer, but he wanted resources of invention to lay open the stores of nature or the human heart with the same radiant light that Shakespeare has done. However fine or profound the thought, we know what was coming, whereas the effect of reading Shakespeare is 'like the eye of vassalage encountering majesty'. Chaucer's mind was consecutive, rather than discursive. He arrived at truth through a certain process; Shakespeare saw everything by intuition, Chaucer had great variety of power, but he could do only one thing at once. He set himself to work on a particular subject. His ideas were kept separate, labelled, ticketed and parcelled out in a set form, in pews and compartments by themselves. They did not play into one another's hands. They did not re-act upon one another, as the blower's breath moulds the yielding glass. There is something hard and dry in them. What is the most wonderful thing in Shakespeare's faculties is their excessive sociability, and how they gossiped and compared notes together.

We must conclude this criticism; and we will do it with a quotation or two. One of the most beautiful passages in Chaucer's tale is the description of Cresseide's first avowal of her love:

And as the new abashed nightingale,
That stinteth first when she beginneth sing,
When that she heareth any herde's tale,

Or in the hedges any wight stirring,
And, after, sicker doth her voice outring;
Right so Cresseide, when that her dread stent,
Opened her heart, and told him her intent.

See also the two next stanzas, and particularly that divine one beginning

Her armes small, her back both straight and soft, &c.

Compare this with the following speech of Troilus to Cressida in the play.

O, that I thought it could be in a woman;
And if it can, I will presume in you,
To feed for aye her lamp and flame of love,
To keep her constancy in plight and youth,
Out-living beauties outward, with a mind
That doth renew swifter than blood decays.
Or, that persuasion could but thus convince me,
That my integrity and truth to you
Might be affronted with the match and weight
Of such a winnow'd purity in love;
How were I then uplifted! But alas,
I am as true as Truth's simplicity,
And simpler than the infancy of Truth.

These passages may not seem very characteristic at first sight, though we think they are so. We will give two, that cannot be mistaken. Patroclus says to Achilles;

—Rouse yourself; and the weak wanton Cupid
Shall from your neck unloose his amorous fold,
And like a dew-drop from the lion's mane,
Be shook to air.

Troilus, addressing the God of Day on the approach of the morning that parts him from Cressida, says with much scorn:

What! proffer'st thou thy light here for to sell?
Go, sell it them that smalle seles grave.

If nobody but Shakespeare could have written the former, nobody but Chaucer would have thought of the latter.—Chaucer was the most literal of poets, as Richardson was of prose-writers.

ANTONY AND CLEOPATRA

This is a very noble play. Though not in the first class of Shakespeare's productions, it stands next to them, and is, we think, the finest of his historical plays, that is, of those in which he made poetry the organ of history, and assumed a certain tone of character and sentiment, in conformity to known facts, instead of trusting to his observations of general nature or to the unlimited indulgence of his own fancy. What he has added to the history, is upon a par with it. His genius was, as it were, a match for history as well as nature, and could grapple at will with either. This play is full of that pervading comprehensive power by which the poet could always make himself master of time and circumstances. It presents a fine picture of Roman pride and Eastern magnificence: and in the struggle between the two, the empire of the world seems suspended, 'like the swan's down-feather:

> That stands upon the swell at full of tide,
> And neither way inclines.'

The characters breathe, move, and live. Shakespeare does not stand reasoning on what his characters would do or say, but at once BECOMES them, and speaks and acts for them. He does not present us with groups of stage-puppets or poetical machines making set speeches on human life, and acting from a calculation of ostensible motives, but he brings living men and women on the scene, who speak and act from real feelings, according to the ebbs and flows of passion, without the least tincture of the pedantry of logic or rhetoric. Nothing is made out by inference and analogy, by climax and antithesis, but everything takes place just as it would have done in reality, according to the occasion.—The character of Cleopatra is a masterpiece. What an extreme contrast it affords to Imogen! One would think it almost impossible for the same person to have drawn both. She is voluptuous, ostentatious, conscious, boastful of her charms, haughty, tyrannical, fickle. The luxurious pomp and gorgeous extravagance of the Egyptian queen are displayed in all their force and lustre, as well as the irregular grandeur of the soul of Mark Antony. Take only the first four lines that they speak as an example of the regal style of love-making.

Cleopatra. If it be love, indeed, tell me how much?

Antony. There's beggary in the love that can be reckon'd.

Cleopatra. I'll set a bourn how far to be belov'd.

Antony. Then must thou needs find out new heav'n, new earth.

The rich and poetical description of her person, beginning:

> The barge she sat in, like a burnish'd throne,
> Burnt on the water; the poop was beaten gold,
> Purple the sails, and so perfumed, that
> The winds were love-sick—

seems to prepare the way for, and almost to justify the subsequent infatuation of Antony when in the sea-fight at Actium, he leaves the battle, and 'like a doting mallard' follows her flying sails.

Few things in Shakespeare (and we know of nothing in any other author like them) have more of that local truth of imagination and character than the passage in which Cleopatra is represented conjecturing what were the employments of Antony in his absence. 'He's speaking now, or murmuring—WHERE'S MY SERPENT OF OLD NILE?' Or again, when she says to Antony, after the defeat at Actium, and his summoning up resolution to risk another fight—'It is my birthday; I had thought to have held it poor; but since my lord is Antony again, I will be Cleopatra.' Perhaps the finest burst of all is Antony's rage after his final defeat when he comes in, and surprises the messenger of Caesar kissing her hand:

> To let a fellow that will take rewards,
> And say, God quit you, be familiar with
> My play-fellow, your hand; this kingly seal,
> And plighter of high hearts.

It is no wonder that he orders him to be whipped; but his low condition is not the true reason: there is another feeling which lies deeper, though Antony's pride would not let him show it, except by his rage; he suspects the fellow to be Caesar's proxy.

Cleopatra's whole character is the triumph of the voluptuous, of the love of pleasure and the power of giving it, over every other consideration. Octavia is a dull foil to her, and Fulvia a shrew and shrill-tongued. What a picture do those lines give of her:

> Age cannot wither her, nor custom stale
> Her infinite variety. Other women cloy
> The appetites they feed, but she makes hungry
> Where most she satisfies.

What a spirit and fire in her conversation with Antony's messenger who brings her the unwelcome news of his marriage with Octavia! How all the pride of beauty and of high rank breaks out in her promised reward to him:

> —There's gold, and here
> My bluest veins to kiss!

She had great and unpardonable faults, but the beauty of her death almost redeems them. She learns from the depth of despair the strength of her affections. She keeps her queen-like state in the last disgrace, and her sense of the pleasurable in the last moments of her life. She tastes a luxury in death. After applying the asp, she says with fondness:

> Dost thou not see my baby at my breast,
> That sucks the nurse asleep?
> As sweet as balm, as soft as air, as gentle.
> Oh Antony!

It is worth while to observe that Shakespeare has contrasted the extreme magnificence of the descriptions in this play with pictures of extreme suffering and physical horror, not less striking—partly perhaps to excuse the effeminacy of Mark Antony to whom they are related as having happened, but more to preserve a certain balance of feeling in the mind. Caesar says, hearing of his conduct at the court of Cleopatra:

> —Antony,
> Leave thy lascivious wassails. When thou once
> Wert beaten from Mutina, where thou slew'st
> Hirtius and Pansa, consuls, at thy heel
> Did famine follow, whom thou fought'st against,
> Though daintily brought up, with patience more
> Than savages could suffer. Thou did'st drink
> The stale of horses, and the gilded puddle
> Which beast would cough at. Thy palate then did deign
> The roughest berry on the rudest hedge,
> Yea, like the stag, when snow the pasture sheets,
> The barks of trees thou browsed'st. On the Alps,
> It is reported, thou did'st eat strange flesh,
> Which some did die to look on: and all this,
> It wounds thine honour, that I speak it now,
> Was borne so like a soldier, that thy cheek
> So much as lank'd not.

The passage after Antony's defeat by Augustus where he is made to say:

> Yes, yes; he at Philippi kept
> His sword e'en like a dancer; while I struck
> The lean and wrinkled Cassius, and 'twas I
> That the mad Brutus ended,

is one of those fine retrospections which show us the winding and eventful march of human life. The jealous attention which has been paid to the unities both of time and place has taken away the principle of perspective in the drama, and all the interest which objects derive from distance, from contrast, from privation, from change of fortune, from long-cherished passion; and contracts our view of life from a strange and romantic dream, long, obscure, and infinite, into a smartly contested, three hours' inaugural disputation on its merits by the different candidates for theatrical applause.

The latter scenes of ANTONY AND CLEOPATRA are full of the changes of accident and passion. Success and defeat follow one another with startling rapidity. For-tune sits upon her wheel more blind and giddy than usual. This precarious state and the approaching dissolution of his greatness are strikingly displayed in the dialogue between Antony and Eros:

Antony. Eros, thou yet behold'st me?

Eros. Ay, noble lord.

60

Antony. Sometime we see a cloud that's dragonish,
  A vapour sometime, like a bear or lion,
  A towered citadel, a pendant rock,
  A forked mountain, or blue promontory
  With trees upon't, that nod unto the world
  And mock our eyes with air. Thou hast seen these signs,
  They are black vesper's pageants.

Eros. Ay, my lord.

  Antony. That which is now a horse, even with a thought
  The rack dislimns, and makes it indistinct
  As water is in water.

Eros. It does, my lord.

  Antony. My good knave, Eros, now thy captain is
  Even such a body, &c.

This is, without doubt, one of the finest pieces of poetry in Shakespeare. The splendour of the imagery, the semblance of reality, the lofty range of picturesque objects hanging over the world, their evanescent nature, the total uncertainty of what is left behind, are ' just like the mouldering schemes of human greatness. It is finer than Cleopatra's passionate lamentation over his fallen grandeur, because it is more dim, unstable, unsubstantial. Antony's headstrong presumption and infatuated determination to yield to Cleopatra's wishes to fight by sea instead of land, meet a merited punishment; and the extravagance of his resolutions, increasing with the desperateness of his circumstances, is well commented upon by Enobarbus:

  —I see men's judgements are
  A parcel of their fortunes, and things outward
  Do draw the inward quality after them
  To suffer all alike.

The repentance of Enobarbus after his treachery to his master is the most affecting part of the play. He cannot recover from the blow which Antony's generosity gives him, and he dies broken-hearted 'a master-leaver and a fugitive'.

Shakespeare's genius has spread over the whole play a richness like the overflowing of the Nile.

HAMLET

This is that Hamlet the Dane, whom we read of in our youth, and whom we seem almost to remember in our after-years; he who made that famous soliloquy on life, who gave the advice to the players, who thought 'this goodly frame, the earth, a sterile promontory, and this brave o'er-hanging firmament, the air, this majestical roof fretted with golden fire, a foul and pestilent congregation of vapours'; whom 'man delighted not, nor woman neither'; he who talked with the grave-diggers, and moralized on Yorick's skull; the schoolfellow of Rosencraus and Guildenstern at Wittenberg; the friend of Horatio; the lover of Ophelia; he that was mad and sent to England; the slow avenger of his father's death; who lived at the court of Horwendillus five hundred years before we were born, but all whose thoughts we seem to know as well as we do our own, because we have read them in Shakespeare.

Hamlet is a name: his speeches and sayings but the idle coinage of the poet's brain. What then, are they not real? They are as real as our own thoughts. Their reality is in the reader's mind. It is WE who are Hamlet. This play has a prophetic truth, which is above that of history. Whoever has become thoughtful and melancholy through his own mishaps or those of others; whoever has borne about with him the clouded brow of reflection, and thought himself 'too much i' th' sun'; whoever has seen the golden lamp of day dimmed by envious mists rising in his own breast, and could find in the world before him only a dull blank with nothing left remarkable in it; whoever has known "the pangs of despised love, the insolence of office, or the spurns which patient merit of the unworthy takes"; he who has felt his mind sink within him, and sadness cling to his heart like a malady, who has had his hopes blighted and his youth staggered by the apparitions of strange things; who cannot be well at ease, while he sees evil hovering near him like a spectre; whose powers of action have been eaten up by thought, he to whom the universe seems infinite, and himself nothing; whose bitterness of soul makes him careless of consequences, and who goes to a play as his best resource to shove off, to a second remove, the evils of life by a mock-presentation of them—this is the true Hamlet.

We have been so used to this tragedy that we hardly know how to criticize it any more than we should know how to describe our own faces. But we must make such observations as we can. It is the one of Shakespeare's plays that we think of oftenest, because it abounds most in striking reflections on human life, and because the distresses of Hamlet are transferred, by the turn of his mind, to the general account of humanity. Whatever happens to him, we apply to ourselves, because he applies it so himself as a means of general reasoning. He is a great moralizer; and what makes him worth attending to is, that he moralizes on his own feelings and experience. He is not a commonplace pedant. If Lear shows the greatest depth of passion, Hamlet is the most remarkable for the ingenuity, originality, and unstudied development of character. Shakespeare had more magnanimity than any other poet, and he has shown more of it in this play than in any other. There is no attempt to force an interest: everything is left for time and circumstances to unfold. The attention is excited without effort, the incidents succeed each other as matters of course, the characters think and speak and act just as they might do, if left entirely to themselves. There is no set purpose, no straining at a point. The observations are suggested by the passing scene—the gusts of passion come and go like sounds of music borne on the wind. The whole play is an exact transcript of what might be supposed to have taken place at the court of Denmark, at the remote period of time fixed upon, before the modern refinements in morals and manners were heard of. It would have been interesting enough to have been admitted as a bystander in such a scene, at such a time, to have heard and seen something of what was going on. But here we are more than spectators. We have not only 'the outward pageants and the signs of grief; but 'we have that within which passes show'. We read the thoughts of the heart, we catch the passions living as they rise. Other dramatic writers give us very fine versions and paraphrases of nature: but Shakespeare, together with his own comments, gives us the original text, that we may judge for ourselves. This is a very great advantage.

The character of Hamlet is itself a pure effusion of genius. It is not a character marked by strength of will or even of passion, but by refinement of thought and sentiment. Hamlet is as little of the hero as a man can well be: but he is a young and princely novice, full of high enthusiasm and quick sensibility—the sport of circumstances, questioning with fortune and refining on his own feelings, and forced from the natural bias of his disposition by the strangeness of his situation. He seems incapable of deliberate action, and is only hurried into extremities on the spur of the occasion, when he has no time to reflect, as in the scene where he kills Polonius, and again, where he alters the letters which Rosencraus and Guildenstern are taking with them to England, purporting his death. At other times, when he is most bound to act, he remains puzzled, undecided, and sceptical, dallies with his purposes, till the occasion is lost, and always finds some pretence to relapse into indolence and thoughtfulness again. For this reason he refuses to kill the King when he is at his prayers, and by a refinement in malice, which is in truth only an excuse for his own want of resolution, defers his revenge to some more fatal opportunity, when he shall be engaged in some act 'that has no relish of salvation in it':

> He kneels and prays,
> And now I'll do't, and so he goes to heaven,
> And so am I reveng'd; THAT WOULD BE SCANN'D.
> He kill'd my father, and for that,
> I, his sole son, send him to heaven.
> Why this is reward, not revenge.
> Up sword and know thou a more horrid time,
> When he is drunk, asleep, or in a rage.

He is the prince of philosophical speculators, and because he cannot have his revenge perfect, according to the most refined idea his wish can form, he misses it altogether. So he scruples to trust the suggestions of the Ghost, contrives the scene of the play to have surer proof of his uncle's guilt, and then rests satisfied with this confirmation of his suspicions, and the success of his experiment, instead of acting upon it. Yet he is sensible of his own weakness, taxes himself with it, and tries to reason himself out of it:

> How all occasions do inform against me,
> And spur my dull revenge! What is a man,
> If his chief good and market of his time
> Be but to sleep and feed? A beast; no more.
> Sure he that made us with such large discourse,
> Looking before and after, gave us not
> That capability and god-like reason

To rust in us unus'd: now whether it be
Bestial oblivion, or some craven scruple
Of thinking too precisely on th' event,—
A thought which quarter'd, hath but one part wisdom,
And ever three parts coward;—I do not know
Why yet I live to say, this thing's to do;
Sith I have cause, and will, and strength, and means
To do it. Examples gross as earth excite me:
Witness this army of such mass and charge,
Led by a delicate and tender prince,
Whose spirit with divine ambition puff'd,
Makes mouths at the invisible event,
Exposing what is mortal and unsure
To all that fortune, death, and danger dare,
Even for an egg-shell. 'Tis not to be great,
Never to stir without great argument;
But greatly to find quarrel in a straw,
When honour's at the stake. How stand I then,
That have a father kill'd, a mother stain'd,
Excitements of my reason and my blood,
And let all sleep, while to my shame I see
The imminent death of twenty thousand men,
That for a fantasy and trick of fame,
Go to their graves like beds, fight for a plot
Whereon the numbers cannot try the cause,
Which is not tomb enough and continent
To hide the slain?—O, from this time forth,
My thoughts be bloody or be nothing worth.

Still he does nothing; and this very speculation on his own infirmity only affords him another occasion for indulging it. It is not for any want of attachment to his father or abhorrence of his murder that Hamlet is thus dilatory, but it is more to his taste to indulge his imagination in reflecting upon the enormity of the crime and refining on his schemes of vengeance, than to put them into immediate practice. His ruling passion is to think, not to act: and any vague pretence that flatters this propensity instantly diverts him from his previous purposes.

The moral perfection of this character has been called in question, we think, by those who did not understand it. It is more interesting than according to rules: amiable, though not faultless. The ethical delineations of 'that noble and liberal casuist' (as Shakespeare has been well called) do not exhibit the drab-coloured quakerism of morality. His plays are not copied either from The Whole Duty of Man, or from The Academy of Compliments! We confess, we are a little shocked at the want of refinement in those who are shocked at the want of refinement in Hamlet. The want of punctilious exactness in his behaviour either partakes of the 'license of the time', or else belongs to the very excess of intellectual refinement in the character, which makes the common rules of life, as well as his own purposes, sit loose upon him. He may be said to be amenable only to the tribunal of his own thoughts, and is too much taken up with the airy world of contemplation to lay as much stress as he ought on the practical consequences of things. His habitual principles of action are unhinged and out of joint with the time. His conduct to Ophelia is quite natural in his circumstances. It is that of assumed severity only. It is the effect of disappointed hope, of bitter regrets, of affection suspended, not obliterated, by the distractions of the scene around him! Amidst the natural and preternatural horrors of his situation, he might be excused in delicacy from carrying on a regular courtship. When 'his father's spirit was in arms', it was not a time for the son to make love in. He could neither marry Ophelia, nor wound her mind by explaining the cause of his alienation, which he durst hardly trust himself to think of. It would have taken him years to have come to a direct explanation on the point. In the harassed state of his mind, he could not have done otherwise than he did. His conduct does not contradict what he says when he sees her funeral:

> I loved Ophelia: forty thousand brothers
> Could not with all their quantity of love
> Make up my sum.

Nothing can be more affecting or beautiful than the Queen's apostrophe to Ophelia on throwing flowers into the grave:

> —Sweets to the sweet, farewell.
> I hop'd thou should'st have been my Hamlet's wife:
> I thought thy bride-bed to have deck'd, sweet maid,
> And not have strew'd thy grave.

Shakespeare was thoroughly a master of the mixed motives of human character, and he here shows us the Queen, who was so criminal in some respects, not without sensibility and affection in other relations of life.—Ophelia is a character almost too exquisitely touching to be dwelt upon. Oh rose of May, oh flower too soon faded! Her love, her madness, her death, are described with the truest touches of tenderness and pathos. It is a character which nobody but Shakespeare could have drawn in the way that he has done, and to the conception of which there is not even the smallest approach, except in some of the old romantic ballads. Her brother, Laertes, is a character we do not like so well; he is too hot and choleric, and somewhat rodomontade. Polonius is a perfect character in its kind; nor is there any foundation for the objections which have been made to the consistency of this part. It is said that he acts very foolishly and talks very sensibly. There is no inconsistency in that. Again, that he talks wisely at one time and foolishly at another; that his advice to Laertes is very sensible, and his advice to the King and Queen on the subject of Hamlet's madness very ridiculous. But he gives the one as a father, and is sincere in it; he gives the other as a mere courtier, a busy-body, and is accordingly officious, garrulous, and impertinent. In short, Shakespeare has been accused of inconsistency in this and other characters, only because he has kept up the distinction which there is in nature, between the understandings and the moral habits of men, between the absurdity of their ideas and the absurdity of their motives. Polonius is not a fool, but he makes himself so. His folly, whether in his actions or speeches, comes under the head of impropriety of intention.

We do not like to see our author's plays acted, and least of all, Hamlet. There is no play that suffers so much in being transferred to the stage. Hamlet himself seems hardly capable of being acted. Mr. Kemble unavoidably fails in this character from a want of ease and variety. The character of Hamlet is made up of undulating lines; it has the yielding flexibility of 'a wave o' th' sea'. Mr. Kemble plays it like a man in armour, with a determined inveteracy of purpose, in one undeviating straight line, which is as remote from the natural grace and refined susceptibility of the character as the sharp angles and abrupt starts which Mr. Kean introduces into the part. Mr. Kean's Hamlet is as much too splenetic and rash as Mr. Kemble's is too deliberate and formal. His manner is too strong and pointed. He throws a severity, approaching to virulence into the common observations and answers. There is nothing of this in Hamlet. He is, as it were, wrapped up in his reflections, and only THINKS ALOUD. There should therefore be no attempt to impress what he says upon others by a studied exaggeration of emphasis or manner; no TALKING AT his hearers. There should be as much of the gentleman and scholar as possible infused into the part, and as little of the actor, A pensive air of sadness should sit reluctantly upon his brow, but no appearance of fixed and sullen gloom. He is full of weakness and melancholy, but there is no harshness in his nature. He is the most amiable of misanthropes.

THE TEMPEST.

There can be little doubt that Shakespeare was the most universal genius that ever lived. 'Either for tragedy, comedy, history, pastoral, pastoral-comical, historical-pastoral, scene individable or poem unlimited, he is the only man. Seneca cannot be too heavy, nor Plautus too light for him.' He has not only the same absolute command over our laughter and our tears, all the resources of passion, of wit, of thought, of observation, but he has the most unbounded range of fanciful invention, whether terrible or playful, the same insight into the world of imagination that he has into the world of reality; and over all there presides the same truth of character and nature, and the same spirit of humanity. His ideal beings are as true and natural as his real characters; that is, as consistent with themselves, or if we suppose such beings to exist at all, they could not act, speak, or feel otherwise than as he makes them. He has invented for them a language, manners, and sentiments of their own, from the tremendous imprecations of the Witches in MACBETH, when they do 'a deed without a name', to the sylph-like expressions 'of Ariel, who 'does his spiriting gently'; the mischievous tricks and gossiping of Robin Goodfellow, or the uncouth gabbling and emphatic gesticulations of Caliban in this play.

THE TEMPEST is one of the most original and perfect of Shakespeare's productions, and he has shown in it all the variety of his powers. It is full of grace and grandeur. The human and imaginary characters, the dramatic and the grotesque, are blended together with the greatest art, and without any appearance of it. Though he has here given 'to airy nothing a local habitation and a name', yet that part which is only the fantastic creation of his mind, has the same palpable texture, and coheres 'semblably' with the rest. As the preternatural part has the air of reality, and almost haunts the imagination with a sense of truth, the real characters and events partake of the wildness of a dream. The stately magician, Prospero, driven from his dukedom, but around whom (so potent is his art) airy spirits throng numberless to do his bidding; his daughter Miranda ('worthy of that name') to whom all the power of his art points, and who seems the goddess of the isle; the princely Ferdinand, cast by fate upon the haven of his happiness in this idol of his love; the delicate Ariel; the savage Caliban, half brute, half demon; the drunken ship's crew—are all connected parts of the story, and can hardly be spared from the place they fill. Even the local scenery is of a piece and character with the subject. Prospero's enchanted island seems to have risen up out of the sea; the airy music, the tempest-tossed vessel, the turbulent waves, all have the effect of the landscape background of some fine picture. Shakespeare's pencil is (to use an allusion of his own) 'like the dyer's hand, subdued to what it works in'. Everything in him, though it partakes of 'the liberty of wit', is also subjected to 'the law' of the understanding. For instance, even the drunken sailors, who are made reeling-ripe, share, in the disorder of their minds and bodies, in the tumult of the elements, and seem on shore to be as much at the mercy of chance as they were before at the mercy of the winds and waves. These fellows with their sea-wit are the least to our taste of any part of the play: but they are as like drunken sailors as they can be, and are an indirect foil to Caliban, whose figure acquires a classical dignity in the comparison.

The character of Caliban is generally thought (and justly so) to be one of the author's masterpieces. It is not indeed pleasant to see this character on the stage any more than it is to see the God Pan personated there. But in itself it is one of the wildest and most abstracted of all Shakespeare's characters, whose deformity whether of body or mind is redeemed by the power and truth of the imagination displayed in it. It is the essence of grossness, but there is not a particle of vulgarity in it. Shakespeare has described the brutal mind of Caliban in contact with the pure and original forms of nature; the character grows out of the soil where it is rooted uncontrolled, uncouth and wild, uncramped by any of the meannesses of custom. It is 'of the earth, earthy'. It seems almost to have been dug out of the ground, with a soul instinctively superadded to it answering to its wants and origin. Vulgarity is not natural coarseness, but conventional coarseness, learnt from others, contrary to, or without an entire conformity of natural power and disposition; as fashion is the commonplace affectation of what is elegant and refined without any feeling of the essence of it. Schlegel, the admirable German critic on Shakespeare observes that Caliban is a poetical character, and 'always speaks in blank verse'. He first comes in thus:

> Caliban. As wicked dew as e'er my mother brush'd
>   With raven's feather from unwholesome fen,
>   Drop on you both: a south-west blow on ye,
>   And blister you all o'er!

> Prospero. For this, be sure, to-night thou shalt have cramps,
>   Side-stitches that shall pen thy breath up; urchins
>   Shall for that vast of night that they may work,
>   All exercise on thee: thou shalt be pinch'd
>   As thick as honey-combs, each pinch more stinging
>   Than bees that made 'em.

> Caliban. I must eat my dinner.
>   This island's mine by Sycorax my mother,
>   Which thou tak'st from me. When thou camest first,
>   Thou strok'dst me, and mad'st much of me; would'st give me
>   Water with berries in 't; and teach me how
>   To name the bigger light and how the less
>   That burn by day and night; and then I lov'd thee,
>   And show'd thee all the qualities o' th' isle,
>   The fresh springs, brine-pits, barren place and fertile:
>   Curs'd be I that I did so! All the charms
>   Of Sycorax, toads, beetles, bats, light on you!
>   For I am all the subjects that you have,
>   Who first was mine own king; and here you sty me
>   In this hard rock, whiles you do keep from me
>   The rest o' th' island.

And again, he promises Trinculo his services thus, if he will free him from his drudgery.

> I'll show thee the best springs; I'll pluck thee berries,
>   I'll fish for thee, and get thee wood enough.
>   I pr'ythee let me bring thee where crabs grow,
>   And I with my long nails will dig thee pig-nuts:

68

Show thee a jay's nest, and instruct thee how
To snare the nimble marmozet: I'll bring thee
To clust'ring filberds; and sometimes I'll get thee
Young scamels from the rock.

In conducting Stephano and Trinculo to Prospero's cell, Caliban shows the superiority of natural capacity over greater knowledge and greater folly; and in a former scene, when Ariel frightens them with his music, Caliban to encourage them accounts for it in the eloquent poetry of the senses:

Be not afraid, the isle is full of noises,
Sounds, and sweet airs, that give delight and hurt not.
Sometimes a thousand twanging instruments
Will hum about mine ears, and sometimes voices,
That if I then had waked after long sleep,
Would make me sleep again; and then in dreaming,
The clouds methought would open, and show riches
Ready to drop upon me: when I wak'd
I cried to dream again.

This is not more beautiful than it is true. The poet here shows us the savage with the simplicity of a child, and makes the strange monster amiable. Shakespeare had to paint the human animal rude and without choice in its pleasures, but not without the sense of pleasure or some germ of the affections. Master Barnardine in Measure for Measure, the savage of civilized life, is an admirable philosophical counterpart to Caliban.

Shakespeare has, as it were by design, drawn off from Caliban the elements of whatever is ethereal and refined, to compound them in the unearthly mould of Ariel. Nothing was ever more finely conceived than this contrast between the material and the spiritual, the gross and delicate. Ariel is imaginary power, the swiftness of thought personified. When told to make good speed by Prospero, he says, 'I drink the air before me.' This is something like Puck's boast on a similar occasion, 'I'll put a girdle round about the earth in forty minutes.' But Ariel differs from Puck in having a fellow-feeling in the interests of those he is employed about. How exquisite is the following dialogue between him and Prospero!

Ariel. Your charm so strongly works 'em,
    That if you now beheld them, your affections
  Would become tender.

Prospero. Dost thou think so, spirit?

Ariel. Mine would, sir, were I human.

Prospero. And mine shall.
  Hast thou, which art but air, a touch, a feeling
  Of their afflictions, and shall not myself,

One of their kind, that relish all as sharply,
Passion'd as they, be kindlier moved than thou art?

It has been observed that there is a peculiar charm in the songs introduced in Shakespeare, which, without conveying any distinct images, seem to recall all the feelings connected with them, like snatches of half-forgotten music heard indistinctly and at intervals. There is this effect produced by Ariel's songs, which (as we are told) seem to sound in the air, and as if the person playing them were invisible. We shall give one instance out of many of this general power.

Enter Ferdinend; and Ariel invisible, playing and singing.

Ariel's Song

> Come unto these yellow sands,
> And then take hands;
> Curt'sied when you have, and kiss'd,
> (The wild waves whist;)
> Foot it featly here and there;
> And sweet sprites the burden bear.
> [Burden dispersedly.]
> Hark, hark! bowgh-wowgh: the watch-dogs bark,
>   Bowgh-wowgh.

> Ariel. Hark, hark! I hear
>   The strain of strutting chanticleer
>   Cry cock-a-doodle-doo.

> Ferdinand. Where should this music be? in air or earth?
> It sounds no more: and sure it waits upon
> Some god o' th' island. Sitting on a bank
> Weeping against the king my father's wreck,
> This music crept by me upon the waters,
> Allaying both their fury and my passion
> With its sweet air; thence I have follow'd it,
> Or it hath drawn me rather:—but 'tis gone.—
> No, it begins again.

Ariel's Song

> Full fathom Eve thy father lies,
>   Of his bones are coral made:
> Those are pearls that were his eyes,
>   Nothing of him that doth fade,
> But doth suffer a sea change,
> Into something rich and strange.
> Sea-nymphs hourly ring his knell—

Hark! I now I hear them, ding-dong bell.
   [Burden ding-dong.]

 Ferdinand. The ditty does remember my drown'd father.
  This is no mortal business, nor no sound
  That the earth owns: I hear it now above me.

The courtship between Ferdinand and Miranda is one of the chief beauties of this play. It is the very purity of love. The pretended interference of Prospero with it heightens its interest, and is in character with the magician, whose sense of preternatural power makes him arbitrary, tetchy, and impatient of opposition.

The Tempest is a finer play than the Midsummer Night's Dream, which has sometimes been compared with it; but it is not so fine a poem. There are a greater number of beautiful passages in the latter. Two of the most striking in The Tempest are spoken by Prospero. The one is that admirable one when the vision which he has conjured up disappears, beginning, 'The cloud-capp'd towers, the gorgeous palaces,' &c., which has so often been quoted that every schoolboy knows it by heart; the other is that which Prospero makes in abjuring his art:

Ye elves of hills, brooks, standing lakes, and groves,
And ye that on the sands with printless foot
Do chase the ebbing Neptune, and do fly him
When he comes back; you demi-puppets, that
By moonshine do the green sour ringlets make,
Whereof the ewe not bites; and you whose pastime
Is to make midnight mushrooms, that rejoice
To hear the solemn curfew, by whose aid
(Weak masters tho' ye be) I have be-dimm'd
The noon-tide sun, call'd forth the mutinous winds,
And 'twixt the green sea and the azur'd vault
Set roaring war; to the dread rattling thunder
Have I giv'n fire, and rifted Jove's stout oak
With his own bolt; the strong-bas'd promontory
Have I made shake, and by the spurs pluck'd up
The pine and cedar: graves at my command
Have wak'd their sleepers; op'd, and let 'em forth
By my so potent art. But this rough magic
I here abjure; and when I have requir'd
Some heav'nly music, which ev'n now I do,
(To work mine end upon their senses that
This airy charm is for) I'll break my staff,
Bury it certain fadoms in the earth,
And deeper than did ever plummet sound,
I'll drown my book.

We must not forget to mention among other things in this play, that Shakespeare has anticipated nearly all the arguments on the Utopian schemes of modern philosophy:

Gonzalo. Had I the plantation of this isle, my lord—Antonio. He'd sow't with nettle-seed. Sebastian. Or docks or mallows. Gonzalo. And were the king on't, what would I do? Sebastian. 'Scape being drunk, for want of wine. Gonzalo. I' th' commonwealth I would by contraries Execute all things: for no kind of traffic Would I admit; no name of magistrate; Letters should not be known; wealth, poverty, And use of service, none; contract, succession, Bourn, bound of land, tilth, vineyard, none; No use of metal, corn, or wine, or oil; No occupation, all men idle, all, And women too; but innocent and pure: No sov'reignty. Sebastian. And yet he would be king on't. Antonio. The latter end of his commonwealth forgets the beginning. Gonzalo. All things in common nature should produce Without sweat or endeavour. Treason, felony, Sword, pike, knife, gun, or need of any engine Would I not have; but nature should bring forth, Of its own kind, all foison, all abundance To feed my innocent people! Sebastian. No marrying 'mong his subjects? Antonio. None, man; all idle; whores and knaves. Gonzalo. I would with such perfection govern, sir, T' excel the golden age. Sebastian. Save his majesty!

THE MIDSUMMER NIGHT'S DREAM

Bottom the Weaver is a character that has not had justice done him. He is the most romantic of mechanics. And what a list of companions he has—Quince the Carpenter, Snug the Joiner, Flute the Bellows- mender, Snout the Tinker, Starveling the Tailor; and then again, what a group of fairy attendants, Puck, Peaseblossom, Cobweb, Moth, and Mustard-seed! It has been observed that Shakespeare's characters are constructed upon deep physiological principles; and there is something in this play which looks very like it. Bottom the Weaver, who takes the lead of

> This crew of patches, rude mechanicals,
> That work for bread upon Athenian stalls,

follows a sedentary trade, and he is accordingly represented as conceited, serious, and fantastical. He is ready to undertake anything and everything, as if it was as much a matter of course as the motion of his loom and shuttle. He is for playing the tyrant, the lover, the lady, the lion. 'He will roar that it shall do any man's heart good to hear him'; and this being objected to as improper, he still has a resource in his good opinion of himself, and 'will roar you an 'twere any nightingale'. Snug the Joiner is the moral man of the piece, who proceeds by measurement and discretion in all things. You see him with his rule and compasses in his hand. 'Have you the lion's part written? Pray you, if it be, give it me, for I am slow of study.'—'You may do it extempore,' says Quince, 'for it is nothing but roaring.' Starveling the Tailor keeps the peace, and objects to the lion and the drawn sword. 'I believe we must leave the killing out when all's done.' Starveling, however, does not start the objections himself, but seconds them when made by others, as if he had not spirit to express his fears without encouragement. It is too much to suppose all this intentional; but it very luckily falls out so. Nature includes all that is implied in the most subtle analytical distinctions; and the same distinctions will be found in Shakespeare. Bottom, who is not only chief actor, but stage-manager for the occasion, has a device to obviate the danger of frightening the ladies: 'Write me a prologue, and let the prologue seem to say, we will do no harm with our swords, and that Pyramus is not killed indeed; and for better assurance, tell them that I, Pyramus, am not Pyramus, but Bottom the Weaver; this will put them out of fear.' Bottom seems to have understood the subject of dramatic illusion at least as well as any modern essayist. If our holiday mechanic rules the roast among his fellows, he is no less at home in his new character of an ass, 'with amiable cheeks, and fair large ears'. He instinctively acquires a most learned taste, and grows fastidious in the choice of dried peas and bottled hay. He is quite familiar with his new attendants, and assigns them their parts with all due gravity. 'Monsieur Cobweb, good Monsieur, get your weapon in your hand, and kill me a red-hipt humble-bee on the top of a thistle, and, good Monsieur, bring me the honey-bag.' What an exact knowledge is here shown of natural history!

Puck, or Robin Goodfellow, is the leader of the fairy band. He is the Ariel of the MIDSUMMER'S NIGHT DREAM; and yet as unlike as can be to the Ariel in THE TEMPEST. No other poet could have made two such different characters out of the same fanciful materials and situations. Ariel is a minister of retribution, who is touched with a sense of pity at the woes he inflicts. Puck is a mad-cap sprite, full of wantonness and mischief, who laughs at those whom he misleads—'Lord, what fools these mortals be!' Ariel cleaves the air, and executes his mission with the zeal of a winged messenger; Puck is borne along on his fairy errand like the light and glittering gossamer before the breeze. He is, indeed, a most Epicurean little gentleman, dealing in quaint devices and faring in dainty delights. Prospero and his world of spirits are a set of moralists; but with Oberon and his fairies we are launched at once into the empire of the butterflies. How beautifully is this race of beings contrasted with the men and women actors in the scene, by a single epithet which Titania gives to the latter, 'the human mortals'! It is astonishing that Shakespeare should be considered, not only by foreigners, but by many of our own critics, as a gloomy and heavy writer, who painted nothing but 'gorgons and hydras, and chimeras dire'. His subtlety exceeds that of all other dramatic writers, insomuch that a celebrated person of the present day said that he regarded him rather as a metaphysician than a poet. His delicacy and sportive gaiety are infinite. In the MIDSUMMER'S NIGHT DREAM alone, we should imagine, there is more sweetness and beauty of description than in the whole range of French poetry put together. What we mean is this, that we will produce out of that single play ten passages, to which we do not think any ten passages in the works of the French poets can be opposed, displaying equal fancy and imagery. Shall we mention the remonstrance of Helena to Hermia, or Titania's description of her fairy train, or her disputes with Oberon about the Indian boy, or Puck's account of himself and his employments, or the Fairy Queen's exhortation to the elves to pay due attendance upon her favourite, Bottom; or Hippolita's description of a chace, or Theseus's answer? The two last are as heroical and spirited as the others are full of luscious tenderness. The reading of this play is like wandering in a grove by moonlight: the descriptions breathe a sweetness like odours thrown from beds of flowers.

Titania's exhortation to the fairies to wait upon Bottom, which is remarkable for a certain cloying sweetness in the repetition of the rhymes, is as follows:

> Be kind and courteous to this gentleman.
> Hop in his walks, and gambol in his eyes,
> Feed him with apricocks and dewberries,
> With purple grapes, green figs and mulberries;
> The honey-bags steal from the humble bees,
> And for night tapers crop their waxen thighs,
> And light them at the fiery glow-worm's eyes,
> To have my love to bed, and to arise:
> And pluck the wings from painted butterflies,
> To fan the moon-beams from his sleeping eyes;
> Nod to him, elves, and do him courtesies.

The sounds of the lute and of the trumpet are not more distinct than the poetry of the foregoing passage, and of the conversation between Theseus and Hippolita:

> Theseus. Go, one of you, find out the forester,
>   For now our observation is perform'd;
>   And since we have the vaward of the day,
>   My love shall hear the music of my hounds.
>   Uncouple in the western valley, go,
>   Dispatch, I say, and find the forester.
>   We will, fair Queen, up to the mountain's top,

And mark the musical confusion
Of hounds and echo in conjunction.

Hippolita. I was with Hercules and Cadmus once,
  When in a wood of Crete they bay'd the bear
  With hounds of Sparta; never did I hear
  Such gallant chiding. For besides the groves,
  The skies, the fountains, every region near
  Seena'd all one mutual cry. I never heard
  So musical a discord, such sweet thunder.

Theseus. My hounds are bred out of the Spartan kind,
  So flew'd, so sanded, and their heads are hung
  With ears that sweep away the morning dew;
  Crook-knee'd and dew-lap'd, like Thessalian bulls,
  Slow in pursuit, but matched in mouth like bells,
  Each under each. A cry more tuneable
  Was never halloo'd to, nor cheer'd with hom,
  In Crete, in Sparta, nor in Thessaly: Judge when you hear.

Even Titian never made a hunting-piece of a gusto so fresh and lusty, and so near the first ages of the world as this.

It had been suggested to us, that the MIDSUMMER'S NIGHT DREAM would do admirably to get up as a Christmas after-piece; and our prompter proposed that Mr. Kean should play the part of Bottom, as worthy of his great talents. He might, in the discharge of his duty, offer to play the lady like any of our actresses that he pleased, the lover or the tyrant like any of our actors that he pleased, and the lion like 'the most fearful wild-fowl living'. The carpenter, the tailor, and joiner, it was thought, would hit the galleries. The young ladies in love would interest the side-boxes; and Robin Goodfellow and his companions excite a lively fellow-feeling in the children from school. There would be two courts, an empire within an empire, the Athenian and the Fairy King and Queen, with their attendants, and with all their finery. What an opportunity for processions, for the sound of trumpets and glittering of spears! What a fluttering of urchins' painted wings; what a delightful profusion of gauze clouds and airy spirits floating on them!

Alas, the experiment has been tried, and has failed; not through the fault of Mr. Kean, who did not play the part of Bottom, nor of Mr. Liston, who did, and who played it well, but from the nature of things. The Midsummer Night's Dream, when acted, is converted from a delightful fiction into a dull pantomime. All that is finest in the play is lost in the representation. The spectacle was grand; but the spirit was evaporated, the genius was fled.—Poetry and the stage do not agree well together. The attempt to reconcile them in this instance fails not only of effect, but of decorum. The IDEAL can have no place upon the stage, which is a picture without perspective; everything there is in the foreground. That which was merely an airy shape, a dream, a passing thought, immediately becomes an unmanageable reality. Where all is left to the imagination (as is the case in reading) every circumstance, near or remote, has an equal chance of being kept in mind, and tells according to the mixed impression of all that has been suggested.

But the imagination cannot sufficiently qualify the actual impressions of the senses. Any offence given to the eye is not to be got rid of by explanation. Thus Bottom's head in the play is a fantastic illusion, produced by magic spells: on the stage, it is an ass's head, and nothing more; certainly a very strange costume for a gentleman to appear in. Fancy cannot be embodied any more than a simile can be painted; and it is as idle to attempt it as to personate Wall or Moonshine. Fairies are not incredible, but fairies six feet high are so. Monsters are not shocking, if they are seen at a proper distance. When ghosts appear at midday, when apparitions stalk along Cheapside, then may the MIDSUMMER'S NIGHT DREAM be represented without injury at Covent Garden or at Drury Lane. The boards of a theatre and the regions of fancy are not the same thing.

ROMEO AND JULIET

ROMEO AND JULIET is the only tragedy which Shakespeare has written entirely on a love-story. It is supposed to have been his first play, and it deserves to stand in that proud rank. There is the buoyant spirit of youth in every line, in the rapturous intoxication of hope, and in the bitterness of despair. It has been said of ROMEO AND JULIET by a great critic, that 'whatever is most intoxicating in the odour of a southern spring, languishing in the song of the nightingale, or voluptuous in the first opening of the rose, is to be found in this poem'. The description is true; and yet it does not answer to our idea of the play. For if it has the sweetness of the rose, it has its freshness too; if it has the languor of the nightingale's song, it has also its giddy transport; if it has the softness of a southern spring, it is as glowing and as bright. There is nothing of a sickly and sentimental cast. Romeo and Juliet are in love, but they are not love-sick. Everything speaks the very soul of pleasure, the high and healthy pulse of the passions: the heart beats, the blood circulates and mantles throughout. Their courtship is not an insipid interchange of sentiments lip-deep, learnt at second-hand from poems and plays,—made up of beauties of the most shadowy kind, of 'fancies wan that hang the pensive head', of evanescent smiles and sighs that breathe not, of delicacy that shrinks from the touch and feebleness that scarce supports itself, an elaborate vacuity of thought, and an artificial dearth of sense, spirit, truth, and nature!—It is the reverse of all this. It is Shakespeare all over, and Shakespeare when he was young.

We have heard it objected to ROMEO AND JULIET that it is founded on an idle passion between a boy and a girl, who have scarcely seen and can have but little sympathy or rational esteem for one another, who have had no experience of the good or ills of life, and whose raptures or despair must be therefore equally groundless and fantastical. Whoever objects to the youth of the parties in this play as 'too unripe and crude' to pluck the sweets of love, and wishes to see a first-love carried on into a good old age, and the passions taken at the rebound, when their force is spent, may find all this done in the Stranger and in other German plays, where they do things by contraries, and transpose nature to inspire sentiment and create philosophy. Shakespeare proceeded in a more straightforward and, we think, effectual way. He did not endeavour to extract beauty from wrinkles, or the wild throb of passion from the last expiring sigh of indifference. He did not 'gather grapes of thorns nor figs of thistles'. It was not his way. But he has given a picture of human life, such as it is in the order of nature. He has founded the passion of the two lovers not on the pleasures they had experienced, but on all the pleasures they had NOT experienced. All that was to come of life was theirs. At that untried source of promised happiness they slaked their thirst, and the first eager draught made them drunk with love and joy. They were in full possession of their senses and their affections. Their hopes were of air, their desires of fire. Youth is the season of love, because the heart is then first melted in tenderness from the touch of novelty, and kindled to rapture, for it knows no end of its enjoyments or its wishes. Desire has no limit but itself. Passion, the love and expectation of pleasure, is infinite, extravagant, inexhaustible, till experience comes to check and kill it. Juliet exclaims on her first interview with Romeo:

My bounty is as boundless as the sea,
My love as deep.

And why should it not? What was to hinder the thrilling tide of pleasure, which had just gushed from her heart, from flowing on without stint or measure, but experience which she was yet without? What was to abate the transport of the first sweet sense of pleasure, which her heart and her senses had just tasted, but indifference which she was yet a stranger to? What was there to check the ardour of hope, of faith, of constancy, just rising in her breast, but disappointment which she had not yet felt? As are the desires and the hopes of youthful passion, such is the keenness of its disappointments, and their baleful effect. Such is the transition in this play from the highest bliss to the lowest despair, from the nuptial couch to an untimely grave. The only evil that even in apprehension befalls the two lovers is the loss of the greatest possible felicity; yet this loss is fatal to both, for they had rather part with life than bear the thought of surviving all that had made life dear to them. In all this, Shakespeare has but followed nature, which existed in his time, as well as now. The modern philosophy, which reduces the whole theory of the mind to habitual impressions, and leaves the natural impulses of passion and imagination out of the account, had not then been discovered; or if it had, would have been little calculated for the uses of poetry.

It is the inadequacy of the same false system of philosophy to account for the strength of our earliest attachments, which has led Mr. Wordsworth to indulge in the mystical visions of Platonism in his Ode on the Progress of Life. He has very admirably described the vividness of our impressions in youth and childhood, and how 'they fade by degrees into the light of common day', and he ascribes the change to the supposition of a pre-existent state, as if our early thoughts were nearer heaven, reflections of former trails of glory, shadows of our past being. This is idle. It is not from the knowledge of the past that the first impressions of things derive their gloss and splendour, but from our ignorance of the future, which fills the void to come with the warmth of our desires, with our gayest hopes, and brightest fancies. It is the obscurity spread before it that colours the prospect of life with hope, as it is the cloud which reflects the rainbow. There is no occasion to resort to any mystical union and transmission of feeling through different states of being to account for the romantic enthusiasm of youth; nor to plant the root of hope in the grave, nor to derive it from the skies. Its root is in the heart of man: it lifts its head above the stars. Desire and imagination are inmates of the human breast. The heaven 'that lies about us in our infancy' is only a new world, of which we know nothing but what we wish it to be, and believe all that we wish. In youth and boyhood, the world we live in is the world of desire, and of fancy: it is experience that brings us down to the world of reality. What is it that in youth sheds a dewy light round the evening star? That makes the daisy look so bright? That perfumes the hyacinth? That embalms the first kiss of love? It is the delight of novelty, and the seeing no end to the pleasure that we fondly believe is still in store for us. The heart revels in the luxury of its own thoughts, and is unable to sustain the weight of hope and love that presses upon it.—The effects of the passion of love alone might have dissipated Mr. Wordsworth's theory, if he means anything more by it than an ingenious and poetical allegory. THAT at least is not a link in the chain let down from other worlds; 'the purple light of love' is not a dim reflection of the smiles of celestial bliss. It does not appear till the middle of life, and then seems like 'another morn risen on midday'. In this respect the soul comes into the world 'in utter nakedness'. Love waits for the ripening of the youthful blood. The sense of pleasure precedes the love of pleasure, but with the sense of pleasure, as soon as it is felt, come thronging infinite desires and hopes of pleasure, and love is mature as soon as born. It withers and it dies almost as soon!

This play presents a beautiful coup d'oeil of the progress of human life. In thought it occupies years, and embraces the circle of the affections from childhood to old age. Juliet has become a great girl, a young woman since we first remember her a little thing in the idle prattle of the nurse. Lady Capulet was about her age when she became a mother, and old Capulet somewhat impatiently tells his younger visitors:

—I've seen the day,
That I have worn a visor, and could tell
A whispering tale in a fair lady's ear,
Such as would please: 'tis gone, 'tis gone, 'tis gone.

Thus one period of life makes way for the following, and one generation pushes another off the stage. One of the most striking passages to show the intense feeling of youth in this play is Capulet's invitation to Paris to visit his entertainment.

At my poor house, look to behold this night
Earth-treading stars that make dark heav'n light;
Such comfort as do lusty young men feel
When well-apparel'd April on the heel
Of limping winter treads, even such delight
Among fresh female-buds shall you this night
Inherit at my house.

The feelings of youth and of the spring are here blended together like the breath of opening flowers. Images of vernal beauty appear to have floated before the author's mind, in writing this poem, in profusion. Here is another of exquisite beauty, brought in more by accident than by necessity. Montague declares of his son smit with a hopeless passion, which he will not reveal:

But he, his own affection's counsellor,
Is to himself so secret and so close,
So far from sounding and discovery,
As is the bud bit with an envious worm,
Ere he can spread his sweet leaves to the air,
Or dedicate his beauty to the sun.

This casual description is as full of passionate beauty as when Romeo dwells in frantic fondness on 'the white wonder of his Juliet's hand'. The reader may, if he pleases, contrast the exquisite pastoral simplicity of the above lines with the gorgeous description of Juliet when Romeo first sees her at her father's house, surrounded by company and artificial splendour.

What lady's that which doth enrich the hand
Of yonder knight?
O she doth teach the torches to burn bright;

Her beauty hangs upon the cheek of night,
Like a rich jewel in an Aethiop's ear.

It would be hard to say which of the two garden scenes is the finest, that where he first converses with his love, or takes leave of her the morning after their marriage. Both are like a heaven upon earth: the blissful bowers of Paradise let down upon this lower world. We will give only one passage of these well-known scenes to show the perfect refinement and delicacy of Shakespeare's conception of the female character. It is wonderful how Collins, who was a critic and a poet of great sensibility, should have encouraged the common error on this subject by saying—'But stronger Shakespeare felt for man alone'.

The passage we mean is Juliet's apology for her maiden boldness.

Thou know'st the mask of night is on my face;
Else would a maiden blush bepaint my cheek
For that which thou hast heard me speak to-night.
Fain would I dwell on form, fain, fain deny
What I have spoke—but farewell compliment:
Dost thou love me? I know thou wilt say, aye,
And I will take thee at thy word—Yet if thou swear'st,
Thou may'st prove false; at lovers' perjuries
They say Jove laughs. Oh gentle Romeo,
If thou dost love, pronounce it faithfully;
Or if thou think I am too quickly won,
I'll frown and be perverse, and say thee nay,
So thou wilt woo: but else not for the world.
In truth, fair Montague, I am too fond;
And therefore thou may'st think my 'haviour light;
But trust me, gentleman, I'll prove more true
Than those that have more cunning to be strange.
I should have been more strange, I must confess,
But that thou over-heard'st, ere I was ware,
My true love's passion; therefore pardon me,
And not impute this yielding to light love,
Which the dark night hath so discovered.

In this and all the rest her heart, fluttering between pleasure, hope, and fear, seems to have dictated to her tongue, and 'calls true love spoken simple modesty'. Of the same sort, but bolder in virgin innocence, is her soliloquy after her marriage with Romeo.

Gallop apace, you fiery-footed steeds,
Towards Phoebus' mansion; such a wagoner
As Phaeton would whip you to the west,
And bring in cloudy night immediately.
Spread thy close curtain, love-performing night;
That run-aways' eyes may wink; and Romeo

Leap to these arms, untalked of, and unseen!—-
Lovers can see to do their amorous rites
By their own beauties: or if love be blind,
It best agrees with night.—Come, civil night,
Thou sober-suited matron, all in black,
And learn me how to lose a winning match,
Play'd for a pair of stainless maidenhoods:
Hood my unmann'd blood bating in my cheeks,
With thy black mantle; till strange love, grown bold,
Thinks true love acted, simple modesty.
Come night!—Come, Romeo! come, thou day in night;
For thou wilt lie upon the wings of night
Whiter than new snow on a raven's back.—-
Come, gentle night; come, loving, black-brow'd night,
Give me my Romeo; and when he shall die,
Take him and cut him out in little stars,
And he will make the face of heaven so fine,
That all the world shall be in love with night,
And pay no worship to the garish sun.—-
O, I have bought the mansion of a love,
But not possess'd it; and though I am sold,
Not yet enjoy'd: so tedious is this day,
As is the night before some festival
To an impatient child, that hath new robes,
And may not wear them.

We the rather insert this passage here, inasmuch as we have no doubt it has been expunged from the Family Shakespeare. Such critics do not perceive that the feelings of the heart sanctify, without disguising, the impulses of nature. Without refinement themselves, they confound modesty with hypocrisy. Not so the German critic, Schlegel. Speaking of Romeo and Juliet, he says, 'It was reserved for Shakespeare to unite purity of heart and the glow of imagination, sweetness and dignity of manners and passionate violence, in one ideal picture.' The character is indeed one of perfect truth and sweetness. It has nothing forward, nothing coy, nothing affected or coquettish about it;—it is a pure effusion of nature. It is as frank as it is modest, for it has no thought that it wishes to conceal. It reposes in conscious innocence on the strength of its affections. Its delicacy does not consist in coldness and reserve, but in combining warmth of imagination and tenderness of heart with the most voluptuous sensibility. Love is a gentle flame that rarefies and expands her whole being. What an idea of trembling haste and airy grace, borne upon the thoughts of love, does the Friar's exclamation give of her, as she approaches his cell to be married:

Here comes the lady. Oh, so light of foot
Will ne'er wear out the everlasting flint:
A lover may bestride the gossamer,
That idles in the wanton summer air,
And yet not fall, so light is vanity.

The tragic part of this character is of a piece with the rest. It is the heroic founded on tenderness and delicacy. Of this kind are her resolution to follow the Friar's advice, and the conflict in her bosom between apprehension and love when she comes to take the sleeping poison. Shakespeare is blamed for the mixture of low characters. If this is a deformity, it is the source of a thousand beauties. One instance is the contrast between the guileless simplicity of Juliet's attachment to her first love, and the convenient policy of the nurse in advising her to marry Paris, which excites such indignation in her mistress. 'Ancient damnation! oh most wicked fiend', &c.

Romeo is Hamlet in love. There is the same rich exuberance of passion and sentiment in the one, that there is of thought and sentiment in the other. Both are absent and self-involved, both live out of themselves in a world of imagination. Hamlet is abstracted from everything; Romeo is abstracted from everything but his love, and lost in it. His 'frail thoughts dally with faint surmise', and are fashioned out of the suggestions of hope, 'the flatteries of sleep'. He is himself only in his Juliet; she is his only reality, his heart's true home and idol. The rest of the world is to him a passing dream. How finely is this character portrayed where he recollects himself on seeing Paris slain at the tomb of Juliet!

> What said my man when my betossed soul
> Did not attend him as we rode? I think
> He told me Paris should have married Juliet.

And again, just before he hears the sudden tidings of her death:

> If I may trust the flattery of sleep,
> My dreams presage some joyful news at hand;
> My bosom's lord sits lightly on his throne,
> And all this day an unaccustom'd spirit
> Lifts me above the ground with cheerful thoughts.
> I dreamt my lady came and found me dead,
> (Strange dream! that gives a dead man leave to think)
> And breath'd such life with kisses on my lips,
> That I reviv'd and was an emperor.
> Ah me! how sweet is love itself possessed,
> When but love's shadows are so rich in joy!

Romeo's passion for Juliet is not a first love: it succeeds and drives out his passion for another mistress, Rosaline, as the sun hides the stars. This is perhaps an artifice (not absolutely necessary) to give us a higher opinion of the lady, while the first absolute surrender of her heart to him enhances the richness of the prize. The commencement, progress, and ending of his second passion are however complete in themselves, not injured, if they are not bettered by the first. The outline of the play is taken from an Italian novel; but the dramatic arrangement of the different scenes between the lovers, the more than dramatic interest in the progress of the story, the development of the characters with time and circumstances, just according to the degree and kind of interest excited, are not inferior to the expression of passion and nature. It has been ingeniously remarked among other proofs of skill in the contrivance of the fable, that the improbability of the main incident in the piece, the administering of the sleeping-potion, is softened and obviated from the beginning by the introduction of the Friar on his first appearance culling simples and descanting on their virtues. Of the passionate scenes in this tragedy, that between the Friar and Romeo when he is told of his sentence of banishment, that between Juliet and the Nurse when she hears of it, and of the death of her cousin Tybalt (which bear no proportion in her mind, when passion after the first shock of surprise throws its weight into the scale of her affections), and the last scene at the tomb, are among the most natural and overpowering. In all of these it is not merely the force of any one passion that is given, but the slightest and most unlooked-for transitions from one to another, the mingling currents of every different feeling rising up and prevailing in turn, swayed by the master-mind of the poet, as the waves undulate beneath the gliding storm. Thus when Juliet has by her complaints encouraged the Nurse to say, 'Shame come to Romeo', she instantly repels the wish, which she had herself occasioned, by answering:

Blister'd be thy tongue
For such a wish, he was not born to shame.
Upon his brow shame is ashamed to sit,
For 'tis a throne where honour may be crown'd
Sole monarch of the universal earth!
O, what a beast was I to chide him so!

Nurse. Will you speak well of him that kill'd your cousin?

Juliet. Shall I speak ill of him that is my husband?
Ah my poor lord, what tongue shall smooth thy name,
When I, thy three-hours' wife, have mangled it?

And then follows on the neck of her remorse and returning fondness, that wish treading almost on the brink of impiety, but still held back by the strength of her devotion to her lord, that 'father, mother, nay, or both were dead', rather than Romeo banished. If she requires any other excuse, it is in the manner in which Romeo echoes her frantic grief and disappointment in the next scene at being banished from her.—Perhaps one of the finest pieces of acting that ever was witnessed on the stage, is Mr. Kean's manner of doing this scene and his repetition of the word, BANISHED. He treads close indeed upon the genius of his author.

A passage which this celebrated actor and able commentator on Shakespeare (actors are the best commentators on the poets) did not give with equal truth or force of feeling was the one which Romeo makes at the tomb of Juliet, before he drinks the poison.

—Let me peruse this face—
Mercutio's kinsman! noble county Paris!
What said my man, when my betossed soul
Did not attend him as we rode! I think,
He told me, Paris should have married Juliet!
Said he not so? or did I dream it so?
Or am I mad, hearing him talk of Juliet,
To think it was so?—O, give me thy hand,

One writ with me in sour misfortune's book!
I'll bury thee in a triumphant grave—
For here lies Juliet.

. . .

—O, my love! my wife!
Death that hath suck'd the honey of thy breath,
Hath had no power yet upon thy beauty:
Thou art not conquer'd; beauty's ensign yet
Is crimson in thy lips, and in thy cheeks,
And Death's pale flag is not advanced there.—
Tybalt, ly'st thou there in thy bloody sheet?
O, what more favour can I do to thee,
Than with that hand that cut thy youth in twain,
To sunder his that was thine enemy?
Forgive me, cousin! Ah, dear Juliet,
Why art thou yet so fair! I will believe
That unsubstantial death is amorous;
And that the lean abhorred monster keeps
Thee here in dark to be his paramour.
For fear of that, I will stay still with thee;
And never from this palace of dim night
Depart again: here, here will I remain
With worms that are thy chamber-maids; O, here
Will I set up my everlasting rest;
And shake the yoke of inauspicious stars
From this world-wearied flesh.—Eyes, look your last!
Arms, take your last embrace! and lips, O you
The doors of breath, seal with a righteous kiss
A dateless bargain to engrossing death!—
Come, bitter conduct, come unsavoury guide!
Thou desperate pilot, now at once run on
The dashing rocks my sea-sick weary bark!
Here's to my love!—[Drinks.] O, true apothecary!
Thy drugs are quick.—Thus with a kiss I die.

The lines in this speech describing the loveliness of Juliet, who is supposed to be dead, have been compared to those in which it is said of Cleopatra after her death, that she looked 'as she would take another Antony in her strong toil of grace;' and a question has been started which is the finest, that we do not pretend to decide. We can more easily decide between Shakespeare and any other author, than between him and himself.—Shall we quote any more passages to show his genius or the beauty of ROMEO AND JULIET? At that rate, we might quote the whole. The late Mr. Sheridan, on being shown a volume of the Beauties of Shakespeare, very properly asked— 'But where are the other eleven?' The character of Mercutio in this play is one of the most mercurial and spirited of the productions of Shakespeare's comic muse.

LEAR

We wish that we could pass this play over, and say nothing about it. All that we can say must fall far short of the subject; or even of what we ourselves conceive of it. To attempt to give a description of the play itself or of its effect upon the mind, is mere impertinence: yet we must say something.—It is then the best of all Shakespeare's plays, for it is the one in which he was the most in earnest. He was here fairly caught in the web of his own imagination. The passion which he has taken as his subject is that which strikes its root deepest into the human heart; of which the bond is the hardest to be unloosed; and the cancelling and tearing to pieces of which gives the greatest revulsion to the frame. This depth of nature, this force of passion, this tug and war of the elements of our being, this firm faith in filial piety, and the giddy anarchy and whirling tumult of the thoughts at finding this prop failing it, the contrast between the fixed, immoveable basis of natural affection, and the rapid, irregular starts of imagination, suddenly wrenched from all its accustomed holds and resting-places in the soul, this is what Shakespeare has given, and what nobody else but he could give. So we believe.—The mind of Lear staggering between the weight of attachment and the hurried movements of passion is like a tall ship driven about by the winds, buffeted by the furious waves, but that still rides above the storm, having its anchor fixed in the bottom of the sea; or it is like the sharp rock circled by the eddying whirlpool that foams and beats against it, or like the solid promontory pushed from its basis by the force of an earthquake.

The character of Lear itself is very finely conceived for the purpose. It is the only ground on which such a story could be built with the greatest truth and effect. It is his rash haste, his violent impetuosity, his blindness to everything but the dictates of his passions or affections, that produces all his misfortunes, that aggravates his impatience of them, that enforces our pity for him. The part which Cordelia bears in the scene is extremely beautiful: the story is almost told in the first words she utters. We see at once the precipice on which the poor old king stands from his own extravagant and credulous importunity, the indiscreet simplicity of her love (which, to be sure, has a little of her father's obstinacy in it) and the hollowness of her sisters' pretensions. Almost the first burst of that noble tide of passion, which runs through the play, is in the remonstrance of Kent to his royal master on the injustice of his sentence against his youngest daughter—'Be Kent unmannerly, when Lear is mad!' This manly plainness which draws down on him the displeasure of the unadvised king is worthy of the fidelity with which he adheres to his fallen fortunes. The true character of the two eldest daughters, Regan and Gonerill (they are so thoroughly hateful that we do not even like to repeat their names) breaks out in their answer to Cordelia who desires them to treat their father well—'Prescribe not us our duties'—their hatred of advice being in proportion to their determination to do wrong, and to their hypocritical pretensions to do right. Their deliberate hypocrisy adds the last finishing to the odiousness of their characters. It is the absence of this detestable quality that is the only relief in the character of Edmund the Bastard, and that at times reconciles us to him. We are not tempted to exaggerate the guilt of his conduct, when he himself gives it up as a bad business, and writes himself down 'plain villain'. Nothing more can be said about it. His religious honesty in this respect is admirable. One speech of his is worth a million. His father, Gloster, whom he has just deluded with a forged story of his brother Edgar's designs against his life, accounts for his unnatural behaviour and the strange depravity of the times from the late eclipses in the sun and moon. Edmund, who is in the secret, says when he is gone: 'This is the excellent foppery of the world, that when we are sick in fortune (often the surfeits of our own behaviour) we make guilty of our disasters the sun, the moon, and stars: as if we were villains on necessity; fools by heavenly compulsion; knaves, thieves, and treacherous by spherical predominance; drunkards, liars, and adulterers by an enforced obedience of planetary influence; and all that we are evil in, by a divine thrusting on. An admirable evasion of whoremaster man, to lay his goatish disposition on the charge of a star! My father compounded with my mother under the Dragon's tale, and my nativity was under Ursa Major: so that it follows, I am rough and lecherous. I should have been what I am, had the maidenliest star in the firmament twinkled on my bastardizing.'— The whole character, its careless, light-hearted villany, contrasted with the sullen, rancorous malignity of Regan and Gonerill, its connexion with the conduct of the under-plot, in which Gloster's persecution of one of his sons and the ingratitude of another, form a counterpart to the mistakes and misfortunes of Lear—his double amour with the two sisters, and the share which he has in bringing about the fatal catastrophe, are all managed with an uncommon degree of skill and power.

It has been said, and we think justly, that the third act of OTHELLO, and the three first acts of LEAR, are Shakespeare's great masterpieces in the logic of passion: that they contain the highest examples not only of the force of individual passion, but of its dramatic vicissitudes and striking effects arising from the different circumstances and characters of the persons speaking. We see the ebb and flow of the feeling, its pauses and feverish starts, its impatience of opposition, its accumulating force when it has time to recollect itself, the manner in which it avails itself of every passing word or gesture, its haste to repel insinuation, the alternate contraction and dilatation of the soul, and all 'the dazzling fence of controversy' in this mortal combat with poisoned weapons, aimed at the heart, where each wound is fatal. We have seen in OTHELLO, how the unsuspecting frankness and impetuous passions of the Moor are played upon and exasperated by the artful dexterity of Iago. In the present play, that which aggravates the sense of sympathy in the reader, and of uncontrollable anguish in the swollen heart of Lear, is the petrifying indifference, the cold, calculating, obdurate selfishness of his daughters. His keen passions seem whetted on their stony hearts. The contrast would be too painful, the shock too great, but for the intervention of the Fool, whose well-timed levity comes in to break the continuity of feeling when it can no longer be borne, and to bring into play again the fibres of the heart just as they are growing rigid from over- strained excitement. The imagination is glad to take refuge in the half-comic, half-serious comments of the Fool, just as the mind under the extreme anguish of a surgical operation vents itself in sallies of wit. The character was also a grotesque ornament of the barbarous times, in which alone the tragic ground-work of the story could be laid. In another point of view it is indispensable, inasmuch as while it is a diversion to the too great intensity of our disgust, it carries the pathos to the highest pitch of which it is capable, by showing the pitiable weakness of the old king's conduct and its irretrievable consequences in the most familiar point of view. Lear may well 'beat at the gate which let his folly in', after, as the Fool says, 'he has made his daughters his mothers'. The character is dropped in the third act to make room for the entrance of Edgar as Mad Tom, which well accords with the increasing bustle and wildness of the incidents; and nothing can be more complete than the distinction between Lear's real and Edgar's assumed madness, while the resemblance in the cause of their distresses, from the severing of the nearest ties of natural affection, keeps up a unity of interest. Shakespeare's mastery over his subject, if it was not art, was owing to a knowledge of the connecting links of the passions, and their effect upon the mind, still more wonderful than any systematic adherence to rules, and that anticipated and outdid all the efforts of the most refined art, not inspired and rendered instinctive by genius.

One of the most perfect displays of dramatic power is the first interview between Lear and his daughter, after the designed affronts upon him, which till one of his knights reminds him of them, his sanguine temperament had led him to overlook. He returns with his train from hunting, and his usual impatience breaks out in his first words, 'Let me not stay a jot for dinner; go, get it ready.' He then encounters the faithful Kent in disguise, and retains him in his service; and the first trial of his honest duty is to trip up the heels of the officious Steward who makes so prominent and despicable a figure through the piece. On the entrance of Gonerill the following dialogue takes place:

Lear. How now, daughter? what makes that frontlet on?
  Methinks, you are too much of late i' the frown.

Fool. Thou wast a pretty fellow, when thou had'st no
  need to care for her frowning; now thou art an O without
  a figure: I am better than thou art now; I am a fool, thou
  art nothing.—Yes, forsooth, I will hold my tongue; [To
  Gonerill.] so your face bids me, though you say nothing.
  Mum, mum.

  He that keeps nor crust nor crum,
  Weary of all, shall want some—
  That's a sheal'd peascod! [Pointing to Lear.]

Gonerill. Not only, sir, this your all-licens'd fool,
  But other of your insolent retinue
  Do hourly carp and quarrel; breaking forth
  In rank and not-to-be-endured riots.
  I had thought, by making this well known unto you,
  To have found a safe redress; but now grow fearful,
  By what yourself too late have spoke and done,
  That you protect this course, and put it on
  By your allowance; which if you should, the fault
  Would not 'scape censure, nor the redresses sleep,
  Which in the tender of a wholesome weal,
  Might in their working do you that offence,
  (Which else were shame) that then necessity
  Would call discreet proceeding.

Fool. For you trow, nuncle,
  The hedge sparrow fed the cuckoo so long,
  That it had its head bit off by its young.
  So out went the candle, and we were left darkling.

Lear. Are you our daughter?

Gonerill. Come, sir,
  I would, you would make use of that good wisdom
  Whereof I know you are fraught; and put away
  These dispositions, which of late transform you
  From what you rightly are.

Fool. May not an ass know when the cart draws the
  horse?—Whoop, Jug, I love thee.

Lear. Does any here know me?—Why, this is not
  Lear:
  Does Lear walk thus? speak thus?—Where are his eyes?
  Either his notion weakens, or his discernings
  Are lethargy'd—Ha! waking?—'Tis not so.—
  Who is it that can tell me who I am?—Lear's shadow?
  I would learn that: for by the marks
  Of sov'reignty, of knowledge, and of reason,
  I should be false persuaded I had daughters.—
  Your name, fair gentlewoman?

Gonerill. Come, sir:
  This admiration is much o' the favour
  Of other your new pranks. I do beseech you
  To understand my purposes aright:
  As you are old and reverend, you should be wise:
  Here do you keep a hundred knights and squires;
  Men so disorder'd, so debauch'd, and bold,
  That this our court, infected with their manners,
  Shows like a riotous inn: epicurism and lust
  Make it more like a tavern, or a brothel,
  Than a grac'd palace. The shame itself doth speak
  For instant remedy: be then desir'd
  By her, that else will take the thing she begs,
  A little to disquantity your train;
  And the remainder, that shall still depend,
  To be such men as may besort your age,
  And know themselves and you.

Lear. Darkness and devils!
  Saddle my horses; call my train together.—
  Degenerate Bastard! I'll not trouble thee;
  Yet have I left a daughter.

Gonerill. You strike my people, and your disorder'd rabble
  Make servants of their betters.

Enter Albany

    Lear. Woe, that too late repents—O, sir, are you come?
    Is it your will? speak, sir.—Prepare my horses.—
           [To Albany.]
    Ingratitude! thou marble-hearted fiend,
    More hideous, when thou show'st thee in a child,
    Than the sea-monster!

Albany. Pray, sir, be patient.

    Lear. Detested kite! thou liest. [To Gonerill.]
    My train are men of choice and rarest parts,
    That all particulars of duty know;
    And in the most exact regard support
    The worships of their name.—O most small fault,
    How ugly didst thou in Cordelia show!
    Which, like an engine, wrench'd my frame of nature
    From the fixt place; drew from my heart all love,
    And added to the gall. O Lear, Lear, Lear!
    Beat at the gate, that let thy folly in,
           [Striking his head.]
    And thy dear judgement out!—Go, go, my people!

Albany. My lord, I am guiltless, as I am ignorant
    Of what hath mov'd you.

    Lear. It may be so, my lord—
    Hear, nature, hear: dear goddess, hear!
    Suspend thy purpose, if thou didst intend
    To make this creature fruitful!
    Into her womb convey sterility;
    Dry up in her the organs of increase;
    And from her derogate body never spring
    A babe to honour her! If she must teem,
    Create her child of spleen: that it may live,
    To be a thwart disnatur'd torment to her!
    Let it stamp wrinkles in her brow of youth;
    With cadent tears fret channels in her cheeks;
    Turn all her mother's pains, and benefits,
    To laughter and contempt; that she may feel
    How sharper than a serpent's tooth it is
    To have a thankless child!—Away, away!
    [Exit.]

Albany. Now, gods, that we adore, whereof comes this?

Gonerill. Never afflict yourself to know the cause;
  But let his disposition have that scope
  That dotage gives it.

Re-enter Lear

Lear. What, fifty of my followers at a clap!
  Within a fortnight!

Albany. What's the matter, sir?

Lear. I'll tell thee; life and death! I am asham'd
  That thou hast power to shake my manhood thus:
     [To Gonerill.]
  That these hot tears, which break from me perforce,
  Should make thee worth them.—Blasts and fogs upon thee!
  The untented woundings of a father's curse
  Pierce every sense about thee!—Old fond eyes,
  Beweep this cause again, I'll pluck you out;
  And cast you, with the waters that you lose,
  To temper clay.—Ha! is it come to this?
  Let it be so:—Yet have I left a daughter,
  Who, I am sure, is kind and comfortable;
  When she shall hear this of thee, with her nails
  She'll flay thy wolfish visage. Thou shalt find
  That I'll resume the shape, which thou dost think
  I have cast off forever.

[Exeunt Lear, Kent, and Attendants.]

This is certainly fine: no wonder that Lear says after it, 'O let me not be mad, not mad, sweet heavens,' feeling its effects by anticipation: but fine as is this burst of rage and indignation at the first blow aimed at his hopes and expectations, it is nothing near so fine as what follows from his double disappointment, and his lingering efforts to see which of them he shall lean upon for support and find comfort in, when both his daughters turn against his age and weakness. It is with some difficulty that Lear gets to speak with his daughter Regan, and her husband, at Gloster's castle. In concert with Gonerill they have left their own home on purpose to avoid him. His apprehensions are fast alarmed by this circumstance, and when Gloster, whose guests they are, urges the fiery temper of the Duke of Cornwall as an excuse for not importuning him a second time, Lear breaks out:

Vengeance! Plague! Death! Confusion!
Fiery? What fiery quality? Why, Gloster,
I'd speak with the Duke of Cornwall and his wife.

Afterwards, feeling perhaps not well himself, he is inclined to admit their excuse from illness, but then recollecting that they have set his messenger (Kent) in the stocks, all his suspicions are roused again, and he insists on seeing them.

Enter Cornwall, Regan, Gloster, and Servants.

Lear. Good-morrow to you both.

Cornwall. Hail to your grace!

[Kent is set at liberty.]

Regan. I am glad to see your highness.

  Lear. Regan, I think you are; I know what reason
  I have to think so; if thou should'st not be glad,
  I would divorce me from thy mother's tomb,
  Sepulch'ring an adultress.—O, are you free?
      [To Kent.]
  Some other time for that.—Beloved Regan,
  Thy sister's naught: O Regan, she hath tied
  Sharp-tooth'd unkindness, like a vulture, here—
      [Points to his heart.]
  I can scarce speak to thee; thou'lt not believe,
  Of how deprav'd a quality—o Regan!

  Regan. I pray you, sir, take patience; I have hope
  You less know how to value her desert,
  Than she to scant her duty.

Lear. Say, how is that?

  Regan. I cannot think my sister in the least
  Would fail her obligation; if, sir, perchance,
  She have restrain'd the riots of your followers,
  'Tis on such ground, and to such wholesome end,
  As clears her from all blame.

Lear. My curses on her!

  Regan. O, sir, you are old;
  Nature in you stands on the very verge
  Of her confine: you should be rul'd, and led
  By some discretion, that discerns your state
  Better than you yourself: therefore, I pray you,
  That to our sister you do make return;
  Say, you have wrong'd her, sir.

Lear. Ask her forgiveness?
  Do you but mark how this becomes the use?
  Dear daughter, I confess that I am old;
  Age is unnecessary; on my knees I beg,
  That you'll vouchsafe me raiment, bed, and food.

  Regan. Good sir, no more; these are unsightly tricks:
  Return you to my sister.

  Lear. Never, Regan:
  She hath abated me of half my train;
  Look'd blank upon me; struck me with her tongue,
  Most serpent-like, upon the very heart:—
  All the stor'd vengeances of heaven fall
  On her ungrateful top! Strike her young bones,
  You taking airs, with lameness!

Cornwall. Fie, sir, fie!

  Lear: You nimble lightnings, dart your blinding flames
  Into her scornful eyes! Infect her beauty,
  You fen-suck'd fogs, drawn by the powerful sun,
  To fall, and blast her pride!

  Regan. O the blest gods!
  So will you wish on me, when the rash mood is on.

  Lear. No, Regan, thou shalt never have my curse;
  Thy tender-hefted nature shall not give
  Thee o'er to harshness; her eyes are fierce, but thine
  Do comfort, and not burn: 'Tis not in thee
  To grudge my pleasures, to cut off my train,
  To bandy hasty words, to scant my sizes,
  And, in conclusion, to oppose the bolt
  Against my coming in: thou better know'st
  The offices of nature, bond of childhood,
  Effects of courtesy, dues of gratitude;
  Thy half o' the kingdom thou hast not forgot,
  Wherein I thee endow'd.

Regan. Good sir, to the purpose. [Trumpets within]

Lear. Who put my man i' the stocks?

Cornwall. What trumpet's that?

Enter Steward

Regan. I know't, my sister's; this approves her letter,
  That she would soon be here.—Is your lady come?

Lear. This is a slave, whose easy-borrow'd pride
  Dwells in the fickle grace of her he follows:—
  Out, varlet, from my sight!

Cornwall. What means your grace?

Lear. Who stock'd my servant? Regan, I have good hope
  Thou did'st not know on't.—Who comes here? O heavens,

Enter Gonerill

  If you do love old men, if your sweet sway
  Allow obedience, if yourselves are old,
  Make it your cause; send down, and take my part!—
  Art not asham'd to look upon this beard?—
    [To Gonerill.]
  O, Regan, wilt thou take her by the hand?

Gonerill. Why not by the hand, sir? How have I
  offended?
  All's not offence, that indiscretion finds,
  And dotage terms so.

Lear. O, sides, you are too tough!
  Will you yet hold?—How came my man i' the stocks?

Cornwall. I set him there, sir: but his own disorders
  Deserv'd much less advancement.

Lear. You! did you?

Regan. I pray you, father, being weak, seem so.
  If, till the expiration of your month,
  You will return and sojourn with my sister,
  Dismissing half your train, come then to me;
  I am now from home, and out of that provision
  Which shall be needful for your entertainment.

Lear. Return to her, and fifty men dismiss'd?
  No, rather I abjure all roofs, and choose
  To be a comrade with the wolf and owl—
  To wage against the enmity o' the air,
  Necessity's sharp pinch!—Return with her!
  Why, the hot-blooded France, that dowerless took
  Our youngest born, I could as well be brought

To knee his throne, and squire-like pension beg
To keep base life afoot.—Return with her!
Persuade me rather to be slave and sumpter
To this detested groom. [Looking on the Steward.]

Gonerill. At your choice, sir.

Lear. Now, I pr'ythee, daughter, do not make me mad;
I will not trouble thee, my child; farewell:
We'll no more meet, no more see one another:—
But yet thou art my flesh, my blood, my daughter;
Or, rather, a disease that's in my flesh,
Which I must needs call mine: thou art a bile,
A plague-sore, an embossed carbuncle,
In my corrupted blood. But I'll not chide thee:
Let shame come when it will, I do not call it:
I did not bid the thunder-bearer shoot,
Nor tell tales of thee to high-judging Jove:
Mend when thou canst; be better, at thy leisure:
I can be patient; I can stay with Regan,
I, and my hundred knights.

Regan. Not altogether so, sir;
I look'd not for you yet, nor am provided
For your fit welcome: Give ear, sir, to my sister;
For those that mingle reason with your passion
Must be content to think you old, and so—
But she knows what she does.

Lear. Is this well spoken now?

Regan. I dare avouch it, sir: What, fifty followers?
Is it not well? What should you need of more?
Yea, or so many? Sith that both charge and danger
Speak 'gainst so great a number? How, in one house,
Should many people, under two commands,
Hold amity? Tis hard; almost impossible.

Gonerill. Why might you not, my lord, receive attendance
From those that she calls servants, or from mine?

Regan. Why not, my lord? If then they chanc'd to slack you,
We would control them: if you will come to me
(For now I spy a danger) I entreat you
To bring but five-and-twenty; to no more
Will I give place, or notice.

Lear. I gave you all—

Regan. And in good time you gave it.

Lear. Made you my guardians, my depositaries;
But kept a reservation to be follow'd
With such a number: what, must I come to you
With five-and-twenty, Regan! said you so?

Regan. And speak it again, my lord; no more with me.

Lear. Those wicked creatures yet do look well-favour'd,
When others are more wicked; not being the worst,
Stands in some rank of praise:—I'll go with thee;
    [To Gonerill.]
Thy fifty yet doth double five-and-twenty,
And thou art twice her love.

Gonerill. Hear me, my lord;
What need you five-and-twenty, ten, or five,
To follow in a house, where twice so many
Have a command to tend you?

Regan. What need one?

Lear. O, reason not the need: our basest beggars
Are in the poorest thing superfluous:
Allow not nature more than nature needs,
Man's life is cheap as beast's: thou art a lady;
If only to go warm were gorgeous,
Why, nature needs not what thou gorgeous wear'st;
Which scarcely keeps thee warm.—But, for true need—
You heavens, give me that patience which I need!
You see me here, you gods; a poor old man,
As full of grief as age; wretched in both!
If it be you that stir these daughters' hearts
Against their father, fool me not so much
To bear it tamely; touch me with noble anger!
O, let no woman's weapons, water-drops,
Stain my man's cheeks!—No, you unnatural hags,
I will have such revenges on you both,
That all the world shall—I will do such things—
What they are, yet I know not; but they shall be
The terrors of the earth. You think, I'll weep:
No, I'll not weep:—
I have full cause of weeping; but this heart
Shall break into a hundred thousand flaws,

Or e'er I'll weep:—O, fool, I shall go mad!
   [Exeunt Lear, Gloster, Kent, and Fool.]

If there is anything in any author like this yearning of the heart, these throes of tenderness, this profound expression of all that can be thought and felt in the most heart-rending situations, we are glad of it; but it is in some author that we have not read.

The scene in the storm, where he is exposed to all the fury of the elements, though grand and terrible, is not so fine, but the moralizing scenes with Mad Tom, Kent, and Gloster, are upon a par with the former. His exclamation in the supposed trial-scene of his daughters, 'See the little dogs and all, Tray, Blanch, and Sweetheart, see they bark at me,' his issuing his orders, 'Let them anatomize Regan, see what breeds about her heart,' and his reflection when he sees the misery of Edgar, 'Nothing but his unkind daughters could have brought him to this,' are in a style of pathos, where the extremest resources of the imagination are called in to lay open the deepest movements of the heart, which was peculiar to Shakespeare. In the same style and spirit is his interrupting the Fool who asks, 'whether a madman be a gentleman or a yeoman', by answering 'A king, a king!'

The indirect part that Gloster takes in these scenes where his generosity leads him to relieve Lear and resent the cruelty of his daughters, at the very time that he is himself instigated to seek the life of his son, and suffering under the sting of his supposed ingratitude, is a striking accompaniment to the situation of Lear. Indeed, the manner in which the threads of the story are woven together is almost as wonderful in the way of art as the carrying on the tide of passion, still varying and unimpaired, is on the score of nature. Among the remarkable instances of this kind are Edgar's meeting with his old blind father; the deception he practises upon him when he pretends to lead him to the top of Dover-cliff—'Come on, sir, here's the place,' to prevent his ending his life and miseries together; his encounter with the perfidious Steward whom he kills, and his finding the letter from Gonerill to his brother upon him which leads to the final catastrophe, and brings the wheel of Justice 'full circle home' to the guilty parties. The bustle and rapid succession of events in the last scenes is surprising. But the meeting between Lear and Cordelia is by far the most affecting part of them. It has all the wildness of poetry, and all the heartfelt truth of nature. The previous account of her reception of the news of his unkind treatment, her involuntary reproaches to her sisters, 'Shame, ladies, shame,' Lear's backwardness to see his daughter, the picture of the desolate state to which he is reduced, 'Alack,'tis he; why he was met even now, as mad as the vex'd sea, singing aloud,' only prepare the way for and heighten our expectation of what follows, and assuredly this expectation is not disappointed when through the tender care of Cordelia he revives and recollects her.

Cordelia. How does my royal lord? How fares your majesty!

  Lear. You do me wrong, to take me out o' the grave:
   Thou art a soul in bliss; but I am bound
   Upon a wheel of fire, that mine own tears
   Do scald like molten lead.

Cordelia. Sir, do you know me?

Lear. You are a spirit I know: when did you die?

Cordelia. Still, still, far wide!

Physician. He's scarce awake; let him alone awhile.

  Lear. Where have I been? Where am I?—Fair daylight?—
  I am mightily abus'd.—I should even die with pity,
  To see another thus.—I know not what to say.—
  I will not swear these are my hands:—let's see;
  I feel this pin prick. 'Would I were assur'd
  Of my condition.

  Cordelia. O, look upon me, sir,
  And hold your hands in benediction o'er me:—
  No, sir, you must not kneel.

  Lear. Pray, do not mock me:
  I am a very foolish fond old man,
  Fourscore and upward;
  Not an hour more, nor less: and, to deal plainly,
  I fear, I am not in my perfect mind.
  Methinks, I shou'd know you, and know this man;
  Yet I am doubtful: for I am mainly ignorant
  What place this is; and all the skill I have
  Remembers not these garments; nor I know not
  Where I did lodge last night: do not laugh at me;
  For, as I am a man, I think this lady
  To be my child Cordelia.

Cordelia. And so I am, I am!

Almost equal to this in awful beauty is their consolation of each other when, after the triumph of their enemies, they are led to prison.

  Cordelia. We are not the first,
  Who, with best meaning, have incurr'd the worst.
  For thee, oppressed king, am I cast down;
  Myself could else out-frown false fortune's frown.—
  Shall we not see these daughters, and these sisters?

  Lear. No, no, no, no! Come, let's away to prison:
  We two alone will sing like birds i' the cage:
  When thou dost ask me blessing, I'll kneel down,
  And ask of thee forgiveness: so we'll live,
  And pray, and sing, and tell old tales, and laugh
  At gilded butterflies, and hear poor rogues

97

Talk of court news; and we'll talk with them too—
Who loses, and who wins; who's in, who's out;—
And take upon us the mystery of things,
As if we were God's spies: and we'll wear out,
In a wall'd prison, packs and sects of great ones,
That ebb and flow by the moon.

Edmund. Take them away.

  Lear. Upon such sacrifices, my Cordelia,
    The gods themselves throw incense.

The concluding events are sad, painfully sad; but their pathos is extreme. The oppression of the feelings is relieved by the very interest we take in the misfortunes of others, and by the reflections to which they give birth. Cordelia is hanged in prison by the orders of the bastard Edmund, which are known too late to be countermanded, and Lear dies broken-hearted, lamenting over her.

  Lear. And my poor fool is hang'd! No, no, no life:
    Why should a dog, a horse, a rat, have life.
    And thou no breath at all? O, thou wilt come no more,
    Never, never, never, never, never!—
    Pray you, undo this button: thank you, sir.—-

He dies, and indeed we feel the truth of what Kent says on the occasion—

  Vex not his ghost: O, let him pass! he hates him,
    That would upon the rack of the rough world
    Stretch him out longer.

Yet a happy ending has been contrived for this play, which is approved of by Dr. Johnson and condemned by Schlegel. A better authority than either, on any subject in which poetry and feeling are concerned, has given it in favour of Shakespeare, in some remarks on the acting of Lear, with which we shall conclude this account.

The Lear of Shakespeare cannot be acted. The contemptible machinery with which they mimic the storm which he goes out in, is not more inadequate to represent the horrors of the real elements than any actor can be to represent Lear. The greatness of Lear is not in corporal dimension, but in intellectual; the explosions of his passions are terrible as a volcano: they are storms turning up and disclosing to the bottom that rich sea, his mind, with all its vast riches. It is his mind which is laid bare. This case of flesh and blood seems too insignificant to be thought on; even as he himself neglects it. On the stage we see nothing but corporal infirmities and weakness, the impotence of rage; while we read it, we see not Lear, but we are Lear;—we are in his mind, we are sustained by a grandeur, which baffles the malice of daughters and storms; in the aberrations of his reason, we discover a mighty irregular power of reasoning, immethodized from the ordinary purposes of life, but exerting its powers, as the wind blows where it listeth, at will on the corruptions and abuses of mankind. What have looks or tones to do with that sublime identification of his age with that of THE HEAVENS THEMSELVES, when in his reproaches to them for conniving at the injustice of his children, he reminds them that "they themselves are old!" What gesture shall we appropriate to this? What has the voice or the eye to do with such things? But the play is beyond all art, as the tamperings with it show: it is too hard and stony; it must have love-scenes, and a happy ending. It is not enough that Cordelia is a daughter, she must shine as a lover too. Tate has put his hook in the nostrils of this Leviathan, for Garrick and his followers, the showmen of the scene, to draw it about more easily. A happy ending!—as if the living martyrdom that Lear had gone through,—the flaying of his feelings alive, did not make a fair dismissal from the stage of life the only decorous thing for him. If he is to live and be happy after, if he could sustain this world's burden after, why all this pudder and preparation—why torment us with all this unnecessary sympathy? As if the childish pleasure of getting his gilt robes and sceptre again could tempt him to act over again his misused station—as if at his years and with his experience anything was left but to die.' [Footnote: See an article, called 'Theatralia', in the second volume of the Reflector, by Charles Lamb.]

Four things have struck us in reading LEAR:

1. That poetry is an interesting study, for this reason, that it relates to whatever is most interesting in human life. Whoever therefore has a contempt for poetry, has a contempt for himself and humanity.

2. That the language of poetry is superior to the language of painting; because the strongest of our recollections relate to feelings, not to faces.

3. That the greatest strength of genius is shown in describing the strongest passions: for the power of the imagination, in works of invention, must be in proportion to the force of the natural impressions, which are the subject of them.

4. That the circumstance which balances the pleasure against the pain in tragedy is, that in proportion to the greatness of the evil, is our sense and desire of the opposite good excited; and that our sympathy with actual suffering is lost in the strong impulse given to our natural affections, and carried away with the swell-ing tide of passion, that gushes from and relieves the heart.

RICHARD II

RICHARD II is a play little known compared with RICHARD III, which last is a play that every unfledged candidate for theatrical fame chooses to strut and fret his hour upon the stage in; yet we confess that we prefer the nature and feeling of the one to the noise and bustle of the other; at least, as we are so often forced to see it acted. In RICHARD II the weakness of the king leaves us leisure to take a greater interest in the misfortunes of the man. 'After the first act, in which the arbitrariness of his behaviour only proves his want of resolution, we see him staggering under the unlooked-for blows of fortune, bewailing his loss of kingly power; not preventing it, sinking under the aspiring genius of Bolingbroke, his authority trampled on, his hopes failing him, and his pride crushed and broken down under insults and injuries, which his own misconduct had provoked, but which he has not courage or manliness to resent. The change of tone and behaviour in the two competitors for the throne according to their change of fortune, from the capricious sentence of banishment passed by Richard upon Bolingbroke, the suppliant offers and modest pretensions of the latter on his return, to the high and haughty tone with which he accepts Richard's resignation of the crown after the loss of all his power, the use which he makes of the deposed king to grace his triumphal progress through the streets of London, and the final intimation of his wish for his death, which immediately finds a servile executioner, is marked throughout with complete effect and without the slightest appearance of effort. The steps by which Bolingbroke mounts the throne are those by which Richard sinks into the grave. We feel neither respect nor love for the deposed monarch; for he is as wanting in energy as in principle: but we pity him, for he pities himself. His heart is by no means hardened against himself, but bleeds afresh at every new stroke of mischance, and his sensibility, absorbed in his own person, and unused to misfortune, is not only tenderly alive to its own sufferings, but without the fortitude to bear them. He is, however, human in his distresses; for to feel pain, and sorrow, weakness, disappointment, remorse and anguish, is the lot of humanity, and we sympathize with him accordingly. The sufferings of the man make us forget that he ever was a king.

The right assumed by sovereign power to trifle at its will with the happiness of others as a matter of course, or to remit its exercise as a matter of favour, is strikingly shown in the sentence of banishment so unjustly pronounced on Bolingbroke and Mowbray, and in what Bolingbroke says when four years of his banishment are taken off, with as little reason:

> How long a time lies in one little word!
> Four lagging winters and four wanton springs
> End in a word: such is the breath of kings.

A more affecting image of the loneliness of a state of exile can hardly be given than by what Bolingbroke afterwards observes of his having 'sighed his English breath in foreign clouds'; or than that conveyed in Mowbray's complaint at being banished for life.

> The language I have learned these forty years,
> My native English, now I must forego;
> And now my tongue's use is to me no more
> Than an unstringed viol or a harp,

Or like a cunning instrument cas'd up,
Or being open, put into his hands
That knows no touch to tune the harmony.
I am too old to fawn upon a nurse,
Too far in years to be a pupil now.—

How very beautiful is all this, and at the same time how very
ENGLISH too!

RICHARD II may be considered as the first of that series of English historical plays, in which 'is hung armour of the invincible knights of old', in which their hearts seem to strike against their coats of mail, where their blood tingles for the fight, and words are but the harbingers of blows. Of this state of accomplished barbarism the appeal of Bolingbroke and Mowbray is an admirable specimen. Another of these 'keen encounters of their wits', which serve to whet the talkers' swords, is where Aumerle answers in the presence of Bolingbroke to the charge which Bagot brings against him of being an accessory in Gloster's death.

  Fitzwater. If that thy valour stand on sympathies,
    There is my gage, Aumerle, in gage to thine;
    By that fair sun that shows me where thou stand'st
    I heard thee say, and vauntingly thou spak'st it,
    That thou wert cause of noble Gloster's death.
    If thou deny'st it twenty times thou liest,
    And I will turn thy falsehood to thy heart
    Where it was forged, with my rapier's point.

Aumerle. Thou dar'st not, coward, live to see the day,

Fitzwater. Now, by my soul, I would it were this hour.

Aumerle. Fitzwater, thou art damn'd to hell for this.

  Percy. Aumerle, thou liest; his honour is as true,
    In this appeal, as thou art all unjust;
    And that thou art so, there I throw my gage
    To prove it on thee, to th' extremest point
    Of mortal breathing. Seize it, if thou dar'st.

  Aumerle. And if I do not, may my hands rot off,
    And never brandish more revengeful steel
    Over the glittering helmet of my foe.
    Who sets me else? By heav'n, I'll throw at all.
    I have a thousand spirits in my breast,
    To answer twenty thousand such as you.

  Surrey. My lord Fitzwater, I remember well
    The very time Aumerle and you did talk.

Fitzwater. My lord, 'tis true: you were in presence then;
    And you can witness with me, this is true.

Surrey. As false, by heav'n, as heav'n itself is true.

Fitzwater, Surrey, thou liest.

  Surrey. Dishonourable boy,
    That lie shall lie so heavy on my sword,
    That it shall render vengeance and revenge,
    Till thou the lie-giver and that lie rest
    In earth as quiet as thy father's skull.
    In proof whereof, there is mine honour's pawn:
    Engage it to the trial, if thou dar'st.

  Fitzwater. How fondly dost thou spur a forward horse:
    If I dare eat or drink or breathe or live,
    I dare meet Surrey in a wilderness,
    And spit upon him, whilst I say he lies,
    And lies, and lies: there is my bond of faith,
    To tie thee to thy strong correction.
    As I do hope to thrive in this new world,
    Aumerle is guilty of my true appeal.

The truth is, that there is neither truth nor honour in all these noble persons: they answer words with words, as they do blows with blows, in mere self-defence: nor have they any principle whatever but that of courage in maintaining any wrong they dare commit, or any falsehood which they find it useful to assert. How different were these noble knights and 'barons bold' from their more refined descendants in the present day, who instead of deciding questions of right by brute force, refer everything to convenience, fashion, and good breeding! In point of any abstract love of truth or justice, they are just the same now that they were then.

The characters of old John of Gaunt and of his brother York, uncles to the King, the one stern and foreboding, the other honest, good- natured, doing all for the best, and therefore doing nothing, are well kept up. The speech of the former, in praise of England, is one of the most eloquent that ever was penned. We should perhaps hardly be disposed to feed the pampered egotism of our countrymen by quoting this description, were it not that the conclusion of it (which looks prophetic) may qualify any improper degree of exultation.

    This royal throne of kings, this sceptered isle,
    This earth of Majesty, this seat of Mars,
    This other Eden, demi-Paradise,
    This fortress built by nature for herself
    Against infection and the hand of war;
    This happy breed of men, this little world,
    This precious stone set in the silver sea,
    Which serves it in the office of a wall

(Or as a moat defensive to a house)
Against the envy of less happy lands:
This nurse, this teeming womb of royal kings,
Fear'd for their breed and famous for their birth,
Renown'd for their deeds, as far from home,
For Christian service and true chivalry,
As is the sepulchre in stubborn Jewry
Of the world's ransom, blessed Mary's son;
This land of such dear souls, this dear dear land,
Dear for her reputation through the world,
Is now leas'd out (I die pronouncing it)
Like to a tenement or pelting farm.
England bound in with the triumphant sea,
Whose rocky shore beats back the envious surge
Of wat'ry Neptune, is bound in with shame,
With inky-blots and rotten parchment bonds.
That England, that was wont to conquer others,
Hath made a shameful conquest of itself.

The character of Bolingbroke, afterwards Henry IV, is drawn with a masterly hand:—patient for occasion, and then steadily availing himself of it, seeing his advantage afar off, but only seizing on it when he has it within his reach, humble, crafty, bold, and aspiring, encroaching by regular but slow degrees, building power on opinion, and cementing opinion by power. His disposition is first unfolded by Richard himself, who however is too self-willed and secure to make a proper use of his knowledge.

Ourself and Bushy, Bagot here and Green,
Observed his courtship of the common people;
How he did seem to dive into their hearts,
With humble and familiar courtesy,
What reverence he did throw away on slaves;
Wooing poor craftsmen with the craft of smiles,
And patient under-bearing of his fortune,
As 'twere to banish their affections with him.
Off goes his bonnet to an oyster-wench;
A brace of draymen bid God speed him well,
And had the tribute of his supple knee,
With thanks my countrymen, my loving friends;
As were our England in reversion his,
And he our subjects' next degree in hope.

Afterwards, he gives his own character to Percy, in these words:

I thank thee, gentle Percy, and be sure
I count myself in nothing else so happy,
As in a soul rememb'ring my good friends;

103

And as my fortune ripens with thy love,
It shall be still thy true love's recompense.

We know how he afterwards kept his promise. His bold assertion of his own rights, his pretended submission to the king, and the ascendancy which he tacitly assumes over him without openly claiming it, as soon as he has him in his power, are characteristic traits of this ambitious and politic usurper. But the part of Richard himself gives the chief interest to the play. His folly, his vices, his misfortunes, his reluctance to part with the crown, his fear to keep it, his weak and womanish regrets, his starting tears, his fits of hectic passion, his smothered majesty, pass in succession before us, and make a picture as natural as it is affecting. Among the most striking touches of pathos are his wish, 'O that I were a mockery king of snow to melt away before the sun of Bolingbroke', and the incident of the poor groom who comes to visit him in prison, and tells him how 'it yearned his heart that Bolingbroke upon his coronation day rode on Roan Barbary. We shall have occasion to return hereafter to the character of Richard II in speaking of Henry VI. There is only one passage more, the description of his entrance into London with Bolingbroke, which we should like to quote here, if it had not been so used and worn out, so thumbed and got by rote, so praised and painted; but its beauty surmounts all these considerations.

Duchess. My lord, you told me you would tell the rest,
  When weeping made you break the story off
  Of our two cousins coming into London.

York. Where did I leave?

Duchess. At that sad stop, my lord,
  Where rude misgovern'd hands, from window tops,
  Threw dust and rubbish on king Richard's head.

York. Then, as I said, the duke, great Bolingbroke,
  Mounted upon a hot and fiery steed,
  Which his aspiring rider seem'd to know,
  With slow, but stately pace, kept on his course,
  While all tongues cried—God save thee, Bolingbroke!
  You would have thought the very windows spake,
  So many greedy looks of young and old
  Through casements darted their desiring eyes
  Upon his visage; and that all the walls,
  With painted imag'ry, had said at once—
  Jesu preserve thee! welcome, Bolingbroke!
  Whilst he, from one side to the other turning,
  Bare-headed, lower than his proud steed's neck,
  Bespake them thus—I thank you, countrymen:
  And thus still doing thus he pass'd along.

Duchess. Alas, poor Richard! where rides he the while?

York. As in a theatre, the eyes of men,
  After a well-grac'd actor leaves the stage,
  Are idly bent on him that enters next,
  Thinking his prattle to be tedious:
  Even so, or with much more contempt, men's eyes
  Did scowl on Richard; no man cried God save him!
  No joyful tongue gave him his welcome home:
  But dust was thrown upon his sacred head!
  Which with such gentle sorrow he shook off—
  His face still combating with tears and smiles,
  The badges of his grief and patience—
  That had not God, for some strong purpose, steel'd
  The hearts of men, they must perforce have melted.
  And barbarism itself have pitied him.

HENRY IV

IN TWO PARTS

If Shakespeare's fondness for the ludicrous sometimes led to faults in his tragedies (which was not often the case), he has made us amends by the character of Falstaff. This is perhaps the most substantial comic character that ever was invented. Sir John carries a most portly presence in the mind's eye; and in him, not to speak it profanely, 'we behold the fullness of the spirit of wit and humour bodily'. We are as well acquainted with his person as his mind, and his jokes come upon us with double force and relish from the quantity of flesh through which they make their way, as he shakes his fat sides with laughter, or 'lards the lean earth as he walks along'. Other comic characters seem, if we approach and handle them, to resolve themselves into air, 'into thin air'; but this is embodied and palpable to the grossest apprehension: it lies 'three fingers deep upon the ribs', it plays about the lungs and the diaphragm with all the force of animal enjoyment. His body is like a good estate to his mind, from which he receives rents and revenues of profit and pleasure in kind, according to its extent, and the richness of the soil. Wit is often a meagre substitute for pleasurable sensation; an effusion of spleen and petty spite at the comforts of others, from feeling none in itself. Falstaff's wit is an emanation of a fine constitution; an exuberance of good-humour and good-nature; an overflowing of his love of laughter, and good-fellowship; a giving vent to his heart's ease and over-contentment with himself and others. He would not be in character, if he were not so fat as he is; for there is the greatest keeping in the boundless luxury of his imagination and the pampered self-indulgence of his physical appetites. He manures and nourishes his mind with jests, as he does his body with sack and sugar. He carves out his jokes, as he would a capon, or a haunch of venison, where there is cut and come again; and pours out upon them the oil of gladness. His tongue drops fatness, and in the chambers of his brain 'it snows of meat and drink'. He keeps up perpetual holiday and open house, and we live with him in a round of invitations to a rump and dozen.—Yet we are not to suppose that he was a mere sensualist. All this is as much in imagination as in reality. His sensuality does not engross and stupify his other faculties, but 'ascends me into the brain, clears away all the dull, crude vapours that environ it, and makes it full of nimble, fiery, and delectable shapes'. His imagination keeps up the ball after his senses have done with it. He seems to have even a greater enjoyment of the freedom from restraint, of good cheer, of his ease, of his vanity, in the ideal exaggerated descriptions which he gives of them, than in fact. He never fails to enrich his discourse with allusions to eating and drinking, but we never see him at table. He carries his own larder about with him, and he is himself 'a tun of man'. His pulling out the bottle in the field of battle is a joke to show his contempt for glory accompanied with danger, his systematic adherence to his Epicurean philosophy in the most trying circumstances. Again, such is his deliberate exaggeration of his own vices, that it does not seem quite certain whether the account of his hostess's bill, found in his pocket, with such an out-of-the-way charge for capons and sack with only one halfpenny-worth of bread, was not put there by himself as a trick to humour the jest upon his favourite propensities, and as a conscious caricature of himself. He is represented as a liar, a braggart, a coward, a glutton, &c., and yet we are not offended but delighted with him; for he is all these as much to amuse others as to gratify himself, He openly assumes all these characters to show the humorous part of them. The unrestrained indulgence of his own ease, appetites, and convenience, has neither malice nor hypocrisy in it. In a word, he is an actor in himself almost as much as upon the stage, and we no more object to the character of Falstaff in a moral point of view than we should think of bringing an excellent comedian, who should represent him to the life, before one of the police offices. We only consider the number of pleasant lights in which he puts certain foibles (the more pleasant as they are opposed to the received rules and necessary restraints of society) and do not trouble ourselves about the consequences resulting from them, for no mischievous consequences do result. Sir John is old as well as fat, which gives a melancholy retrospective tinge to the character; and by the disparity between his inclinations and his capacity for enjoyment, makes it still more ludicrous and fantastical.

The secret of Falstaff's wit is for the most part a masterly presence of mind, an absolute self-possession, which nothing can disturb. His repartees are involuntary suggestions of his self-love; instinctive evasions of everything that threatens to interrupt the career of his triumphant jollity and self-complacency. His very size floats him out of all his difficulties in a sea of rich conceits; and he turns round on the pivot of his convenience, with every occasion and at a moment's warning. His natural repugnance to every unpleasant thought or circumstance of itself makes light of objections, and provokes the most extravagant and licentious answers in his own justification. His indifference to truth puts no check upon his invention, and the more improbable and unexpected his contrivances are, the more happily does he seem to be delivered of them, the anticipation of their effect acting as a stimulus to the gaiety of his fancy. The success of one adventurous sally gives him spirits to undertake another: he deals always in round numbers, and his exaggerations and excuses are 'open, palpable, monstrous as the father that begets them'. His dissolute carelessness of what he says discovers itself in the first dialogue with the Prince.

Falstaff. By the lord, thou say'st true, lad; and is not mine hostess of the tavern a most sweet wench?

P. Henry. As the honey of Hibla, my old lad of the castle; and is not a buff-jerkin a most sweet robe of durance?

Falstaff. How now, how now, mad wag, what in thy quips and thy quiddities? what a plague have I to do with a buff-jerkin?

P. Henry. Why, what a pox have I to do with mine hostess of the tavern?

In the same scene he afterwards affects melancholy, from pure satisfaction of heart, and professes reform, because it is the farthest thing in the world from his thoughts. He has no qualms of conscience, and therefore would as soon talk of them as of anything else when the humour takes him.

Falstaff. But Hal, I pr'ythee trouble me no more with vanity. I would to God thou and I knew where a commodity of good names were to be bought: an old lord of council rated me the other day in the street about you, sir; but I mark'd him not, and yet he talked very wisely, and in the street too.

P. Henry. Thou didst well, for wisdom cries out in the street, and no man regards it.

Falstaff. O, thou hast damnable iteration, and art indeed able to corrupt a saint. Thou hast done much harm unto me, Hal; God forgive thee for it. Before I knew thee, Hal, I knew nothing, and now I am, if a man should speak truly, little better than one of the wicked. I must give over this life, and I will give it over, by the lord; an I do not, I am a villain. I'll be damn'd for never a king's son in Christendom,

P. Henry. Where shall we take a purse to-morrow. Jack?

Falstaff. Where thou wilt, lad, I'll make one; an I do not, call me villain, and baffle me.

P. Henry. I see good amendment of life in thee, from praying to purse-taking.

Falstaff. Why, Hal, 'tis my vocation, Hal. 'Tis no sin for a man to labour in his vocation.

Of the other prominent passages, his account of his pretended resistance to the robbers, 'who grew from four men in buckram into eleven' as the imagination of his own valour increased with his relating it, his getting off when the truth is discovered by pretending he knew the Prince, the scene in which in the person of the old king he lectures the prince and gives himself a good character, the soliloquy on honour, and description of his new- raised recruits, his meeting with the chief justice, his abuse of the Prince and Poins, who overhear him, to Doll Tearsheet, his reconciliation with Mrs. Quickly who has arrested him for an old debt and whom he persuades to pawn her plate to lend him ten pounds more, and the scenes with Shallow and Silence, are all inimitable. Of all of them, the scene in which Falstaff plays the part, first, of the King, and then of Prince Henry, is the one that has been the most often quoted. We must quote it once more in illustration of our remarks.

Falstaff. Harry, I do not only marvel where thou spendeth thy time, but also how thou art accompanied: for though the camomile, the more it is trodden on, the faster it grows, yet youth, the more it is wasted, the sooner it wears. That thou art my son, I have partly thy mother's word, partly my own opinion; but chiefly, a villainous trick of thine eye, and a foolish hanging of thy nether lip, that doth warrant me. If then thou be son to me, here lies the point;— Why, being son to me, art thou so pointed at? Shaft the blessed sun of heaven prove a micher, and eat blackberries? A question not to be ask'd. Shall the son of England prove a thief, and take purses? a question not to be ask'd. There is a thing, Harry, which thou hast often heard of, and it is known to many in our land by the name of pitch: this pitch, as ancient writers do report, doth defile; so doth the company thou keepest: for, Harry, now I do not speak to thee in drink, but in tears; not in pleasure, but in passion; not in words only, but in woes also:—and yet there is a virtuous man, whom I have often noted in thy company, but I know not his name.

P. Henry. What manner of man, an it like your majesty?

Falstaff. A goodly portly man, i'faith, and a corpulent; of a cheerful look, a pleasing eye, and a most noble carriage; and, as I think, his age some fifty, or, by'r-lady, inclining to threescore; and now I do remember me, his name is Falstaff: if that man should be lewdly given, he deceiveth me; for, Harry, I see virtue in his looks. If then the fruit may be known by the tree, as the tree by the fruit, then peremptorily I speak it, there is virtue in that Falstaff: him keep with, the rest banish. And tell me now, thou naughty varlet, tell me, where hast thou been this month?

P. Henry. Dost thou speak like a king? Do thou stand for me, and
I'll play my father.

Falstaff. Depose me? if thou dost it half so gravely, so majestically, both in word and matter, hang
me up by the heels for a rabbit-sucker, or a poulterer's hare.

P. Henry. Well, here I am set.

Falstaff. And here I stand:—judge, my masters.

P. Henry. Now, Harry, whence come you?

Falstaff. My noble lord, from Eastcheap.

P. Henry. The complaints I hear of thee are grievous.

Falstaff. S'blood, my lord, they are false:—nay, I'll tickle ye for a young prince, i'faith.

P. Henry. Swearest thou, ungracious boy? henceforth ne'er look on me. Thou art violently
carried away from grace: there is a devil haunts thee, in the likeness of a fat old man; a tun of
man is thy companion. Why dost thou converse with that trunk of humours, that bolting-hutch
of beastliness, that swoln parcel of dropsies, that huge bombard of sack, that stuft cloak-bag of
guts, that roasted Manning-tree ox with the pudding in his belly, that reverend vice, that grey
iniquity, that father ruffian, that vanity in years? wherein is he good, but to taste sack and drink
it? wherein neat and cleanly, but to carve a capon and eat it? wherein cunning, but in craft?
wherein crafty, but in villainy? wherein villainous, but in all things? wherein worthy, but in
nothing?

Falstaff. I would, your grace would take me with you: whom means your grace?

P. Henry. That villainous, abominable mis-leader of youth, Falstaff, that old white-bearded Satan.

Falstaff. My lord, the man I know.

P. Henry. I know thou dost.

Falstaff. But to say, I know more harm in him than in myself, were to say more than I know. That
he is old (the more the pity) his white hairs do witness it: but that he is (saving your reverence)
a whore-master, that I utterly deny. If sack and sugar be a fault, God help the wicked! if to be old
and merry be a sin, then many an old host that I know is damned: if to be fat be to be hated, then
Pharaoh's lean kine are to be loved. No, my good lord; banish Peto, banish Bardolph, banish
Poins; but for sweet Jack Falstaff, kind Jack Falstaff, true Jack Falstaff, valiant Jack Falstaff, and
therefore more valiant, being as he is, old Jack Falstaff, banish not him thy Harry's company;
banish plump Jack, and banish all the world.

P. Henry. I do, I will.

[Knocking; and Hostess and Bardolph go out.]

Re-enter Bardolph, running.

Bardolph. O, my lord, my lord; the sheriff, with a most monstrous watch, is at the door.

Falstaff. Out, you rogue! play out the play: I have much to say in the behalf of that Falstaff.

One of the most characteristic descriptions of Sir John is that which Mrs. Quickly gives of him when he asks her, 'What is the gross sum that I owe thee?'

Hostess. Marry, if thou wert an honest man, thyself, and the money too. Thou didst swear to me upon a parcel-gilt goblet, sitting in my Dolphin-chamber, at the round table, by a sea-coal fire on Wednesday in Whitsunweek, when the prince broke thy head for likening his father to a singing man of Windsor; thou didst swear to me then, as I was washing thy wound, to marry me, and make me my lady thy wife. Canst thou deny it? Did not goodwife Keech, the butcher's wife, come in then, and call me gossip Quickly? coming in to borrow a mess of vinegar; telling us, she had a good dish of prawns; whereby thou didst desire to eat some; whereby I told thee, they were ill for a green wound? And didst thou not, when she was gone down stairs, desire me to be no more so familiarity with such poor people; saying, that ere long they should call me madam? And didst thou not kiss me, and bid me fetch thee thirty shillings? I put thee now to thy book-oath; deny it, if thou canst.

This scene is to us the most convincing proof of Falstaff's power of gaining over the goodwill of those he was familiar with, except indeed Bardolph's somewhat profane exclamation on hearing the account of his death, 'Would I were with him, wheresoe'er he is, whether in heaven or hell.'

One of the topics of exulting superiority over others most common in Sir John's mouth is his corpulence and the exterior marks of good living which he carries about him, thus 'turning his vices into commodity'. He accounts for the friendship between the Prince and Poins, from 'their legs being both of a bigness'; and compares Justice Shallow to 'a man made after supper of a cheese-paring'. There cannot be a more striking gradation of character than that between Falstaff and Shallow, and Shallow and Silence. It seems difficult at first to fall lower than the squire; but this fool, great as he is, finds an admirer and humble foil in his cousin Silence. Vain of his acquaintance with Sir John, who makes a butt of him, he exclaims, 'Would, cousin Silence, that thou had'st seen that which this knight and I have seen!'—'Aye, Master Shallow, we have heard the chimes at midnight,' says Sir John. To Falstaff's observation, 'I did not think Master Silence had been a man of this mettle', Silence answers, 'Who, I? I have been merry twice and once ere now.' What an idea is here conveyed of a prodigality of living? What good husbandry and economical self-denial in his pleasures? What a stock of lively recollections? It is curious that Shakespeare has ridiculed in Justice Shallow, who was 'in some authority under the king', that disposition to unmeaning tautology which is the regal infirmity of later times, and which, it may be supposed, he acquired from talking to his cousin Silence, and receiving no answers.

Falstaff. You have here a goodly dwelling, and a rich.

Shallow. Barren, barren, barren; beggars all, beggars all, Sir John: marry, good air. Spread Davy, spread Davy. Well said, Davy.

Falstaff. This Davy serves you for good uses.

Shallow. A good varlet, a good varlet, a very good varlet. By the mass, I have drank too much sack at supper. A good varlet. Now sit down, now sit down. Come, cousin.

The true spirit of humanity, the thorough knowledge of the stuff we are made of, the practical wisdom with the seeming fooleries in the whole of the garden-scene at Shallow's country-seat, and just before in the exquisite dialogue between him and Silence on the death of old Double, have no parallel anywhere else. In one point of view, they are laughable in the extreme; in another they are equally affecting, if it is affecting to show what a little thing is human life, what a poor forked creature man is!

The heroic and serious part of these two plays founded on the story of Henry IV is not inferior to the comic and farcical. The characters of Hotspur and Prince Henry are two of the most beautiful and dramatic, both in themselves and from contrast, that ever were drawn. They are the essence of chivalry. We like Hotspur the best upon the whole, perhaps because he was unfortunate.— The characters of their fathers, Henry IV and old Northumberland, are kept up equally well. Henry naturally succeeds by his prudence and caution in keeping what he has got; Northumberland fails in his enterprise from an excess of the same quality, and is caught in the web of his own cold, dilatory policy. Owen Glendower is a masterly character. It is as bold and original as it is intelligible and thoroughly natural. The disputes between him and Hotspur are managed with infinite address and insight into nature. We cannot help pointing out here some very beautiful lines, where Hotspur describes the fight between Glendower and Mortimer.

—When on the gentle Severn's sedgy bank,
In single opposition hand to hand,
He did confound the best part of an hour
In changing hardiment with great Glendower:
Three times they breath'd, and three times did they drink,
Upon agreement, of swift Severn's flood;
Who then affrighted with their bloody looks,
Ran fearfully among the trembling reeds,
And hid his crisp head in the hollow bank,
Blood-stained with these valiant combatants.

The peculiarity and the excellence of Shakespeare's poetry is, that it seems as if he made his imagination the hand-maid of nature, and nature the plaything of his imagination. He appears to have been all the characters, and in all the situations he describes. It is as if either he had had all their feelings, or had lent them all his genius to express themselves. There cannot be stronger instances of this than Hotspur's rage when Henry IV forbids him to speak of Mortimer, his insensibility to all that his father and uncle urge to calm him, and his fine abstracted apostrophe to honour, 'By heaven methinks it were an easy leap to pluck bright honour from the moon,' &c. After all, notwithstanding the gallantry, generosity, good temper, and idle freaks of the mad-cap Prince of Wales, we should not have been sorry if Northumberland's force had come up in time to decide the fate of the battle at Shrewsbury; at least, we always heartily sympathize with Lady Percy's grief when she exclaims:

111

Had my sweet Harry had but half their numbers,
To-day might I (hanging on Hotspur's neck)
Have talked of Monmouth's grave.

The truth is, that we never could forgive the Prince's treatment of Falstaff; though perhaps Shakespeare knew what was best, according to the history, the nature of the times, and of the man. We speak only as dramatic critics. Whatever terror the French in those days might have of Henry V, yet to the readers of poetry at present, Falstaff is the better man of the two. We think of him and quote him oftener.

HENRY V

Henry V is a very favourite monarch with the English nation, and he appears to have been also a favourite with Shakespeare, who labours hard to apologize for the actions of the king, by showing us the character of the man, as 'the king of good fellows'. He scarcely deserves this honour. He was fond of war and low company:—we know little else of him. He was careless, dissolute, and ambitious—idle, or doing mischief. In private, he seemed to have no idea of the common decencies of life, which he subjected to a kind of regal license; in public affairs, he seemed to have no idea of any rule of right or wrong, but brute force, glossed over with a little religious hypocrisy and archiepiscopal advice. His principles did not change with his situation and professions. His adventure on Gadshill was a prelude to the affair of Agincourt, only a bloodless one; Falstaff was a puny prompter of violence and outrage, compared with the pious and politic Archbishop of Canterbury, who gave the king carte blanche, in a genealogical tree of his family, to rob and murder in circles of latitude and longitude abroad—to save the possessions of the Church at home. This appears in the speeches in Shakespeare, where the hidden motives that actuate princes and their advisers in war and policy are better laid open than in speeches from the throne or woolsack. Henry, because he did not know how to govern his own kingdom, determined to make war upon his neighbours. Because his own title to the crown was doubtful, he laid claim to that of France. Because he did not know how to exercise the enormous power, which had just dropped into his hands, to any one good purpose, he immediately undertook (a cheap and obvious resource of sovereignty) to do all the mischief he could. Even if absolute monarchs had the wit to find out objects of laudable ambition, they could only 'plume up their wills' in adhering to the more sacred formula of the royal prerogative, 'the right divine of kings to govern wrong', because will is only then triumphant when it is opposed to the will of others, because the pride of power is only then shown, not when it consults the rights and interests of others, but when it insults and tramples on all justice and all humanity. Henry declares his resolution 'when France is his, to bend it to his awe, or break it all to pieces'—a resolution worthy of a conqueror, to destroy all that he cannot enslave; and what adds to the joke, he lays all the blame of the consequences of his ambition on those who will not submit tamely to his tyranny. Such is the history of kingly power, from the beginning to the end of the world—with this difference, that the object of war formerly, when the people adhered to their allegiance, was to depose kings; the object latterly, since the people swerved from their allegiance, has been to restore kings, and to make common cause against mankind. The object of our late invasion and conquest of France was to restore the legitimate monarch, the descendant of Hugh Capet, to the throne: Henry V in his time made war on and deposed the descendant of this very Hugh Capet, on the plea that he was a usurper and illegitimate. What would the great modern catspaw of legitimacy and restorer of divine right have said to the claim of Henry and the title of the descendants of Hugh Capet? Henry V, it is true, was a hero, a king of England, and the conqueror of the king of France. Yet we feel little love or admiration for him. He was a hero, that is, he was ready to sacrifice his own life for the pleasure of destroying thousands of other lives: he was a king of England, but not a constitutional one, and we only like kings according to the law; lastly, he was a conqueror of the French king, and for this we dislike him less than if he had conquered the French people. How then do we like him? We like him in the play. There he is a very amiable monster, a very splendid pageant. As we like to gaze at a panther or a young lion in their cages in the Tower, and catch a pleasing horror from their glistening eyes, their velvet paws, and dreadless roar, so we take a very romantic, heroic, patriotic, and poetical delight in the boasts and feats of our younger Harry, as they appear on the stage and are confined to lines of ten syllables; where no blood follows the stroke that wounds our ears, where no harvest bends beneath horses' hoofs, no city flames, no little child is butchered, no dead men's bodies are found piled on heaps and festering the next morning—in the orchestra!

So much for the politics of this play; now for the poetry. Perhaps one of the most striking images in all Shakespeare is that given of war in the first lines of the Prologue.

> O for a muse of fire, that would ascend
> The brightest heaven of invention,
> A kingdom for a stage, princes to act,
> And monarchs to behold the swelling scene!
> Then should the warlike Harry, like himself,
> Assume the port of Mars, and AT HIS HEELS
> LEASH'D IN LIKE HOUNDS, SHOULD FAMINE, SWORD, AND FIRE
> CROUCH FOR EMPLOYMENT.

Rubens, if he had painted it, would not have improved upon this simile. The conversation between the Archbishop of Canterbury and the Bishop of Ely relating to the sudden change in the manners of Henry V is among the well-known BEAUTIES of Shakespeare. It is indeed admirable both for strength and grace. It has sometimes occurred to us that Shakespeare, in describing 'the reformation' of the Prince, might have had an eye to himself—

> Which is a wonder how his grace should glean it,
> Since his addiction was to courses vain,
> His companies unletter'd, rude and shallow,
> His hours fill'd up with riots, banquets, sports;
> And never noted in him any study,
> Any retirement, any sequestration
> From open haunts and popularity.

> Ely. The strawberry grows underneath the nettle,
> And wholesome berries thrive and ripen best
> Neighbour'd by fruit of baser quality:
> And so the prince obscur'd his contemplation
> Under the veil of wildness, which no doubt
> Grew like the summer-grass, fastest by night,
> Unseen, yet crescive in his faculty.

This at least is as probable an account of the progress of the poet's mind as we have met with in any of the Essays on the Learning of Shakespeare.

Nothing can be better managed than the caution which the king gives the meddling Archbishop, not to advise him rashly to engage in the war with France, his scrupulous dread of the consequences of that advice, and his eager desire to hear and follow it.

114

And God forbid, my dear and faithful lord,
That you should fashion, wrest, or bow your reading,
Or nicely charge your understanding soul
With opening titles miscreate, whose right
Suits not in native colours with the truth.
For God doth know how many now in health
Shall drop their blood, in approbation
Of what your reverence shall incite us to.

Therefore take heed how you impawn your person,
How you awake our sleeping sword of war;
We charge you in the name of God, take heed.
For never two such kingdoms did contend
Without much fall of blood, whose guiltless drops
Are every one a woe, a sore complaint
'Gainst him, whose wrong gives edge unto the swords
That make such waste in brief mortality.
Under this conjuration, speak, my lord;
For we will hear, note, and believe in heart,
That what you speak, is in your conscience wash'd,
As pure as sin with baptism.

Another characteristic instance of the blindness of human nature to everything but its own interests is the complaint made by the king of 'the ill neighbourhood' of the Scot in attacking England when she was attacking France.

For once the eagle England being in prey,
To her unguarded nest the weazel Scot
Comes sneaking, and so sucks her princely eggs.

It is worth observing that in all these plays, which give an admirable picture of the spirit of the good old times, the moral inference does not at all depend upon the nature of the actions, but on the dignity or meanness of the persons committing them. 'The eagle England' has a right 'to be in prey', but 'the weazel Scot' has none 'to come sneaking to her nest', which she has left to pounce upon others. Might was right, without equivocation or disguise, in that heroic and chivalrous age. The substitution of right for might, even in theory, is among the refinements and abuses of modern philosophy.

A more beautiful rhetorical delineation of the effects of subordination in a commonwealth can hardly be conceived than the following:

For government, though high and low and lower,
Put into parts, doth keep in one consent,
Congruing in a full and natural close,
Like music.
—Therefore heaven doth divide
The state of man in divers functions,

Setting endeavour in continual motion;
To which is fixed, as an aim or butt,
Obedience; for so work the honey bees;
Creatures that by a rule in nature, teach
The art of order to a peopled kingdom.
They have a king, and officers of sorts:
Where some, like magistrates, correct at home;
Others, like merchants, venture trade abroad;
Others, like soldiers, armed in their stings,
Make boot upon the summer's velvet buds;
Which pillage they with merry march bring home
To the tent-royal of their emperor;
Who, busied in his majesty, surveys
The singing mason building roofs of gold;
The civil citizens kneading up the honey;
The poor mechanic porters crowding in
Their heavy burthens at his narrow gate;
The sad-eyed justice, with his surly hum,
Delivering o'er to executors pale
The lazy yawning drone. I this infer,—
That many things, having full reference
To one consent, may work contrariously:
As many arrows, loosed several ways,
Fly to one mark;
As many several ways meet in one town;
As many fresh streams meet in one salt sea;
As many lines close in the dial's centre;
So may a thousand actions, once a-foot,
End in one purpose, and be all well borne
Without defeat.

HENRY V is but one of Shakespeare's second-rate plays. Yet by quoting passages, like this, from his second-rate plays alone, we might make a volume 'rich with his praise',

As is the oozy bottom of the sea
With sunken wrack and sumless treasuries.

Of this sort are the king's remonstrance to Scroop, Grey, and Cambridge, on the detection of their treason, his address to the soldiers at the siege of Harfleur, and the still finer one before the battle of Agincourt, the description of the night before the battle, and the reflections on ceremony put into the mouth of the king.

O hard condition; twin-born with greatness,
Subjected to the breath of every fool,
Whose sense no more can feel but his own wringing!
What infinite heart's ease must kings neglect,

That private men enjoy? and what have kings,
That privates have not too, save ceremony?
Save general ceremony?
And what art thou, thou idol ceremony?
What kind of god art thou, that suffer'st more
Of mortal griefs, than do thy worshippers?
What are thy rents? what are thy comings-in?
O ceremony, show me but thy worth!
What is thy soul, O adoration?
Art thou aught else but place, degree, and form,
Creating awe and fear in other men?
Wherein thou art less happy, being feared,
Than they in fearing.
What drink'st thou oft, instead of homage sweet,
But poison'd flattery? O, be sick, great greatness,
And bid thy ceremony give thee cure!
Think'st thou, the fiery fever will go out
With titles blown from adulation?
Will it give place to flexure and low bending?
Can'st thou, when thou command'st the beggar's knee,
Command the health of it? No, thou proud dream,
That play'st so subtly with a king's repose,
I am a king, that find thee: and I know,
'Tis not the balm, the sceptre, and the ball,
The sword, the mace, the crown imperial,
The enter-tissu'd robe of gold and pearl,
The farsed title running 'fore the king,
The throne he sits on, nor the tide of pomp
That beats upon the high shore of this world,
No, not all these, thrice-gorgeous ceremony,
Not all these, laid in bed majestical,
Can sleep so soundly as the wretched slave;
Who, with a body fili'd, and vacant mind,
Gets him to rest, cramm'd with distressful bread,
Never sees horrid night, the child of hell:
But, like a lacquey, from the rise to set,
Sweats in the eye of Phoebus, and all night
Sleeps in Elysium; next day, after dawn,
Doth rise, and help Hyperion to his horse;
And follows so the ever-running year
With profitable labour, to his grave:
And, but for ceremony, such a wretch,
Winding up days with toil, and nights with sleep,
Has the forehand and vantage of a king.
The slave, a member of the country's peace,

Enjoys it; but in gross brain little wots,
What watch the king keeps to maintain the peace,
Whose hours the peasant best advantages.

Most of these passages are well known: there is one, which we do not remember to have seen noticed, and yet it is no whit inferior to the rest in heroic beauty. It is the account of the deaths of York and Suffolk.

Exeter. The duke of York commends him to your majesty.

K. Henry. Lives he, good uncle? thrice within this hour,
I saw him down; thrice up again, and fighting;
From helmet to the spur all blood he was.

Exeter. In which array (brave soldier) doth he lie,
Larding the plain; and by his bloody side
(Yoke-fellow to his honour-owing wounds)
The noble earl of Suffolk also lies.
Suffolk first died: and York, all haggled o'er,
Comes to him, where in gore he lay insteep'd,
And takes him by the beard; kisses the gashes,
That bloodily did yawn upon his face;
And cries aloud—Tarry, dear cousin Suffolk!
My soul shall thine keep company to heaven:
Tarry, sweet soul, for mine, then fly a-breast;
As, in this glorious and well-foughten field,
We kept together in our chivalry!
Upon these words I came, and cheer'd him up:
He smil'd me in the face, raught me his hand,
And, with a feeble gripe, says—Dear my lord,
Commend my service to my sovereign.
So did he turn, and over Suffolk's neck
He threw his wounded arm, and kiss'd his lips;
And so, espous'd to death, with blood he seal'd
A testament of noble-ending love.

But we must have done with splendid quotations. The behaviour of the king, in the difficult and doubtful circumstances in which he is placed, is as patient and modest as it is spirited and lofty in his prosperous fortune. The character of the French nobles is also very admirably depicted; and the Dauphin's praise of his horse shows the vanity of that class of persons in a very striking point of view. Shakespeare always accompanies a foolish prince with a satirical courtier, as we see in this instance. The comic parts of HENRY V are very inferior to those of HENRY IV. Falstaff is dead, and without him. Pistol, Nym, and Bardolph are satellites without a sun. Fluellen the Welshman is the most entertaining character in the piece. He is good-natured, brave, choleric, and pedantic. His parallel between Alexander and Harry of Monmouth, and his desire to have 'some disputations' with Captain Macmorris on the discipline of the Roman wars, in the heat of the battle, are never to be forgotten. His treatment of Pistol is as good as Pistol's treatment of his French prisoner. There are two other remarkable prose passages in this play: the conversation of Henry in disguise with the three sentinels on the duties of a soldier, and his courtship of Katherine in broken French. We like them both exceedingly, though the first savours perhaps too much of the king, and the last too little of the lover.

HENRY VI

IN THREE PARTS

During the time of the civil wars of York and Lancaster, England was a perfect bear-garden, and Shakespeare has given us a very lively picture of the scene. The three parts of HENRY VI convey a picture of very little else; and are inferior to the other historical plays. They have brilliant passages; but the general ground-work is comparatively poor and meagre, the style 'flat and unraised'. There are few lines like the following:

> Glory is like a circle in the water;
> Which never ceaseth to enlarge itself,
> Till by broad spreading it disperse to naught.

The first part relates to the wars in France after the death of Henry V and the story of the Maid of Orleans. She is here almost as scurvily treated as in Voltaire's Pucelle. Talbot is a very magnificent sketch: there is something as formidable in this portrait of him, as there would be in a monumental figure of him or in the sight of the armour which he wore. The scene in which he visits the Countess of Auvergne, who seeks to entrap him, is a very spirited one, and his description of his own treatment while a prisoner to the French not less remarkable.

Salisbury. Yet tell'st thou not how thou wert entertain'd.

> Talbot. With scoffs and scorns, and contumelious taunts,
> In open market-place produced they me,
> To be a public spectacle to all.
> Here, said they, is the terror of the French,
> The scarecrow that affrights our children so.
> Then broke I from the officers that led me,
> And with my nails digg'd stones out of the ground,
> To hurl at the beholders of my shame.
> My grisly countenance made others fly,
> None durst come near for fear of sudden death.
> In iron walls they deem'd me not secure:
> So great a fear my name amongst them spread,
> That they suppos'd I could rend bars of steel,
> And spurn in pieces posts of adamant.
> Wherefore a guard of chosen shot I had:
> They walk'd about me every minute-while;
> And if I did but stir out of my bed,
> Ready they were to shoot me to the heart.

The second part relates chiefly to the contests between the nobles during the minority of Henry and the death of Gloucester, the good Duke Humphrey. The character of Cardinal Beaufort is the most prominent in the group: the account of his death is one of our author's masterpieces. So is the speech of Gloucester to the nobles on the loss of the provinces of France by the king's marriage with Margaret of Anjou. The pretensions and growing ambition of the Duke of York, the father of Richard III, are also very ably developed. Among the episodes, the tragi-comedy of Jack Cade, and the detection of the impostor Simcox are truly edifying.

The third part describes Henry's loss of his crown: his death takes place in the last act, which is usually thrust into the common acting play of RICHARD III. The character of Gloucester, afterwards King Richard, is here very powerfully commenced, and his dangerous designs and long-reaching ambition are fully described in his soliloquy in the third act, beginning, 'Aye, Edward will use women honourably.' Henry VI is drawn as distinctly as his high-spirited Queen, and notwithstanding the very mean figure which Henry makes as a king, we still feel more respect for him than for his wife.

We have already observed that Shakespeare was scarcely more remarkable for the force and marked contrasts of his characters than for the truth and subtlety with which he has distinguished those which approached the nearest to each other. For instance, the soul of Othello is hardly more distinct from that of Iago than that of Desdemona is shown to be from Aemilia's; the ambition of Macbeth is as distinct from the ambition of Richard III as it is from the meekness of Duncan; the real madness of Lear is as different from the feigned madness of Edgar [Footnote: There is another instance of the name distinction in Hamlet and Ophelia. Hamlet's pretended madness would make a very good real madness in any other author.] as from the babbling of the fool; the contrast between wit and folly in Falstaff and Shallow is not more characteristic though more obvious than the gradations of folly, loquacious or reserved, in Shallow and Silence; and again, the gallantry of Prince Henry is as little confounded with that of Hotspur as with the cowardice of Falstaff, or as the sensual and philosophic cowardice of the Knight is with the pitiful and cringing cowardice of Parolles. All these several personages were as different in Shakespeare as they would have been in themselves: his imagination borrowed from the life, and every circumstance, object, motive, passion, operated there as it would in reality, and produced a world of men and women as distinct, as true and as various as those that exist in nature. The peculiar property of Shakespeare's imagination was this truth, accompanied with the unconsciousness of nature: indeed, imagination to be perfect must be unconscious, at least in production; for nature is so. We shall attempt one example more in the characters of Richard II and Henry VI.

The characters and situations of both these persons were so nearly alike, that they would have been completely confounded by a commonplace poet. Yet they are kept quite distinct in Shakespeare. Both were kings, and both unfortunate. Both lost their crowns owing to their mismanagement and imbecility; the one from a thoughtless, wilful abuse of power, the other from an indifference to it. The manner in which they bear their misfortunes corresponds exactly to the causes which led to them. The one is always lamenting the loss of his power which he has not the spirit to regain; the other seems only to regret that he had ever been king, and is glad to be rid of the power, with the trouble; the effeminacy of the one is that of a voluptuary, proud, revengeful, impatient of contradiction, and inconsolable in his misfortunes; the effeminacy of the other is that of an indolent, good-natured mind, naturally averse to the turmoils of ambition and the cares of greatness, and who wishes to pass his time in monkish indolence and contemplation.—Richard bewails the loss of the kingly power only as it was the means of gratifying his pride and luxury; Henry regards it only as a means of doing right, and is less desirous of the advantages to be derived from possessing it than afraid of exercising it wrong. In knighting a young soldier, he gives him ghostly advice—

> Edward Plantagenet, arise a knight,
> And learn this lesson, draw thy sword in right.

Richard II in the first speeches of the play betrays his real character. In the first alarm of his pride, on hearing of Bolingbroke's rebellion, before his presumption has met with any check, he exclaims:

> Mock not my senseless conjuration, lords:
> This earth shall have a feeling, and these stones
> Prove armed soldiers, ere her native king
> Shall falter under proud rebellious arms.
> . . . . .
> Not all the water in the rough rude sea
> Can wash the balm from an anointed king;
> The breath of worldly man cannot depose
> The Deputy elected by the Lord.
> For every man that Bolingbroke hath prest,
> To lift sharp steel against our golden crown,
> Heaven for his Richard hath in heavenly pay
> A glorious angel; then if angels fight,
> Weak men must fall; for Heaven still guards the right.

Yet, notwithstanding this royal confession of faith, on the very first news of actual disaster, all his conceit of himself as the peculiar favourite of Providence vanishes into air.

> But now the blood of twenty thousand men
> Did triumph in my face, and they are fled.
> All souls that will be safe fly from my side;
> For time hath set a blot upon my pride.

Immediately after, however, recollecting that 'cheap defence' of the divinity of kings which is to be found in opinion, he is for arming his name against his enemies.

> Awake, thou coward Majesty, thou sleep'st;
> Is not the King's name forty thousand names?
> Arm, arm, my name: a puny subject strikes
> At thy great glory.

King Henry does not make any such vapouring resistance to the loss of his crown, but lets it slip from off his head as a weight which he is neither able nor willing to bear; stands quietly by to see the issue of the contest for his kingdom, as if it were a game at push-pin, and is pleased when the odds prove against him.

122

When Richard first hears of the death of his favourites, Bushy, Bagot, and the rest, he indignantly rejects all idea of any further efforts, and only indulges in the extravagant impatience of his grief and his despair, in that fine speech which has been so often quoted:

Aumerle. Where is the duke my father, with his power?

  K. Richard. No matter where: of comfort no man speak:
    Let's talk of graves, of worms, and epitaphs,
    Make dust our paper, and with rainy eyes
    Write sorrow in the bosom of the earth!
    Let's choose executors, and talk of wills:
    And yet not so—for what can we bequeath,
    Save our deposed bodies to the ground?
    Our lands, our lives, and all are Bolingbroke's,
    And nothing can we call our own but death,
    And that small model of the barren earth,
    Which serves as paste and cover to our bones.
    For heaven's sake let us sit upon the ground,
    And tell sad stories of the death of Kings:
    How some have been depos'd, some slain in war;
    Some haunted by the ghosts they dispossess'd;
    Some poison'd by their wives, some sleeping kili'd;
    All murder'd:—for within the hollow crown,
    That rounds the mortal temples of a king,
    Keeps death his court: and there the antic sits,
    Scoffing his state, and grinning at his pomp!
    Allowing him a breath, a little scene
    To monarchize, be fear'd, and kill with looks;
    Infusing him with self and vain conceit—
    As if this flesh, which walls about our life,
    Were brass impregnable; and, humour'd thus,
    Comes at the last, and, with a little pin,
    Bores through his castle wall, and—farewell king!
    Cover your heads, and mock not flesh and blood
    With solemn reverence; throw away respect,
    Tradition, form, and ceremonious duty,
    For you have but mistook me all this while:
    I live on bread like you, feel want, taste grief,
    Need friends, like you; subjected thus,
    How can you say to me I am a king?

There is as little sincerity afterwards in his affected resignation to his fate, as there is fortitude in this exaggerated picture of his misfortunes before they have happened.

When Northumberland comes back with the message from Bolingbroke, he exclaims, anticipating the result,—

What must the king do now? Must he submit?
The king shall do it: must he be depos'd?
The king shall be contented: must he lose
The name of king? O' God's name let it go.
I'll give my jewels for a set of beads,
My gorgeous palace for a hermitage,
My gay apparel for an almsman's gown,
My figur'd goblets for a dish of wood,
My sceptre for a palmer's walking staff,
My subjects for a pair of carved saints,
And my large kingdom for a little grave—
A little, little grave, an obscure grave.

How differently is all this expressed in King Henry's soliloquy, during the battle with Edward's party:

This battle fares like to the morning's war,
When dying clouds contend with growing light,
What time the shepherd blowing of his nails,
Can neither call it perfect day or night.
Here on this mole-hill will I sit me down;
To whom God will, there be the victory!
For Margaret my Queen, and Clifford too,
Have chid me from the battle; swearing both
They prosper best of all when I am thence.
Would I were dead, if God's good will were so.
For what is in this world but grief and woe?
O God! methinks it were a happy life
To be no better than a homely swain,
To sit upon a hill as I do now,
To carve out dials quaintly, point by point,
Thereby to see the minutes how they run:
How many make the hour full complete,
How many hours bring about the day,
How many days will finish up the year,
How many years a mortal man may live.
When this is known, then to divide the times:
So many hours must I tend my flock,
So many hours must I take my rest,
So many hours must I contemplate,
So many hours must I sport myself;
So many days my ewes have been with young,
So many weeks ere the poor fools will yean,
So many months ere I shall shear the fleece:
So many minutes, hours, weeks, months, and years
Past over, to the end they were created,

124

Would bring white hairs unto a quiet grave.
Ah! what a life were this! how sweet, how lovely!
Gives not the hawthorn bush a sweeter shade
To shepherds looking on their silly sheep,
Than doth a rich embroidered canopy
To kings that fear their subjects' treachery?
O yes it doth, a thousand-fold it doth.
And to conclude, the shepherds' homely curds,
His cold thin drink out of his leather bottle,
His wonted sleep under a fresh tree's shade,
All which secure and sweetly he enjoys,
Is far beyond a prince's delicates,
His viands sparkling in a golden cup,
His body couched in a curious bed,
When care, mistrust, and treasons wait on him.

This is a true and beautiful description of a naturally quiet and contented disposition, and not, like the former, the splenetic effusion of disappointed ambition.

In the last scene of RICHARD II his despair lends him courage: he beats the keeper, slays two of his assassins, and dies with imprecations in his mouth against Sir Pierce Exton, who 'had staggered his royal person'. Henry, when he is seized by the deer- stealers, only reads them a moral lecture on the duty of allegiance and the sanctity of an oath; and when stabbed by Gloucester in the Tower, reproaches him with his crimes, but pardons him his own death.

RICHARD III

RICHARD III may be considered as properly a stageplay: it belongs to the theatre, rather than to the closet. We shall therefore criticize it chiefly with a reference to the manner in which we have seen it performed. It is the character in which Garrick came out: it was the second character in which Mr. Kean appeared, and in which he acquired his fame. Shakespeare we have always with us: actors we have only for a few seasons; and therefore some account of them may be acceptable, if not to our cotemporaries, to those who come after us, if 'that rich and idle personage, Posterity', should deign to look into our writings.

It is possible to form a higher conception of the character of Richard than that given by Mr. Kean: but we cannot imagine any character represented with greater distinctness and precision, more perfectly ARTICULATED in every part. Perhaps indeed there is too much of what is technically called execution. When we first saw this celebrated actor in the part, we thought he sometimes failed from an exuberance of manner, and dissipated the impression of the general character by the variety of his resources. To be complete, his delineation of it should have more solidity, depth, sustained and impassioned feeling, with somewhat less brilliancy, with fewer glancing lights, pointed transitions, and pantomimic evolutions.

The Richard of Shakespeare is towering and lofty; equally impetuous and commanding; haughty, violent, and subtle; bold and treacherous; confident in his strength as well as in his cunning; raised high by his birth, and higher by his talents and his crimes; a royal usurper, a princely hypocrite, a tyrant and a murderer of the house of Plantagenet.

> But I was born so high:
> Our aery buildeth in the cedar's top,
> And dallies with the wind, and scorns the sun.

The idea conveyed in these lines (which are indeed omitted in the miserable medley acted for Richard III) is never lost sight of by Shakespeare, and should not be out of the actor's mind for a moment. The restless and sanguinary Richard is not a man striving to be great, but to be greater than he is; conscious of his strength of will, his power of intellect, his daring courage, his elevated station; and making use of these advantages to commit unheard-of crimes, and to shield himself from remorse and infamy.

If Mr. Kean does not entirely succeed in concentrating all the lines of the character, as drawn by Shakespeare, he gives an animation, vigour, and relief to the part which we have not seen equalled. He is more refined than Cooke; more bold, varied, and original than Kemble in the same character. In some parts he is deficient in dignity, and particularly in the scenes of state business, he has by no means an air of artificial authority. There is at times an aspiring elevation, an enthusiastic rapture in his expectations of attaining the crown, and at others a gloating expression of sullen delight, as if he already clenched the bauble, and held it in his grasp. The courtship scene with Lady Anne is an admirable exhibition of smooth and smiling villainy. The progress of wily adulation, of encroaching humility, is finely marked by his action, voice and eye. He seems, like the first Tempter, to approach his prey, secure of the event, and as if success had smoothed his way before him. The late Mr. Cooke's manner of representing this scene was more vehement, hurried, and full of anxious uncertainty. This, though more natural in general, was

126

less in character in this particular instance. Richard should woo less as a lover than as an actor—to show his mental superiority, and power of making others the playthings of his purposes. Mr. Kean's attitude in leaning against the side of the stage before he comes forward to address Lady Anne, is one of the most graceful and striking ever witnessed on the stage. It would do for Titian to paint. The frequent and rapid transition of his voice from the expression of the fiercest passion to the most familiar tones of conversation was that which gave a peculiar grace of novelty to his acting on his first appearance. This has been since imitated and caricatured by others, and he himself uses the artifice more sparingly than he did. His by-play is excellent. His manner of bidding his friends 'Good night', after pausing with the point of his sword drawn slowly backward and forward on the ground, as if considering the plan of the battle next day, is a particularly happy and natural thought. He gives to the two last acts of the play the greatest animation and effect. He fills every part of the stage; and makes up for the deficiency of his person by what has been sometimes objected to as an excess of action, The concluding scene in which he is killed by Richmond is the most brilliant of the whole. He fights at last like one drunk with wounds; and the attitude in which he stands with his hands stretched out, after his sword is wrested from him, has a preternatural and terrific grandeur, as if his will could not be disarmed, and the very phantoms of his despair had power to kill.— Mr. Kean has since in a great measure effaced the impression of his Richard III by the superior efforts of his genius in Othello (his masterpiece), in the murder-scene in MACBETH, in RICHARD II, in SIR GILES OVERREACH, and lastly in OROONOKO; but we still like to look back to his first performance of this part, both because it first assured his admirers of his future success, and because we bore our feeble but, at that time, not useless testimony to the merits of this very original actor, on which the town was considerably divided for no other reason than because they WERE original.

The manner in which Shakespeare's plays have been generally altered or rather mangled by modern mechanists, is a disgrace to the English stage. The patch-work Richard III which is acted under the sanction of his name, and which was manufactured by Cibber, is a striking example of this remark.

The play itself is undoubtedly a very powerful effusion of Shakespeare's genius. The groundwork of the character of Richard, that mixture of intellectual vigour with moral depravity, in which Shakespeare delighted to show his strength—gave full scope as well as temptation to the exercise of his imagination. The character of his hero is almost everywhere predominant, and marks its lurid track throughout. The original play is, however, too long for representation, and there are some few scenes which might be better spared than preserved, and by omitting which it would remain a complete whole. The only rule, indeed, for altering Shakespeare is to retrench certain passages which may be considered either as superfluous or obsolete, but not to add or transpose anything. The arrangement and development of the story, and the mutual contrast and combination of the dramatis personae, are in general as finely managed as the development of the characters or the expression of the passions.

This rule has not been adhered to in the present instance. Some of the most important and striking passages in the principal character have been omitted, to make room for idle and misplaced extracts from other plays; the only intention of which seems to have been to make the character of Richard as odious and disgusting as possible. It is apparently for no other purpose than to make Gloucester stab King Henry on the stage, that the fine abrupt introduction of the character in the opening of the play is lost in the tedious whining morality of the uxorious king (taken from another play);—we say TEDIOUS, because it interrupts the business of the scene, and loses its beauty and effect by having no intelligible connexion with the previous character of the mild, well-meaning monarch. The passages which the unfortunate Henry has to recite are beautiful and pathetic in themselves, but they have nothing to do with the world that Richard has to 'bustle in'. In the same spirit of vulgar caricature is the scene between Richard and Lady Anne (when his wife) interpolated without any authority, merely to gratify this favourite propensity to disgust and loathing. With the same perverse consistency, Richard, after his last fatal struggle, is raised up by some galvanic process, to utter the imprecation, without any motive but pure malignity, which Shakespeare has so properly put into the mouth of Northumberland on hearing of Percy's death. To make room for these worse than needless additions, many of the most striking passages in the real play have been omitted by the foppery and ignorance of the prompt-book critics. We do not mean to insist merely on passages which are fine as poetry and to the reader, such as Clarence's dream, &c., but on those which are important to the understanding of the character, and peculiarly adapted for stage- effect. We will give the following as instances among several others. The first is the scene where Richard enters abruptly to the queen and her friends to defend himself:

Gloucester. They do me wrong, and I will not endure it.
  Who are they that complain unto the king,
  That I forsooth am stern, and love them not?
  By holy Paul, they love his grace but lightly,
  That fill his ears with such dissentious rumours:
  Because I cannot flatter and look fair,
  Smile in men's faces, smooth, deceive, and cog,
  Duck with French nods, and apish courtesy,
  I must be held a rancorous enemy.
  Cannot a plain man live, and think no harm,
  But thus his simple truth must be abus'd
  With silken, sly, insinuating Jacks?

Gray. To whom in all this presence speaks your grace?

Gloucester. To thee, that hast nor honesty nor grace;
  When have I injur'd thee, when done thee wrong?
  Or thee? or thee? or any of your faction?
  A plague upon you all!

Nothing can be more characteristic than the turbulent pretensions to meekness and simplicity in this address. Again, the versatility and adroitness of Richard is admirably described in the following ironical conversation with Brakenbury:

Brakenbury. I beseech your graces both to pardon me.
  His majesty hath straitly given in charge,
  That no man shall have private conference,
  Of what degree soever, with your brother.

128

Gloucester. E'en so, and please your worship, Brakenbury,
  You may partake of anything we say:
  We speak no treason, man—we say the king
  Is wise and virtuous, and his noble queen
  Well strook in years, fair, and not jealous.
  We say that Shore's wife hath a pretty foot,
  A cherry lip,
  A bonny eye, a passing pleasing tongue;
  That the queen's kindred are made gentlefolks.
  How say you, sir? Can you deny all this?

Brakenbury. With this, my lord, myself have nought to do.

  Gloucester. What, fellow, naught to do with mistress Shore?
  I tell you, sir, he that doth naught with her,
  Excepting one, were best to do it secretly alone.

Brakenbury. What one, my lord?

Gloucester. Her husband, knave—would'st thou betray me?

The feigned reconciliation of Gloucester with the queen's kinsmen is also a masterpiece. One of the finest strokes in the play, and which serves to show as much as anything the deep, plausible manners of Richard, is the unsuspecting security of Hastings, at the very time when the former is plotting his death, and when that very appearance of cordiality and good-humour on which Hastings builds his confidence arises from Richard's consciousness of having betrayed him to his ruin. This, with the whole character of Hastings, is omitted.

Perhaps the two most beautiful passages in the original play are the farewell apostrophe of the queen to the Tower, where the children are shut up from her, and Tyrrel's description of their death. We will finish our quotations with them.

  Queen. Stay, yet look back with me unto the Tower;
  Pity, you ancient stones, those tender babes,
  Whom envy hath immured within your walls;
  Rough cradle for such little pretty ones,
  Rude, rugged nurse, old sullen play-fellow,
  For tender princes! The other passage is the account of their
   death by Tyrrel:

  Dighton and Forrest, whom I did suborn
  To do this piece of ruthless butchery,
  Albeit they were flesh'd villains, bloody dogs,—
  Wept like to children in their death's sad story:
  O thus! quoth Dighton, lay the gentle babes;
  Thus, thus, quoth Forrest, girdling one another
  Within their innocent alabaster arms;

Their lips were four red roses on a stalk,
And in that summer beauty kissed each other;
A book of prayers on their pillow lay,
Which once, quoth Forrest, almost changed my mind:
But oh the devil!—there the villain stopped;
When Dighton thus told on—we smothered
The most replenished sweet work of nature,
That from the prime creation ere she framed.

These are some of those wonderful bursts of feeling, done to the life, to the very height of fancy and nature, which our Shakespeare alone could give. We do not insist on the repetition of these last passages as proper for the stage: we should indeed be loath to trust them in the mouth of almost any actor: but we should wish them to be retained in preference at least to the fantoccini exhibition of the young princes, Edward and York, bandying childish wit with their uncle.

HENRY VIII

This play contains little action or violence of passion, yet it has considerable interest of a more mild and thoughtful cast, and some of the most striking passages in the author's works. The character of Queen Katherine is the most perfect delineation of matronly dignity, sweetness, and resignation, that can be conceived. Her appeals to the protection of the king, her remonstrances to the cardinals, her conversations with her women, show a noble and generous spirit accompanied with the utmost gentleness of nature. What can be more affecting than her answer to Campeius and Wolsey, who come to visit her as pretended friends.

>   —'Nay, forsooth, my friends,
> They that must weigh out my afflictions,
> They that my trust must grow to, live not here;
> They are, as all my comforts are, far hence,
> In mine own country, lords.'

Dr. Johnson observes of this play, that 'the meek sorrows and virtuous distress of Katherine have furnished some scenes, which may be justly numbered among the greatest efforts of tragedy. But the genius of Shakespeare comes in and goes out with Katherine. Every other part may be easily conceived and easily written.' This is easily said; but with all due deference to so great a reputed authority as that of Johnson, it is not true. For instance, the scene of Buckingham led to execution is one of the most affecting and natural in Shakespeare, and one to which there is hardly an approach in any other author. Again, the character of Wolsey, the description of his pride and of his fall, are inimitable, and have, besides their gorgeousness of effect, a pathos, which only the genius of Shakespeare could lend to the distresses of a proud, bad man, like Wolsey. There is a sort of child-like simplicity in the very helplessness of his situation, arising from the recollection of his past overbearing ambition. After the cutting sarcasms of his enemies on his disgrace, against which he bears up with a spirit conscious of his own superiority, he breaks out into that fine apostrophe:

>   Farewell, a long farewell, to all my greatness!
> This is the state of man; to-day he puts forth
> The tender leaves of hope, to-morrow blossoms,
> And bears his blushing honours thick upon him;
> The third day, comes a frost, a killing frost;
> And—when he thinks, good easy man, full surely
> His greatness is a ripening—nips his root,
> And then he falls, as I do. I have ventur'd,
> Like little wanton boys that swim on bladders,
> These many summers in a sea of glory;
> But far beyond my depth: my high-blown pride
> At length broke under me; and now has left me,
> Weary and old with service, to the mercy
> Of a rude stream, that must for ever hide me.
> Vain pomp and glory of the world, I hate ye!
> I feel my heart new open'd; O how wretched

Is that poor man, that hangs on princes' favours!
There is betwixt that smile we would aspire to,
That sweet aspect of princes, and our ruin,
More pangs and fears than war and women have;
And when he falls, he falls like Lucifer,
Never to hope again!—

There is in this passage, as well as in the well-known dialogue with Cromwell which follows, something which stretches beyond commonplace; nor is the account which Griffiths gives of Wolsey's death less Shakespearian; and the candour with which Queen Katherine listens to the praise of 'him whom of all men while living she hated most' adds the last graceful finishing to her character.

Among other images of great individual beauty might be mentioned the description of the effect of Ann Boleyn's presenting herself to the crowd at her coronation.

—While her grace sat down
To rest awhile, some half an hour or so,
In a rich chair of state, opposing freely
The beauty of her person to the people.
Believe me, sir, she is the goodliest woman
That ever lay by man. Which when the people
Had the full view of, 'such a noise arose
As the shrouds make at sea in a stiff tempest,
As loud and to as many tunes'.

The character of Henry VIII is drawn with great truth and spirit. It is like a very disagreeable portrait, sketched by the hand of a master. His gross appearance, his blustering demeanour, his vulgarity, his arrogance, his sensuality, his cruelty, his hypocrisy, his want of common decency and common humanity, are marked in strong lines. His traditional peculiarities of expression complete the reality of the picture. The authoritative expletive, 'Ha!' with which ne intimates his indignation or surprise, has an effect like the first startling sound that breaks from a thunder-cloud. He is of all the monarchs in our history the most disgusting: for he unites in himself all the vices of barbarism and refinement, without their virtues. Other kings before him (such as Richard III) were tyrants and murderers out of ambition or necessity: they gained or established unjust power by violent means: they destroyed their or made its tenure insecure. But Henry VIII's power is most fatal to those whom he loves: he is cruel and remorseless to pamper his luxurious appetites: bloody and voluptuous; an amorous murderer; an uxorious debauchee. His hardened insensibility to the feelings of others is strengthened by the most profligate self-indulgence. The religious hypocrisy, under which he masks his cruelty and his lust, is admirably displayed in the speech in which he describes the first misgivings of his conscience and its increasing throes and terrors, which have induced him to divorce his queen. The only thing in his favour in this play is his treatment of Cranmer: there is also another circumstance in his favour, which is his patronage of Hans Holbein.—It has been said of Shakespeare, 'No maid could live near such a man.' It might with as good reason be said, 'No king could live near such a man.' His eye would have penetrated through the pomp of circumstance and the veil of opinion.

As it is, he has represented such persons to the life—his plays are in this respect the glass of history—he has done them the same justice as if he had been a privy counsellor all his life, and in each successive reign. Kings ought never to be seen upon the stage. In the abstract, they are very disagreeable characters: it is only while living that they are 'the best of kings'. It is their power, their splendour, it is the apprehension of the personal consequences of their favour or their hatred that dazzles the imagination and suspends the judgement of their favourites or their vassals; but death cancels the bond of allegiance and of interest; and seen AS THEY WERE, their power and their pretensions look monstrous and ridiculous. The charge brought against modern philosophy as inimical to loyalty is unjust because it might as well be brought lover of kings. We have often wondered that Henry VIII as he is drawn by Shakespeare, and as we have seen him represented in all the bloated deformity of mind and person, is not hooted from the English stage.

KING JOHN

KING JOHN is the last of the historical plays we shall have to speak of; and we are not sorry that it is. If we are to indulge our imaginations, we had rather do it upon an imaginary theme; if we are to find subjects for the exercise of our pity and terror, we prefer seeking them in fictitious danger and fictitious distress. It gives a SORENESS to our feelings of indignation or sympathy, when we know that in tracing the progress of sufferings and crimes we are treading upon real ground, and recollect that the poet's 'dream' DENOTED A FOREGONE CONCLUSION— irrevocable ills, not conjured up by fancy, but placed beyond the reach of poetical justice. That the treachery of King John, the death of Arthur, the grief of Constance, had a real truth in history, sharpens the sense of pain, while it hangs a leaden weight on the heart and the imagination. Something whispers us that we have no right to make a mock of calamities like these, or to turn the truth of things into the puppet and plaything of our fancies. 'To consider thus' may be 'to consider too curiously'; but still we think that the actual truth of the particular events, in proportion as we are conscious of it, is a drawback on the pleasure as well as the dignity of tragedy.

KING JOHN has all the beauties of language and all the richness of the imagination to relieve the painfulness of the subject. The character of King John himself is kept pretty much in the background; it is only marked in by comparatively slight indications. The crimes he is tempted to commit are such as are thrust upon him rather by circumstances and opportunity than of his own seeking: he is here represented as more cowardly than cruel, and as more contemptible than odious. The play embraces only a part of his history. There are however few characters on the stage that excite more disgust and loathing. He has no intellectual grandeur or strength of character to shield him from the indignation which his immediate conduct provokes: he stands naked and defenceless, in that respect, to the worst we can think of him: and besides, we are impelled to put the very worst construction on his meanness and cruelty by the tender picture of the beauty and helplessness of the object of it, as well as by the frantic and heart-rending pleadings of maternal despair. We do not forgive him the death of Arthur because he had too late revoked his doom and tried to prevent it, and perhaps because he has himself repented of his black design, our MORAL SENSE gains courage to hate him the more for it. We take him at his word, and think his purposes must be odious indeed, when he himself shrinks back from them. The scene in which King John suggests to Hubert the design of murdering his nephew is a masterpiece of dramatic skill, but it is still inferior, very inferior to the scene between Hubert and Arthur, when the latter learns the orders to put out his eyes. If anything ever was penned, heart-piercing, mixing the extremes of terror and pity, of that which shocks and that which soothes the mind, it is this scene. We will give it entire, though perhaps it is tasking the reader's sympathy too much.

Enter Hubert and Executioner

  Hubert. Heat me these irons hot, and look you stand
   Within the arras; when I strike my foot
   Upon the bosom of the ground, rush forth
   And bind the boy, which you shall find with me,
   Fast to the chair: be heedful: hence, and watch.

Executioner. I hope your warrant will bear out the deed.

Hubert. Uncleanly scruples! fear not you; look to't.—
  Young lad, come forth; I have to say with you.

Enter Arthur

Arthur. Good morrow, Hubert.

Hubert. Morrow, little Prince.

Arthur. As little prince (having so great a title
  To be more prince) as may be. You are sad.

Hubert. Indeed I have been merrier.

Arthur. Mercy on me!
  Methinks no body should be sad but I;
  Yet I remember when I was in France,
  Young gentlemen would be as sad as night,
  Only for wantonness. By my Christendom,
  So were I out of prison, and kept sheep,
  I should be merry as the day is long.
  And so I would be here, but that I doubt
  My uncle practises more harm to me.
  He is afraid of me, and I of him.
  Is it my fault that I was Geoffery's son?
  Indeed it is not, and I would to heav'n
  I were your son, so you would love me, Hubert.

Hubert. If I talk to him, with his innocent prate
  He will awake my mercy, which lies dead;
  Therefore I will be sudden, and dispatch. [Aside.]

Arthur. Are you sick, Hubert? you look pale to-day?
  In sooth, I would you were a little sick,
  That I might sit all night and watch with you.
  Alas, I love you more than you do me.

Hubert. His words do take possession of my bosom.
  Read here, young Arthur—[Showing a paper.]
  How now, foolish rheum, [Aside.]
  Turning dis-piteous torture out of door!
  I must be brief, lest resolution drop
  Out at mine eyes in tender womanish tears.—
  Can you not read it? Is it not fair writ?

135

Arthur. Too fairly, Hubert, for so foul effect.
    Must you with irons burn out both mine eyes?

Hubert. Young boy, I must.

Arthur. And will you?

Hubert. And I will.

Arthur. Have you the heart? When your head did but ache,
    I knit my handkerchief about your brows,
    (The best I had, a princess wrought it me)
    And I did never ask it you again;
    And with my hand at midnight held your head;
    And, like the watchful minutes to the hour,
    Still and anon cheer'd up the heavy time,
    Saying, what lack you? and where lies your grief?
    Or, what good love may I perform for you?
    Many a poor man's son would have lain still,
    And ne'er have spoke a loving word to you;
    But you at your sick service had a prince.
    Nay, you may think my love was crafty love,
    And call it cunning. Do, and if you will:
    If heav'n be pleas'd that you must use me ill,
    Why then you must.—Will you put out mine eyes?
    These eyes, that never did, and never shall,
    So much as frown on you?

Hubert. I've sworn to do it;
    And with hot irons must I burn them out.

Arthur. Oh if an angel should have come to me,
    And told me Hubert should put out mine eyes,
    I would not have believ'd a tongue but Hubert's.
    Hubert, Come forth; do as I bid you.
    [Stamps, and the men enter.]

Arthur. O save me, Hubert, save me! my eyes are out
    Ev'n with the fierce looks of these bloody men.

Hubert. Give me the iron, I say, and bind him here.

Arthur. Alas, what need you be so boist'rous rough?
    I will not struggle, I will stand stone-still.
    For heav'n's sake, Hubert, let me not be bound!
    Nay, hear me, Hubert, drive these men away,
    And I will sit as quiet as a lamb:

I will not stir, nor wince, nor speak a word,
Nor look upon the iron angrily:
Thrust but these men away, and I'll forgive you,
Whatever torment you do put me to.

Hubert. Go, stand within; let me alone with him.

Executioner. I am best pleas'd to be from such a deed. [Exit.]

Arthur. Alas, I then have chid away my friend.
He hath a stern look, but a gentle heart;
Let him come back, that his compassion may
Give life to yours.

Hubert. Come, boy, prepare yourself.

Arthur. Is there no remedy?

Hubert. None, but to lose your eyes.

Arthur. O heav'n! that there were but a mote in yours,
A grain, a dust, a gnat, a wand'ring hair,
Any annoyance in that precious sense!
Then, feeling what small things are boist'rous there,
Your vile intent must needs seem horrible.

Hubert. Is this your promise? go to, hold your tongue.

Arthur. Let me not hold my tongue; let me not, Hubert;
Or, Hubert, if you will, cut out my tongue,
So I may keep mine eyes. O spare mine eyes!
Though to no use, but still to look on you.
Lo, by my troth, the instrument is cold,
And would not harm me.

Hubert. I can heat it, boy.

Arthur. No, in good sooth, the fire is dead with grief.
Being create for comfort, to be us'd
In undeserv'd extremes; see else yourself,
There is no malice in this burning coal;
The breath of heav'n hath blown its spirit out,
And strew'd repentant ashes on its head.

Hubert. But with my breath I can revive it, boy.

Arthur. All things that you shall use to do me wrong,
Deny their office, only you do lack

137

That mercy which fierce fire and iron extend,
Creatures of note for mercy-lacking uses. '

Hubert. Well, see to live; I will not touch thine eyes
  For all the treasure that thine uncle owns:
  Yet I am sworn, and I did purpose, boy,
  With this same very iron to bum them out.

Arthur. O, now you look like Hubert. All this while
  You were disguised.

Hubert. Peace! no more. Adieu,
  Your uncle must not know but you are dead.
  I'll fill these dogged spies with false reports:
  And, pretty child, sleep doubtless and secure,
  That Hubert, for the wealth of all the world,
  Will not offend thee.

Arthur. O heav'n! I thank you, Hubert.

Hubert. Silence, no more; go closely in with me;
  Much danger do I undergo for thee. [Exeunt.]

His death afterwards, when he throws himself from his prison-walls, excites the utmost pity for his innocence and friendless situation, and well justifies the exaggerated denunciations of Falconbridge to Hubert whom he suspects wrongfully of the deed.

There is not yet so ugly a fiend of hell
As thou shalt be, if thou did'st kill this child.
—If thou did'st but consent
To this most cruel act, do but despair:
And if thou want'st a cord, the smallest thread
That ever spider twisted from her womb
Will strangle thee; a rush will be a beam
To hang thee on: or would'st thou drown thyself,
Put but a little water in a spoon,
And it shall be as all the ocean,
Enough to stifle such a villain up.

The excess of maternal tenderness, rendered desparate by the fickleness of friends and the injustice of fortune, and made stronger in will, in proportion to the want of all other power, was never more finely expressed than in Constance, The dignity of her answer to King Philip, when she refuses to accompany his messenger, 'To me and to the state of my great grief, let kings assemble,' her indignant reproach to Austria for deserting her cause, her invocation to death, 'that love of misery', however fine and spirited, all yield to the beauty of the passage, where, her passion subsiding into tenderness, she addresses the Cardinal in these words:

138

Oh father Cardinal, I have heard you say
That we shall see and know our friends in heav'n:
If that be, I shall see my boy again,
For since the birth of Cain, the first male child,
To him that did but yesterday suspire,
There was not such a gracious creature born.
But now will canker-sorrow eat my bud,
And chase the native beauty from his cheek,
And he will look as hollow as a ghost,
As dim and meagre as an ague's fit,
And so he'll die; and rising so again,
When I shall meet him in the court of heav'n,
I shall not know him; therefore never, never
Must I behold my pretty Arthur more.

K. Philip. You are as fond of grief as of your child.

Constance. Grief fills the room up of my absent child:
Lies in his bed, walks up and down with me;
Puts on his pretty looks, repeats his words,
Remembers me of all his gracious parts,
Stuffs out his vacant garments with his form.
Then have I reason to be fond of grief.

The contrast between the mild resignation of Queen Katherine to her own wrongs, and the wild, uncontrollable affliction of Constance for the wrongs which she sustains as a mother, is no less naturally conceived than it is ably sustained throughout these two wonderful characters.

The accompaniment of the comic character of the Bastard was well chosen to relieve the poignant agony of suffering, and the cold, cowardly policy of behaviour in the principal characters of this play. Its spirit, invention, volubility of tongue, and forwardness in action, are unbounded. Aliquando sufflaminandus erat, says Ben Jonson of Shakespeare. But we should be sorry it Ben Jonson had been his licenser. We prefer the heedless magnanimity of his wit infinitely to all Jonson's laborious caution. The character of the Bastard's comic humour is the same in essence as that of other comic characters in Shakespeare; they always run on with good things and are never exhausted; they are always daring and successful. They have words at will and a flow of wit, like a flow of animal spirits. The difference between Falconbridge and the others is that he is a soldier, and brings his wit to bear upon action, is courageous with his sword as well as tongue, and stimulates his gallantry by his jokes, his enemies feeling the sharpness of his blows and the sting of his sarcasms at the same time. Among his happiest sallies are his descanting on the composition of his own person, his invective against 'commodity, tickling commodity', and his expression of contempt for the Archduke of Austria, who had killed his father, which begins in jest but ends in serious earnest. His conduct at the siege of Angiers shows that his resources were not confined to verbal retorts.—The same exposure of the policy of courts and camps, of kings, nobles, priests, and cardinals, takes place here as in the other plays we have gone through, and we shall not go into a disgusting repetition.

139

This, like the other plays taken from English history, is written in a remarkably smooth and flowing style, very different from some of the tragedies, MACBETH, for instance. The passages consist of a series of single lines, not running into one another. This peculiarity in the versification, which is most common in the three parts of HENRY VI, has been assigned as a reason why those plays were not written by Shakespeare. But the same structure of verse occurs in his other undoubted plays, as in RICHARD II and in KING JOHN. The following are instances:

> That daughter there of Spain, the Lady Blanch,
> Is near to England; look upon the years
> Of Lewis the Dauphin, and that lovely maid.
> If lusty love should go in quest of beauty,
> Where should he find it fairer than in Blanch?
> If zealous love should go in search of virtue,
> Where should he find it purer than in Blanch?
> If love ambitious sought a match of birth,
> Whose veins bound richer blood than Lady Blanch?
> Such as she is, in beauty, virtue, birth,
> Is the young Dauphin every way complete:
> If not complete of, say he is not she;
> And she again wants nothing, to name want,
> If want it be not, that she is not he.
> He is the half part of a blessed man,
> Left to be finished by such as she;
> And she a fair divided excellence,
> Whose fulness of perfection lies in him.
> O, two such silver currents, when they join,
> Do glorify the banks that bound them in;
> And two such shores to two such streams made one,
> Two such controlling bounds, shall you be, kings,
> To these two princes, if you marry them.

Another instance, which is certainly very happy as an example of the simple enumeration of a number of particulars, is Salisbury's remonstrance against the second crowning of the king.

> Therefore to be possessed with double pomp,
> To guard a title that was rich before;
> To gild refined gold, to paint the lily,
> To throw a perfume on the violet,
> To smooth the ice, to add another hue
> Unto the rainbow, or with taper light
> To seek the beauteous eye of heav'n to garnish:
> Is wasteful and ridiculous excess.

TWELFTH NIGHT; OR, WHAT YOU WILL

This is justly considered as one of the most delightful of Shakespeare's comedies. It is full of sweetness and pleasantry. It is perhaps too good-natured for comedy. It has little satire, and no spleen. It aims at the ludicrous rather than the ridiculous. It makes us laugh at the follies of mankind, not despise them, and still less bear any ill-will towards them. Shakespeare's comic genius resembles the bee rather in its power of extracting sweets from weeds or poisons, than in leaving a sting behind it. He gives die most amusing exaggeration of the prevailing foibles of his characters, but in a way that they themselves, instead of being offended at, would almost join in to humour; he rather contrives opportunities for them to show themselves off in the happiest lights, than renders them contemptible in the perverse construction of the wit or malice of others.—There is a certain stage of society in which people become conscious of their peculiarities and absurdities, affect to disguise what they are, and set up pretensions to what they are not. This gives rise to a corresponding style of comedy, the object of which is to detect the disguises of self-love, and to make reprisals on these preposterous assumptions of vanity, by marking the contrast between the real and the affected character as severely as possible, and denying to those who would impose on us for what they are not, even the merit which they have. This is the comedy of artificial life, of wit and satire, such as we see it in Congreve, Wycherley, Vanbrugh, &c. To this succeeds a state of society from which the same sort of affectation and pretence are banished by a greater knowledge of the world or by their successful exposure on the stage; and which by neutralizing the materials of comic character, both natural and artificial, leaves no comedy at all—but the sentimental. Such is our modern comedy. There is a period in the progress of manners anterior to both these, in which the foibles and follies of individuals are of nature's planting, not the growth of art or study; in which they are therefore unconscious of them themselves, or care not who knows them, if they can but have their whim out; and in which, as there is no attempt at imposition, the spectators rather receive pleasure from humouring the inclinations of the persons they laugh at, than wish to give them pain by exposing their absurdity. This may be called the comedy of nature, and it is the comedy which we generally find in Shakespeare.—Whether the analysis here given be just or not, the spirit of his comedies is evidently quite distinct from that of the authors above mentioned, as it is in its essence the same with that of Cervantes, and also very frequently of Moliere, though he was more systematic in his extravagance than Shakespeare. Shakespeare's comedy is of a pastoral and poetical cast. Folly is indigenous to the soil, and shoots out with native, happy, unchecked luxuriance. Absurdity has every encouragement afforded it; and nonsense has room to flourish in. Nothing is stunted by the churlish, icy hand of indifference or severity. The poet runs riot in a conceit, and idolizes a quibble. His whole object is to turn the meanest or rudest objects to a pleasurable account. The relish which he has of a pun, or of the quaint humour of a low character, does not interfere with the delight with which he describes a beautiful image, or the most refined love. The clown's forced jests do not spoil the sweetness of the character of Viola; the same house is big enough to hold Malvolio, the Countess, Maria, Sir Toby, and Sir Andrew Aguecheek. For instance, nothing can fall much lower than this last character in intellect or morals: yet how are his weaknesses nursed and dandled by Sir Toby into something 'high fantastical', when on Sir Andrew's commendation of himself for dancing and fencing, Sir Toby answers: 'Wherefore are these things hid? Wherefore have these gifts a curtain before them? Are they like to take dust like Mistress Moll's picture? Why dost thou not go to church in a galliard, and come home in a coranto? My very walk should be a jig! I would not so much as make water but in a cinque- pace. What dost thou mean? Is this a world to hide virtues in? I did think by the excellent constitution of thy leg, it was framed under the star of a galliard!'—How Sir Toby, Sir Andrew, and the Clown afterwards chirp over their cups, how they 'rouse the night-owl in a catch, able to draw three souls out of one weaver'!—What can be better than Sir Toby's unanswerable answer to Malvolio, 'Dost thou think, because thou art virtuous, there shall be no more cakes and ale?' In a word, the best turn is given to everything, instead of the worst. There is a constant infusion of the romantic and enthusiastic, in proportion as the characters are natural and sincere: whereas, in the more artificial style of comedy, everything gives way to ridicule and indifference, there being nothing left but affectation on one side, and incredulity on the other.—Much as we like Shakespeare's comedies, we cannot agree with Dr. Johnson that they are better than his tragedies; nor do we like them half so well. If his inclination to comedy sometimes led him to trifle with the seriousness of tragedy, the poetical and impassioned passages are the best parts of his comedies. The great and secret charm of TWELFTH NIGHT is the character of Viola. Much as we like catches and cakes and ale, there is something that we like better. We have a friendship for Sir Toby; we patronize Sir Andrew; we have an understanding with the Clown, a sneaking kindness for Maria and her rogueries; we feel a regard for Malvolio, and sympathize with his gravity, his smiles, his cross-garters, his yellow stockings, and imprisonment in the stocks. But there is something that excites in us a stronger feeling than all this—it is Viola's confession of her love.

Duke. What's her history?

  Viola. A blank, my lord, she never told her love:
    She let concealment, like a worm i' th' bud,
    Feed on her damask cheek, she pin'd in thought,
    And with a green and yellow melancholy,
    She sat like Patience on a monument,
    Smiling at grief. Was not this love indeed?
    We men may say more, swear more, but indeed,
    Our shows are more than will; for still we prove
    Much in our vows, but little in our love.

Duke. But died thy sister of her love, my boy?

  Viola. I am all the daughters of my father's house,
    And all the brothers too; and yet I know not.

Shakespeare alone could describe the effect of his own poetry.

  Oh, it came o'er the ear like the sweet south
  That breathes upon a bank of violets,
  Stealing and giving odour.

What we so much admire here is not the image of Patience on a monument, which has been generally quoted, but the lines before and after it. 'They give a very echo to the seat where love is throned.' How long ago it is since we first learnt to repeat them; and still, still they vibrate on the heart, like the sounds which the passing wind draws from the trembling strings of a harp left on some desert shore! There are other passages of not less impassioned sweetness. Such is Olivia's address to Sebastian whom she supposes to have already deceived her in a promise of marriage.

Blame not this haste of mine: if you mean well,
Now go with me and with this holy man
Into the chantry by: there before him,
And underneath that consecrated roof,
Plight me the full assurance of your faith,
THAT MY MOST JEALOUS AND TOO DOUBTFUL SOUL
MAY LIVE AT PEACE.

We have already said something of Shakespeare's songs. One of the most beautiful of them occurs in this play, with a preface of his own to it.

Duke. O fellow, come, the song we had last night.
Mark it, Cesario, it is old and plain;
The spinsters and the knitters in the sun,
And the free maids that weave their thread with bones,
Do use to chaunt it; it is silly sooth,
And dallies with the innocence of love,
Like the old age.

Song

Come away, come away, death,
And in sad cypress let me be laid;
Fly away, fly away, breath;
I am slain by a fair cruel maid.
My shroud of white, stuck all with yew,
O prepare it;
My part of death no one so true
Did share it.

Not a flower, not a flower sweet,
On my black coffin let there be strown;
Not a friend, not a friend greet
My poor corpse, where my bones shall be thrown;
A thousand thousand sighs to save,
Lay me, O! where
Sad true-love never find my grave,
To weep there.

Who after this will say that Shakespeare's genius was only fitted for comedy? Yet after reading other parts of this play, and particularly the garden-scene where Malvolio picks up the letter, if we were to say that his genius for comedy was less than his genius for tragedy, it would perhaps only prove that our own taste in such matters is more saturnine than mercurial.

Enter Maria

Sir Toby. Here comes the little villain:—How now, my
Nettle of India?

Maria. Get ye all three into the box-tree: Malvolio's coming down this walk: he has been yonder i' the sun, practising behaviour to his own shadow this half hour; observe him, for the love of mockery; for I know this letter will make a contemplative idiot of him. Close, in the name of jesting! Lie thou there; for here comes the trout that must be caught with tickling.

[They hide themselves. Maria throws down a letter, and exit.]

Enter Malvolio

Malvolio. 'Tis but fortune; all is fortune. Maria once told me, she did affect me; and I have heard herself come thus near, that, should she fancy, it should be one of my complexion. Besides, she uses me with a more exalted respect than any one else that follows her. What should I think on't?

Sir Toby. Here's an over-weening rogue!

Fabian. O, peace! Contemplation makes a rare turkey- cock of him; how he jets under his advanced plumes!

Sir Andrew. 'Slight, I could so beat the rogue:—

Sir Toby. Peace, I say.

Malvolio. To be Count Malvolio;—

Sir Toby. Ah, rogue!

Sir Andrew. Pistol him, pistol him.

Sir Toby. Peace, peace!

Malvolio. There is example for't; the lady of the Strachy married the yeoman of the wardrobe.

Sir Andrew. Fire on him, Jezebel!

Fabian. O, peace! now he's deeply in; look, how
imagination blows him.

Malvolio. Having been three months married to her, sitting in my chair of state,—

Sir Toby. O for a stone bow, to hit him in the eye!

Malvolio. Calling my officers about me, in my branch'd velvet gown; having come from a day-bed, where I have left Olivia sleeping.

Sir Toby. Fire and brimstone!

Fabian. O peace, peace!

Malvolio. And then to have the humour of state: and after a demure travel of regard,—telling them, I know my place, as I would they should do theirs,—to ask for my kinsman Toby.—

Sir Toby. Bolts and shackles!

Fabian. O, peace, peace, peace! now, now.

Malvolio. Seven of my people, with an obedient start, make out for him; I frown the while; and, perchance, wind up my watch, or play with some rich jewel. Toby approaches; curtsies there to me.

Sir Toby. Shall this fellow live?

Fabian. Though our silence be drawn from us with cares, yet peace.

Malvolio. I extend my hand to him thus, quenching my familiar smile with an austere regard to control.

Sir Toby. And does not Toby take you a blow o' the lips then?

Malvolio. Saying—Cousin Toby, my fortunes having cast me on your niece, give me this prerogative of speech;—

Sir Toby. What, what?

Malvolio. You must amend your drunkenness.

Fabian. Nay, patience, or we break the sinews of our plot.

Malvolio. Besides, you waste the treasure of your time with a foolish knight—

Sir Andrew. That's me, I warrant you.

Malvolio. One Sir Andrew—

Sir Andrew. I knew,'twas I; for many do call me fool.

Malvolio. What employment have we here? [Taking up the letter.]

The letter and his comments on it are equally good. If poor Malvolio's treatment afterwards is a little hard, poetical justice is done in the uneasiness which Olivia suffers on account of her mistaken attachment to Cesario, as her insensibility to the violence of the Duke's passion is atoned for by the discovery of Viola's concealed love of him.

THE TWO GENTLEMEN OF VERONA

This is little more than the first outlines of a comedy loosely sketched in. It is the story of a novel dramatized with very little labour or pretension; yet there are passages of high poetical spirit, and of inimitable quaintness of humour, which are undoubtedly Shakespeare's, and there is throughout the conduct of the fable a careless grace and felicity which marks it for his. One of the editors (we believe, Mr. Pope) remarks in a marginal note to the TWO GENTLEMEN OF VERONA: 'It is observable (I know not for what cause) that the style of this comedy is less figurative, and more natural and unaffected than the greater part of this author's, though supposed to be one of the first he wrote.' Yet so little does the editor appear to have made up his mind upon this subject, that we find the following note to the very next (the second) scene. 'This whole scene, like many others in these plays (some of which I believe were written by Shakespeare, and others interpolated by the players) is composed of the lowest and most trifling conceits, to be accounted for only by the gross taste of the age he lived in: Populo ut placerent. I wish I had authority to leave them out, but I have done all I could, set a mark of reprobation upon them, throughout this edition.' It is strange that our fastidious critic should fall so soon from praising to reprobating. The style of the familiar parts of this comedy is indeed made up of conceits—low they may be for what we know, but then they are not poor, but rich ones. The scene of Launce with his dog (not that in the second, but that in the fourth act) is a perfect treat in the way of farcical drollery and invention; nor do we think Speed's manner of proving his master to be in love deficient in wit or sense, though the style may be criticized as not simple enough for the modern taste.

Valentine. Why, how know you that I am in love?

Speed. Marry, by these special marks; first, you have learned, like Sir Protheus, to wreathe your arms like a malcontent, to relish a love-song like a robin-red-breast, to walk alone like one that had the pestilence, to sigh like a schoolboy that had lost his A B C, to weep like a young wench that had buried her grandam, to fast like one that takes diet, to watch like one that fears robbing, to speak puling like a beggar at Hallowmas. You were wont, when you laughed, to crow like a cock; when you walked, to walk; like one of the lions; when you fasted, it was presently after dinner; when you looked sadly, it was for want of money; and now you are metamorphosed with a mistress, that when I look on you, I can hardly think you my master.

The tender scenes in this play, though not so highly wrought as in some others, have often much sweetness of sentiment and expression. There is something pretty and playful in the conversation of Julia with her maid, when she shows such a disposition to coquetry about receiving the letter from Proteus; and her behaviour afterwards and her disappointment, when she finds him faithless to his vows, remind us at a distance of Imogen's tender constancy. Her answer to Lucetta, who advises her against following her lover in disguise, is a beautiful piece of poetry.

Lucetta. I do not seek to quench your love's hot fire, But qualify the fire's extremes! rage, Lest it should burn above the bounds of reason.

Julia. The more thou damm'st it up, the more it burns; The current that with gentle murmur glides, Thou know'st, being stopp'd, impatiently doth rage; But when his fair course is not hindered, He makes sweet music with th' enamell'd stones, Giving a gentle kiss to every sedge He overtaketh in his pilgrimage: And so by many winding nooks he strays, With willing sport, to the wild ocean.

[Footnote: 'The river wanders at its own sweet will.' Wordsworth.]

Then let me go, and hinder not my course; I'll be as patient as a gentle stream, And make a pastime of each weary step, Till the last step have brought me to my love; And there I'll rest, as after much turmoil, A blessed soul doth in Elysium.

If Shakespeare indeed had written only this and other passages in the TWO GENTLEMEN OF VERONA, he would ALMOST have deserved Milton's praise of him—

And sweetest Shakespeare, Fancy's child, Warbles his native wood- notes wild.

But as it is, he deserves rather more praise than this.

THE MERCHANT OF VENICE

This is a play that in spite of the change of manners and of prejudices still holds undisputed possession of the stage. Shakespeare's malignant has outlived Mr. Cumberland's benevolent Jew. In proportion as Shylock has ceased to be a popular bugbear, 'baited with the rabble's curse', he becomes a half favourite with the philosophical part of the audience, who are disposed to think that Jewish revenge is at least as good as Christian injuries. Shylock is A GOOD HATER; 'a man no less sinned against than sinning'. If he carries his revenge too far, yet he has strong grounds for 'the lodged hate he bears Anthonio', which he explains with equal force of eloquence and reason. He seems the depositary of the vengeance of his race; and though the long habit of brooding over daily insults and injuries has crusted over his temper with inveterate misanthropy, and hardened him against the contempt of mankind, this adds but little to the triumphant pretensions of his enemies. There is a strong, quick, and deep sense of justice mixed up with the gall and bitterness of his resentment. The constant apprehension of being burnt alive, plundered, banished, reviled, and trampled on, might be supposed to sour the most forbearing nature, and to take something from that 'milk of human kindness', with which his persecutors contemplated his indignities. The desire of revenge is almost inseparable from the sense of wrong; and we can hardly help sympathizing with the proud spirit, hid beneath his 'Jewish gaberdine', stung to madness by repeated undeserved provocations, and labouring to throw off the load of obloquy and oppression heaped upon him and all his tribe by one desperate act of 'lawful' revenge, till the ferociousness of the means by which he is to execute his purpose, and the pertinacity with which he adheres to it, turn us against him; but even at last, when disappointed of the sanguinary revenge with which he had glutted his hopes, and exposed to beggary and contempt by the letter of the law on which he had insisted with so little remorse, we pity him, and think him hardly dealt with by his judges. In all his answers and retorts upon his adversaries, he has the best not only of the argument but of the question, reasoning on their own principles and practice. They are so far from allowing of any measure of equal dealing, of common justice or humanity between themselves and the Jew, that even when they come to ask a favour of him, and Shylock reminds them that 'on such a day they spit upon him, another spurned him, another called him dog, and for these courtesies request he'll lend them so much monies'—Anthonio, his old enemy, instead of any acknowledgement of the shrewdness and justice of his remonstrance, which would have been preposterous in a respectable Catholic merchant in those times, threatens him with a repetition of the same treatment—

> I am as like to call thee so again,
> To spit on thee again, to spurn thee too.

After this, the appeal to the Jew's mercy, as if there were any common principle of right and wrong between them, is the rankest hypocrisy, or the blindest prejudice; and the Jew's answer to one of Anthonio's friends, who asks him what his pound of forfeit flesh is good for, is irresistible:

To bait fish withal; if it will feed nothing else, it will feed my revenge. He hath disgrac'd me, and hinder'd me of half a million, laughed at my losses, mock'd at my gains, scorn'd my nation, thwarted my bargains, cool'd my friends, heated mine enemies; and what's his reason? I am a Jew. Hath not a Jew eyes; hath not a Jew hands, organs, dimensions, senses, affections, passions;

fed with the same food, hurt with the same weapons, subject to the same diseases, healed by the same means, warmed and cooled by the same winter and summer that a Christian is? If you prick us, do we not bleed? If you tickle us, do we not laugh? If you poison us, do we not die? And if you wrong us, shall we not revenge? If we are like you in the rest, we will resemble you in that. If a Jew wrong a Christian, what is his humility? revenge. If a Christian wrong a Jew, what should his sufferance be by Christian example? why revenge. The villany you teach me I will execute, and it shall go hard but I will better the instruction.

The whole of the trial scene, both before and after the entrance of Portia, is a masterpiece of dramatic skill. The legal acuteness, the passionate declamations, the sound maxims of jurisprudence, the wit and irony interspersed in it, the fluctuations of hope and fear in the different persons, and the completeness and suddenness of the catastrophe, cannot be surpassed. Shylock, who is his own counsel, defends himself well, and is triumphant on all the general topics that are urged against him, and only Tails through a legal flaw. Take the following as an instance:

Shylock. What judgment shall I dread, doing no wrong? You have among you many a purchas'd slave, Which, like your asses, and your dogs, and mules, You use in abject and in slavish part, Because you bought them:—shall I say to you, Let them be free, marry them to your heirs? Why sweat they under burdens? let their beds Be made as soft as yours, and let their palates Be season'd with such viands? you will answer, The slaves are ours:—so do I answer you: The pound of flesh, which I demand of him, Is dearly bought, is mine, and I will have it; If you deny me, fie upon your law! There is no force in the decrees of Venice: I stand for judgment: answer; shall I have it?

The keenness of his revenge awakes all his faculties; and he beats back all opposition to his purpose, whether grave or gay, whether of wit or argument, with an equal degree of earnestness and self- possession. His character is displayed as distinctly in other less prominent parts of the play, and we may collect from a few sentences the history of his life—his descent and origin, his thrift and domestic economy, his affection for his daughter, whom he loves next to his wealth, his courtship and his first present to Leah, his wife! 'I would not have parted with it' (the ring which he first gave her) 'for a wilderness of monkeys!' What a fine Hebraism is implied in this expression!

Portia is not a very great favourite with us, neither are we in love with her maid, Nerissa. Portia has a certain degree of affectation and pedantry about her, which is very unusual in Shakespeare's women, but which perhaps was a proper qualification for the office of a 'civil doctor', which she undertakes and executes so successfully. The speech about mercy is very well; but there are a thousand finer ones in Shakespeare. We do not admire the scene of the caskets; and object entirely to the Black Prince, Morocchius. We should like Jessica better if she had not deceived and robbed her father, and Lorenzo, if he had not married a Jewess, though he thinks he has a right to wrong a Jew. The dialogue between this newly married couple by moonlight, beginning 'On such a night', &c., is a collection of classical elegancies. Launcelot, the Jew's man, is an honest fellow. The dilemma in which he describes himself placed between his 'conscience and the fiend', the one of which advises him to run away from his master's service and the other to stay in it, is exquisitely humorous.

Gratiano is a very admirable subordinate character, He is the jester of the piece: yet one speech of his, in his own defence, contains a whole volume of wisdom,

Anthonio. I hold the world but as the world, Gratiano, A stage, where every one must play his part; And mine a sad one.

Gratiano. Let me play the fool: With mirth and laughter let old wrinkles come; And let my liver rather heat with wine, Than my heart cool with mortifying groans. Why should a man, whose blood is warm within, Sit like his grandsire cut in alabaster? Sleep when he wakes? and creep into the jaundice By being peevish? I tell thee what, Anthonio—I love thee, and it is my love that speaks;—There are a sort of men, whose visages Do cream and mantle like a standing pond: And do a wilful stillness entertain, With purpose to be drest in an opinion Of wisdom, gravity, profound conceit; As who should say, 'I am Sir Oracle, And when I ope my lips, let no dog bark'! O, my Anthonio, I do know of these, That therefore only are reputed wise, For saying nothing; who, I am very sure, If they should speak, would almost damn those ears, Which hearing them, would call their brothers fools. I'll tell thee more of this another time; But fish not, with this melancholy bait, For this fool's gudgeon, this opinion.

Gratiano's speech on the philosophy of love, and the effect of habit in taking off the force of passion, is as full of spirit and good sense. The graceful winding up of this play in the fifth act, after the tragic business is dispatched, is one of the happiest instances of Shakespeare's knowledge of the principles of the drama. We do not mean the pretended quarrel between Portia and Nerissa and their husbands about the rings, which is amusing enough, but the conversation just before and after the return of Portia to her own house, begining 'How sweet the moonlight sleeps upon this bank', and ending 'Peace! how the moon sleeps with Endymion, and would not be awaked'. There is a number of beautiful thoughts crowded into that short space, and linked together by the most natural transitions.

When we first went to see Mr. Kean in Shylock we expected to see, what we had been used to see, a decrepid old man, bent with age and ugly with mental deformity, grinning with deadly malice, with the venom of his heart congealed in the expression of his countenance, sullen, morose, gloomy, inflexible, brooding over one idea, that of his hatred, and fixed on one unalterable purpose, that of his revenge. We were disappointed, because we had taken our idea from other actors, not from the play. There is no proof there that Shylock is old, but a single line, 'Bassanic and old Shylock, both stand forth,'—which does not imply that he is infirm with age— and the circumstance that he has a daughter marriageable, which does not imply that he is old at all. It would be too much to say that his body should be made crooked and deformed to answer to his mind, which is bowed down and warped with prejudices and passion. That he has but one idea, is not true; he has more ideas than any other person in the piece: and if he is intense and inveterate in the pursuit of his purpose, he shows the utmost elasticity, vigour, and presence of mind, in the means of attaining it. But so rooted was our habitual impression of the part from seeing it caricatured in the representation, that it was only from a careful perusal of the play itself that we saw our error. The stage is not in general the best place to study our author's characters in. It is too often filled with traditional common-place conceptions of the part, handed down from sire to son, and suited to the taste of THE GREAT VULGAR AND THE SMALL.—"Tis an unweeded garden: things rank and gross do merely gender in it!' If a man of genius comes once in an age to clear away the rubbish, to make it fruitful and wholesome, they cry, "Tis a bad school: it may be like nature, it may be like Shakespeare, but it is not like us." Admirable critics!

THE WINTER'S TALE

We wonder that Mr. Pope should have entertained doubts of the genuineness of this play. He was, we suppose, shocked (as a certain critic suggests) at the Chorus, Time, leaping over sixteen years with his crutch between the third and fourth act, and at Antigonus's landing with the infant Perdita on the seacoast of Bohemia. These slips or blemishes, however, do not prove it not to be Shakespeare's; for he was as likely to fall into them as anybody; but we do not know anybody but himself who could produce the beauties. The STUFF of which the tragic passion is composed, the romantic sweetness, the comic humour, are evidently his. Even the crabbed and tortuous style of the speeches of Leontes, reasoning on his own jealousy, beset with doubts and fears, and entangled more and more in the thorny labyrinth, bears every mark of Shakespeare's peculiar manner of conveying the painful struggle of different thoughts and feelings, labouring for utterance, and almost strangled in me birth. For instance:

> Ha' not you seen, Camillo?
> (But that's past doubt; you have, or your eye-glass
> Is thicker than a cuckold's horn) or heard,
> (For to a vision so apparent, rumour
> Cannot be mute) or thought (for cogitation
> Resides not within man that does not think)
> My wife is slippery? If thou wilt, confess,
> Or else be impudently negative,
> To have nor eyes, nor ears, nor thought.—

Here Leontes is confounded with his passion, and does not know which way to turn himself, to give words to the anguish, rage, and apprehension which tug at his breast. It is only as he is worked up into a clearer conviction of his wrongs by insisting on the grounds of his unjust suspicions to Camillo, who irritates him by his opposition, that he bursts out into the following vehement strain of bitter indignation: yet even here his passion staggers, and is as it were oppressed with its own intensity.

> Is whispering nothing?
> Is leaning cheek to cheek? is meeting noses?
> Kissing with inside lip? stopping the career
> Of laughter with a sigh? (a note infallible
> Of breaking honesty!) horsing foot on foot?
> Skulking in corners? wishing clocks more swift?
> Hours, minutes? the noon, midnight? and all eyes
> Blind with the pin and web, but theirs; theirs only,
> That would, unseen, be wicked? is this nothing?
> Why then the world, and all that's in't, is nothing,
> The covering sky is nothing, Bohemia's nothing,
> My wife is nothing!

The character of Hermione is as much distinguished by its saint-like resignation and patient forbearance, as that of Paulina is by her zealous and spirited remonstrances against the injustice done to the queen, and by her devoted attachment to her misfortunes. Hermione's restoration to her husband and her child, after her long separation from them, is as affecting in itself as it is striking in the representation. Camillo, and the old shepherd and his son, are subordinate but not uninteresting instruments in the development of the plot, and though last, not least, comes Autolycus, a very pleasant, thriving rogue; and (what is the best feather in the cap of all knavery) he escapes with impunity in the end.

THE WINTER'S TALE is one of the best-acting of our author's plays. We remember seeing it with great pleasure many years ago. It was on the night that King took leave of the stage, when he and Mrs. Jordan played together in the after-piece of The Wedding-day. Nothing could go off with more eclat, with more spirit, and grandeur of effect. Mrs. Siddons played Hermione, and in the last scene acted the painted statue to the life—with true monumental dignity and noble passion; Mr. Kemble, in Leontes, worked himself up into a very fine classical frenzy; and Bannister, as Autolycus, roared as loud for pity as a sturdy beggar could do who felt none of the pain he counterfeited, and was sound of wind and limb. We shall never see these parts so acted again; or if we did, it would be in vain. Actors grow old, or no longer surprise us by their novelty. But true poetry, like nature, is always young; and we still read the courtship of Florizel and Perdita, as we welcome the return of spring, with the' same feelings as ever.

> Florizel. Thou dearest Perdita,
>   With these forc'd thoughts, I prithee, darken not
>   The mirth o' the feast: or, I'll be thine, my fair,
>   Or not my father's: for I cannot be
>   Mine own, nor anything to any, if
>   I be not thine. To this I am most constant,
>   Tho' destiny say. No. Be merry, gentle;
>   Strangle such thoughts as these, with anything
>   That you behold the while. Your guests are coming:
>   Lift up your countenance; as it were the day
>   Of celebration of that nuptial which
>   We two have sworn shall come.
>
> Perdita. O lady Fortune, Stand you auspicious!
>
> Enter Shepherd, Clown, Mopsa, Dobcas, Servants;
> with Polixenes, and Camillo, disguised.
>
> Florizel. See, your guests approach.
>   Address yourself to entertain them sprightly,
>   And let's be red with mirth.
>
> Shepherd. Fie, daughter! when my old wife liv'd, upon
>   This day, she was both pantler, butler, cook;
>   Both dame and servant: welcom'd all, serv'd all:
>   Would sing her song, and dance her turn: now here
>   At upper end o' the table, now i' the middle:
>   On his shoulder, and his: her face o' fire

With labour; and the thing she took to quench it
She would to each one sip. You are retir d,
As if you were a feasted one, and not
The hostess of the meeting. Pray you, bid
These unknown friends to us welcome; for it is
A way to make us better friends, more known.
Come, quench your blushes; and present yourself
That which you are, mistress o' the feast. Come on,
And bid us welcome to your sheep-shearing,
As your good flock shall prosper.

Perdita. Sir, welcome! [To Polixenes and Camillo.]
It is my father's will I should take on me
The hostess-ship o' the day: you're welcome, sir!
Give me those flowers there, Dorcas.—Reverend sirs,
For you there's rosemary and rue; these keep
Seeming, and savour, all the winter long:
Grace and remembrance be unto you both
And welcome to our shearing!

Polixenes. Shepherdess,
(A fair one are you) well you fit our ages
With flowers of winter.

Perdita. Sir, the year growing ancient,
Not yet on summer's death, nor on the birth
Of trembling winter, the fairest flowers o' the season
Are our carnations, and streak'd gilly-flowers,
Which some call nature's bastards: of that kind
Our rustic garden's barren; and I care not
To get slips of them.

Polixenes. Wherefore, gentle maiden,
Do you neglect them?

Perdita. For I have heard it said
There is an art which in their piedness shares
With great creating nature.

Polixenes. Say, there be: Yet nature is made better by no mean,
But nature makes that mean: so, o'er that art
Which, you say, adds to nature, is an art
That nature makes. You see, sweet maid, we marry
A gentler scion to the wildest stock;
And make conceive a bark of baser kind
By bud of nobler race. This is an art

155

Which does mend nature, change it rather: but
The art itself is nature.

Perdita. So it is.
  [Footnote: The lady, we here see, gives up the
  argument, but keeps her mind.]

Polixenes. Then make your garden rich in gilly-flowers,
  And do not call them bastards.

Perdita. I'll not put
  The dibble in earth, to set one slip of them;
  [Footnote: The lady, we here see, gives up the argument, but
  keeps her mind.]
  No more than, were I painted, I would wish
  This youth should say, 'twere well; and only therefore
  Desire to breed by me.—Here's flowers for you;
  Hot lavender, mints, savory, marjoram;
  The marigold, that goes to bed with the sun,
  And with him rises, weeping: these are flowers
  Of middle summer, and, I think, they are given
  To men of middle age. You are very welcome.

Camillo. I should leave grazing, were I of your flock,
  And only live by gazing.

Perdita. Out, alas!
  You'd be so lean, that blasts of January
  Would blow you through and through. Now my fairest friends.
  I would I had some flowers o' the spring that might
  Become your time of day; and yours, and yours,
  That wear upon your virgin branches yet
  Your maidenheads growing: O Proserpina!
  For the flowers now that frighted thou let'st fall
  From Dis's waggon! daffodils,
  That come before the swallow dares and take
  The winds of March with beauty: violets dim,
  But sweeter than the lids of Juno's eyes,
  Or Cytherea's breath; pale primroses,
  That die unmarried, ere they can behold
  Bright Phoebus in his strength (a malady
  Most incident to maids); bold oxlips, and
  The crown-imperial; lilies of all kinds,
  The fleur-de-lis being one! O, these I lack
  To make you garlands of; and my sweet friend
  To strow him o'er and o'er.

Florizel. What, like a corse?

Perdita. No, like a bank, for love to lie and play on;
  Not like a corse; or if—not to be buried,
  But quick, and in mine arms. Come, take your flowers;
  Methinks, I play as I have seen them do
  In Whitsun pastorals: sure this robe of mine
  Does change my disposition.

Florizel. What you do,
  Still betters what is done. When you speak, sweet,
  I'd have you do it ever: when you sing,
  I'd have you buy and sell so; so give alms;
  Pray so; and for the ordering your affairs,
  To sing them too. When you do dance, I wish you
  A wave o' the sea, that you might ever do
  Nothing but that; move still, still so,
  And own no other function. Each your doing,
  So singular in each particular,
  Crowns what you're doing in the present deeds,
  That all your acts are queens.

Perdita. O Doricles,
  Your praises are too large; but that your youth
  And the true blood, which peeps forth fairly through it,
  Do plainly give you out an unstained shepherd;
  With wisdom I might fear, my Doricles,
  You woo'd me the false way.

Florizel. I think you have
  As little skill to fear, as I have purpose
  To put you to't. But come, our dance, I pray.
  Your hand, my Perdita: so turtles pair,
  That never mean to part.

Perdita. I'll swear for 'em.

Polixenes. This is the prettiest low-bom lass that ever
  Ran on the green-sward; nothing she does, or seems,
  But smacks of something greater than herself,
  Too noble for this place.

Camillo. He tells her something
  That makes her blood look out: good sooth she is
  The queen of curds and cream.

This delicious scene is interrupted by the father of the prince discovering himself to Florizel, and haughtily breaking off the intended match between his son and Perdita. When Polixenes goes out, Perdita says,

> Even here undone!
> I was not much afraid; for once or twice
> I was about to speak; and tell him plainly
> The self-same sun that shines upon his court,
> Hides not his visage from our cottage, but
> Looks on't alike. Wilt please you, sir, be gone?
> [To Florizel.]
> I told you what would come of this. Beseech you,
> Of your own state take care; this dream of mine,
> Being now awake, I'll queen it no inch further,
> But milk my ewes and weep.

As Perdita, the supposed shepherdess, turns out to be the daughter of Hermione, and a princess in disguise, both feelings of the pride of birth and the claims of nature are satisfied by the fortunate event of the story, and the fine romance of poetry is reconciled to the strictest court-etiquette.

ALL'S WELL THAT ENDS WELL

ALL'S WELL THAT ENDS WELL is one of the most pleasing of our author's comedies. The interest is, however, more of a serious than of a comic nature. The character of Helen is one of great sweetness and delicacy. She is placed in circumstances of the most critical kind, and has to court her husband both as a virgin and a wife: yet the most scrupulous nicety of female modesty is not once violated. There is not one thought or action that ought to bring a blush into her cheeks, or that for a moment lessens her in our esteem. Perhaps the romantic attachment of a beautiful and virtuous girl to one placed above her hopes by the circumstances of birth and fortune, was never so exquisitely expressed as in the reflections which she utters when young Roussillon leaves his mother's house, under whose protection she has been brought up with him, to repair to the French king's court.

> Helena. Oh, were that all—I think not on my father,
>   And these great tears grace his remembrance more
>   Than those I shed for him. What was he like?
>   I have forgot him. My imagination
>   Carries no favour in it, but Bertram's.
>   I am undone, there is no living, none,
>   If Bertram be away. It were all one
>   That I should love a bright particular star,
>   And think to wed it; he is so above me:
>   In his bright radiance and collateral light
>   Must I be comforted, not in his sphere.
>   Th' ambition in my love thus plagues itself;
>   The hind that would be mated by the lion,
>   Must die for love. 'Twas pretty, tho' a plague,
>   To see him every hour, to sit and draw
>   His arched brows, his hawking eye, his curls
>   In our heart's table: heart too capable
>   Of every line and trick of his sweet favour.
>   But now he's gone, and my idolatrous fancy
>   Must sanctify his relics.

The interest excited by this beautiful picture of a kind and innocent heart is kept up afterwards by her resolution to follow him to France, the success of her experiment in restoring the king's health, her demanding Bertram in marriage as a recompense, his leaving her in disdain, her interview with him afterwards disguised as Diana, a young lady whom he importunes with his secret addresses, and their final reconciliation when the consequences of her stratagem and the proofs of her love are fully made known. The persevering gratitude of the French king to his benefactress, who cures him of a languishing distemper by a prescription hereditary in her family, the indulgent kindness of the Countess, whose pride of birth yields, almost without struggle, to her affection for Helen, the honesty and uprightness of the good old lord Lafeu, make very interesting parts of the picture. The wilful stubbornness and youthful petulance of Bertram are also very admirably described. The comic part of the play turns on the folly, boasting, and cowardice of Parolles, a parasite and hanger-on of Bertram's, the detection of whose false pretensions to bravery and honour forms a very amusing episode. He is first found out by the old lord Lafeu, who says, 'The soul of this man is in his clothes'; and it is proved afterwards that his heart is in his tongue, and that both are false and hollow. The adventure of the bringing off of his drum' has become proverbial as a satire on all ridiculous and blustering undertakings which the person never means to perform: nor can anything be more severe than what one of the bystanders remarks upon what Parolles says of himself, 'Is it possible he should know what he is, and be that he is?' Yet Parolles himself gives the best solution of the difficulty afterwards when he is thankful to escape with his life and the loss of character; for, so that he can live on, he is by no means squeamish about the loss of pretensions, to which he had sense enough to know he had no real claims, and which he had assumed only as a means to live.

> Parolles. Yet I am thankful; if my heart were great,
> 'Twould burst at this. Captain I'll be no more,
> But I will eat and drink, and sleep as soft
> As captain shall. Simply the thing I am
> Shall make me live; who knows himself a braggart,
> Let him fear this; for it shall come to pass,
> That every braggart shall be found an ass.
> Rust sword, cool blushes, and Parolles live
> Safest in shame; being fool'd, by fool'ry thrive;
> There's place and means for every man alive.
> I'll after them.

The story of ALL'S WELL THAT ENDS WELL, and of several others of Shakespeare's plays, is taken from Boccaccio. The poet has dramatized the original novel with great skill and comic spirit, and has preserved all the beauty of character and sentiment without improving upon it, which was impossible. There is indeed in Boccaccio's serious pieces a truth, a pathos, and an exquisite refinement of sentiment, which is hardly to be met with in any other prose writer whatever. Justice has not been done him by the world. He has in general passed for a mere narrator of lascivious tales or idle jests. This character probably originated in his obnoxious attacks on the monks, and has been kept up by the grossness of mankind, who revenged their own want of refinement on Boccaccio, and only saw in his writings what suited the coarseness of their own tastes. But the truth is, that he has carried sentiment of every kind to its very highest purity and perfection. By sentiment we would here understand the habitual workings of some one powerful feeling, where the heart reposes almost entirely upon itself, without the violent excitement of opposing duties or, untoward circumstances. In this way, nothing ever came up to the story of Frederigo Alberigi and his Falcon. The perseverance in attachment, the spirit of gallantry and generosity displayed in it, has no parallel in the history of heroical sacrifices. The feeling is so unconscious too, and involuntary, is brought out in such small, unlooked-for, and unostentatious circumstances, as to show it to have been woven into the very nature and soul of the author. The story of Isabella is scarcely less fine and is more affecting in the circumstances and in the catastrophe. Dryden has done justice to the impassioned eloquence of the Tancred and Sigismunda; but has not given an adequate idea of the wild preternatural interest of the story of Honoria. Cimon and Iphigene is by no means one of the best, notwithstanding the popularity of the subject. The proof of unalterable affection given in the story of Jeronymo, and the simple touches of nature and picturesque beauty in the story of the two holiday lovers, who were poisoned by tasting of a leaf in the garden at Florence, are perfect masterpieces. The epithet of Divine was well bestowed on this great painter of the human heart. The invention implied in his different tales is immense: but we are not to infer that it is all his own. He probably availed himself of all the common traditions which were floating in his time, and which he was the first to appropriate. Homer appears the most original of all authors—probably for no other reason than that we can trace the plagiarism no further. Boccaccio has furnished subjects to numberless writers since his time, both dramatic and narrative. The story of Griselda is borrowed from his DECAMERON by Chaucer; as is the KNIGHT'S TALE (Palamon and Arcite) from his poem of the THESEID.

LOVE'S LABOUR'S LOST

If we were to part with any of the author's comedies, it should be this. Yet we should be loth to part with Don Adriano de Armado, that mighty potentate of nonsense, or his page, that handful of wit; with Nathaniel the curate, or Holofernes the schoolmaster, and their dispute after dinner on 'the golden cadences of poesy'; with Costard the clown, or Dull the constable. Biron is too accomplished a character to be lost to the world, and yet he could not appear without his fellow courtiers and the king: and if we were to leave out the ladies, the gentlemen would have no mistresses. So that we believe we may let the whole play stand as it is, and we shall hardly venture to 'set a mark of reprobation on it'. Still we have some objections to the style, which we think savours more of the pedantic spirit of Shakespeare's time than of his own genius; more of controversial divinity, and the logic of Peter Lombard, than of the inspiration of the Muse. It transports us quite as much to the manners of the court, and the quirks of courts of law, as to the scenes of nature or the fairyland of his own imagination. Shakespeare has set himself to imitate the tone of polite conversation then prevailing among the fair, the witty, and the learned, and he has imitated it but too faithfully. It is as if the hand of Titian had been employed to give grace to the curls of a full-bottomed periwig, or Raphael had attempted to give expression to the tapestry figures in the House of Lords. Shakespeare has put an excellent description of this fashionable jargon into the mouth of the critical Holofernes 'as too picked, too spruce, too affected, too odd, as it were, too peregrinate, as I may call it'; and nothing can be more marked than the difference when he breaks loose from the trammels he had imposed on himself, 'as light as bird from brake', and speaks in his own person. We think, for instance, that in the following soliloquy the poet has fairly got the start of Queen Elizabeth and her maids of honour;

Biron. O! and I forsooth in love, I that have been love's whip; A very beadle to an amorous sigh: A critic; nay, a night-watch constable, A domineering pedant o'er the boy, Than whom no mortal more magnificent. This whimpled, whining, purblind, wayward boy, This signior Junio, giant dwarf, Dan Cupid, Regent of love-rimes, lord of folded arms, Th' anointed sovereign of sighs and groans: Liege of all loiterers and malcontents, Dread prince of plackets. king of codpieces, Sole imperator, and great general Of trotting parators (O my little heart!) And I to be a corporal of his field, And wear his colours like a tumbler's hoop! What? I love! I sue! I seek a wife! A woman, that is like a German clock, Still a repairing; ever out of frame; And never going aright, being a watch, And being watch'd, that it may still go right? Nay, to be perjur'd, which is worst of all: And among three to love the worst of all, A whitely wanton with a velvet brow, With two pitch balls stuck in her face for eyes; Ay, and by heav'n, one that will do the deed, Though Argus were her eunuch and her guard; And I to sigh for her! to watch for her! To pray for her! Go to; it is a plague That Cupid will impose for my neglect Of his almighty dreadful little might. Well, I will love, write, sigh, pray, sue, and groan: Some men must love my lady, and some Joan.

The character of Biron drawn by Rosaline and that which Biron gives of Boyet are equally happy. The observations on the use and abuse of study, and on the power of beauty to quicken the understanding as well as the senses, are excellent. The scene which has the greatest dramatic effect is that in which Biron, the king, Longaville, and Dumain, successively detect each other and are detected in their breach of their vow and in their profession of attachment to their several mistresses, in which they suppose themselves to be overheard by no one. The reconciliation between these lovers and their sweethearts is also very good, and the penance

162

which Rosaline imposes on Biron, before he can expect to gain her consent to marry him, full of propriety and beauty.

Rosaline. Oft have I heard of you, my lord Biron, Before I saw you: and the world's large tongue Proclaims you for a man replete with mocks; Full of comparisons, and wounding flouts; Which you on all estates will execute, That lie within the mercy of your wit. To weed this wormwood from your faithful brain; And therewithal to win me, if you please, (Without the which I am not to be won) You shall this twelvemonth term from day to day Visit the speechless sick, and still converse With groaning wretches; and your task shall be, With all the fierce endeavour of your wit, T' enforce the pained impotent to smile.

Biron. To move wild laughter in the throat of death? It cannot be: it is impossible: Mirth cannot move a soul in agony.

Rosaline. Why, that's the way to choke a gibing spirit, Whose influence is begot of that loose grace, Which shallow laughing hearers give to fools; A jest's prosperity lies in the ear Of him that hears it; never in the tongue Of him that makes it: then, if sickly ears, Deaf'd with the clamours of their own dear groans, Will hear your idle scorns, continue then, And I will have you, and that fault withal; But, if they will not, throw away that spirit, And I shall find you empty of that fault, Right joyful of your reformation.

Biron. A twelvemonth? Well, befall what will befall, I'll jest a twelvemonth in an hospital.

The famous cuckoo-song closes the play; but we shall add no more criticisms: 'the words of Mercury are harsh after the songs of Apollo'.

MUCH ADO ABOUT NOTHING

This admirable comedy used to be frequently acted till of late years. Mr. Garrick's Benedick was one of his most celebrated characters; and Mrs. Jordan, we have understood, played Beatrice very delightfully. The serious part is still the most prominent here, as in other instances that we have noticed. Hero is the principal figure in the piece, and leaves an indelible impression on the mind by her beauty, her tenderness, and the hard trial of her love. The passage in which Claudio first makes a confession of his affection towards her conveys as pleasing an image of the entrance of love into a youthful bosom as can well be imagined.

> Oh, my lord,
> When you went onward with this ended action,
> I look'd upon her with a soldier's eye,
> That lik'd, but had a rougher task in hand
> Than to drive liking to the name of love;
> But now I am return'd, and that war-thoughts
> Have left their places vacant; in their rooms
> Come thronging soft and delicate desires,
> All prompting me how fair young Hero is,
> Saying, I lik'd her ere I went to wars.

In the scene at the altar, when Claudio, urged on by the villain Don John, brings the charge of incontinence against her, and as it were divorces her in the very marriage-ceremony, her appeals to her own conscious innocence and honour are made with the most affecting simplicity.

> Claudio. No, Leonato,
> I never tempted her with word too large,
> But, as a brother to his sister, show'd
> Bashful sincerity, and comely love.

Hero. And seem'd I ever otherwise to you?

> Claudio. Out on thy seeming, I will write against it:
> You seem to me as Dian in her orb,
> As chaste as is the bud ere it be blown;
> But you are more intemperate in your blood
> Than Veilus, or those pamper'd animals
> That rage in savage sensuality.

Hero. Is my lord well, that he doth speak so wide?

Leonato. Are these things spoken, or do I but dream?

John. Sir, they are spoken, and these things are true.

Benedick. This looks not like a nuptial.

Hero. True! O God!

The justification of Hero in the end, and her restoration to the confidence and arms of her lover, is brought about by one of those temporary consignments to the grave of which Shakespeare seems to have been fond. He has perhaps explained the theory of this predilection in the following lines:

> Friar. She dying, as it must be so maintain'd,
>   Upon the instant that she was accus'd,
>   Shall be lamented, pity'd, and excus'd,
>   Of every hearer: for it so falls out,
>   That what we have we prize not to the worth,
>   While we enjoy it; but being lack'd and lost,
>   Why then we rack the value; then we find
>   The virtue, that possession would not show us
>   Whilst it was ours.—So will it fare with Claudio;
>   When he shall hear she dy'd upon his words,
>   The idea of her love shall sweetly creep
>   Into his study of imagination;
>   And every lovely organ of her life
>   Shall come apparel'd in more precious habit,
>   More moving, delicate, and full of life,
>   Into the eye and prospect of his soul,
>   Than when she liv'd indeed.

The principal comic characters in MUCH ADO ABOUT NOTHING, Benedick and Beatrice, are both essences in their kind. His character as a woman-hater is admirably supported, and his conversion to matrimony is no less happily effected by the pretended story of Beatrice's love for him. It is hard to say which of the two scenes is the best, that of the trick which is thus practised on Benedick, or that in which Beatrice is prevailed on to take pity on him by overhearing her cousin and her maid declare (which they do on purpose) that he is dying of love for her. There is something delightfully picturesque in the manner in which Beatrice is described as coming to hear the plot which is contrived against herself:

> For look where Beatrice, like a lapwing, runs
>   Close by the ground, to hear our conference.

In consequence of what she hears (not a word of which s true) she exclaims when these good-natured informants are gone:

> What fire is in mine ears? Can this be true?
>   Stand I condemn'd for pride and scorn so much?
>   Contempt, farewell! and maiden pride adieu!
>   No glory lives behind the back of such.
>   And, Benedick, love on, I will requite thee;
>   Taming my wild heart to thy loving hand;
>   If thou dost love, my kindness shall incite thee
>   To bind our loves up in an holy band:

165

For others say thou dost deserve; and I
Believe it better than reportingly.

And Benedick, on his part, is equally sincere in his repentance with equal reason, after he has heard the grey-beard, Leonato, and his friend, 'Monsieur Love', discourse of the desperate state of his supposed inamorata.

This can be no trick; the conference was sadly borne.—They have the truth of this from Hero. They seem to pity the lady; it seems her affections have the full bent. Love me! why, it must be requited. I hear how I am censur'd: they say, I will bear myself proudly, if I perceive the love come from her; they say too, that she will rather die than give any sign of affection.—I did never think to marry; I must not seem proud:—happy are they that hear their detractions, and can put them to mending. They say, the lady is fair; 'tis a truth, I can bear them witness: and vir-tuous;— 'tis so, I cannot reprove it; and wise—but for loving me;—by my troth it is no addition to her wit;—nor no great argument of her folly, for I will be horribly in love with her.—I may chance to have some odd quirks and remnants of wit broken on me, because I have rail'd so long against marriage: but doth not the appetite alter? A man loves the meat in his youth, that he cannot endure in his age.—Shall quips, and sentences, and these paper bullets of the brain, awe a man from the career of his humour? No: the world must be peopled. When I said, I would die a bachelor, I did not think I should live till I were marry'd.—Here comes Beatrice; by this day, she's a fair lady: I do spy some marks of love in her.

The beauty of all this arises from the characters of the persons so entrapped. Benedick is a professed and staunch enemy to marriage, and gives very plausible reasons for the faith that is in him. And as to Beatrice, she persecutes him all day with her jests (so that he could hardly think of being troubled with them at night), she not only turns him but all other things into jest, and is proof against everything serious.

Hero. Disdain and scorn ride sparkling in her eyes,
  Misprising what they look on; and her wit
  Values itself so highly, that to her
  All matter else seems weak: she cannot love,
  Nor take no shape nor project of affection,
  She is so self-endeared.

Ursula. Sure, I think so;
  And therefore, certainly, it were not good
  She knew his love, lest she make sport at it.

Hero. Why, you speak truth: I never yet saw man,
  How wise, how noble, young, how rarely featur'd,
  But she would spell him backward: if fair-fac'd,
  She'd swear the gentleman should be her sister;
  If black, why, nature, drawing of an antick,
  Made a foul blot: if tall, a lance ill-headed;
  If low, an agate very vilely cut:
  If speaking, why, a vane blown with all winds;

If silent, why, a block moved with none.
So turns she every man the wrong side out;
And never gives to truth and virtue that
Which simpleness and merit purchaseth.

These were happy materials for Shakespeare to work on, and he has made a happy use of them. Perhaps that middle point of comedy was never more nicely hit in which the ludicrous blends with the tender, and our follies, turning round against themselves in support of our affections, retain nothing but their humanity.

Dogberry and Verges in this play are inimitable specimens of quaint blundering and misprisions of meaning; and are a standing record of that formal gravity of pretension and total want of common understanding, which Shakespeare no doubt copied from real life, and which in the course of two hundred years appear to have ascended from the lowest to the highest offices in the state.

AS YOU LIKE IT

Shakespeare has here converted the forest of Arden into another Arcadia, where they 'fleet the time carelessly, as they did in the golden world'. It is the most ideal of any of this author's plays. It is a pastoral drama in which the interest arises more out of the sentiments and characters than out of the actions or situations. It is not what is done, but what is said, that claims our attention. Nursed in solitude, 'under the shade of melancholy boughs', the imagination grows soft and delicate, and the wit runs riot in idleness, like a spoiled child that is never sent to school. Caprice is and fancy reign and revel here, and stern necessity is banished to the court. The mild sentiments of humanity are strengthened with thought and leisure; the echo of the cares and noise of the world strikes upon the ear of those 'who have felt them knowingly', softened by time and distance. 'They hear the tumult, and are still.' The very air of the place seems to breathe a spirit of philosophical poetry; to stir the thoughts, to touch the heart with pity, as the drowsy forest rustles to the sighing gale. Never was there such beautiful moralizing, equally free from pedantry or petulance.

> And this their life, exempt from public haunts,
> Finds tongues in trees, books in the running brooks,
> Sermons in stones, and good in everything.

Jaques is the only purely contemplative character in Shakespeare. He thinks, and does nothing. His whole occupation is to amuse his mind, and he is totally regardless of his body and his fortunes. He is the prince of philosophical idlers; his only passion is thought; he sets no value upon anything but as it serves as food for reflection. He can 'suck melancholy out of a song, as a weasel sucks eggs'; the motley fool, 'who morals on the time', is the greatest prize he meets with in the forest. He resents Orlando's passion for Rosalind as some disparagement of his own passion for abstract truth; and leaves the Duke, as soon as he is restored to his sovereignty, to seek his brother out, who has quitted it, and turned hermit.

> —Out of these convertites
> There is much matter to be heard and learnt.

Within the sequestered and romantic glades of the Forest of Arden, they find leisure to be good and wise, or to play the fool and fall in love. Rosalind's character is made up of sportive gaiety and natural tenderness: her tongue runs the faster to conceal the pressure at her heart. She talks herself out of breath, only to get deeper in love. The coquetry with which she plays with her lover in the double character which she has to support is managed with the nicest address. How Full of voluble, laughing grace is all her conversation with Orlando:

> —In heedless mazes running
> With wanton haste and giddy cunning.

How full of real fondness and pretended cruelty is her answer to him when he promises to love her 'For ever and a day'!

Say a day without the ever: no, no, Orlando, men are April when they woo, December when they wed: maids are May when they are maids, but the sky changes when they are wives: I will be more jealous of thee than a Barbary cock-pigeon over his hen; more clamorous than a parrot against rain; more newfangled than an ape; more giddy in my desires than a monkey; I will weep for nothing, like Diana in the fountain, and I will do that when you are disposed to be merry; I will laugh like a hyen, and that when you are inclined to sleep.

Orlando. But will my Rosalind do so?

Rosalind. By my life she will do as I do.

The silent and retired character of Celia is a necessary relief to the provoking loquacity of Rosalind, nor can anything be better conceived or more beautifully described than the mutual affection between the two cousins:

> —We still have slept together,
> Rose at an instant, learn'd, play'd, eat together,
> And wheresoe'er we went, like Juno's swans,
> Still we went coupled and inseparable.

The unrequited love of Silvius for Phebe shows the perversity of this passion in the commonest scenes of life, and the rubs and stops which nature throws in its way, where fortune has placed none. Touchstone is not in love, but he will have a mistress as a subject for the exercise of his grotesque humour, and to show his contempt for the passion, by his indifference about the person. He is a rare fellow. He is a mixture of the ancient cynic philosopher with the modern buffoon, and turns folly into wit, and wit into folly, just as the fit takes him. His courtship of Audrey not only throws a degree of ridicule on the state of wedlock itself, but he is equally an enemy to the prejudices of opinion in other respects. The lofty tone of enthusiasm, which the Duke and his companions in exile spread over the stillness and solitude of a country life, receives a pleasant shock from Touchstone's sceptical determination of the question.

Corin. And how like you this shepherd's life, Mr. Touchstone?

> Clown. Truly, shepherd, in respect of itself, it is a good life; but in respect that it is a shepherd's life, it is naught. In respect that it is solitary, I like it very well; but in respect that it is private, it is a very vile life. Now in respect it is in the fields, it pleaseth me well; but in respect it is not in the court, it is tedious. As it is a spare life, took you, it fits my humour; but as there is no more plenty in it, it goes much against my stomach.

Zimmennan's celebrated work on Solitude discovers only half the sense of this passage.

There is hardly any of Shakespeare's plays that contains a greater number of passages that have been quoted in books of extracts, or a greater number of phrases that have become in a manner proverbial. If we were to give all the striking passages, we should give half the play. We will only recall a few of the most delightful to the reader's recollection. Such are the meeting between Orlando and Adam, the exquisite appeal of Orlando to the humanity of the Duke and his company to supply him with food for the old man, and their answer, the Duke's description of a country life, and the account of Jaques moralizing on the wounded deer, his meeting with

Touchstone in the forest, his apology for his own melancholy and his satirical vein, and the well-known speech on the stages of human life, the old song of 'Blow, blow, thou winter's wind', Rosalind's description of the marks of a lover and of the progress of time with different persons, the picture of the snake wreathed round Oliver's neck while the lioness watches her sleeping prey, and Touchstone's lecture to the shepherd, his defence of cuckolds, and panegyric on the virtues of 'an If.—All of these are familiar to the reader: there is one passage of equal delicacy and beauty which may have escaped him, and with it we shall close our account of As You Like it. It is Phebe's description of Ganimed at the end of the third act.

Think not I love him, tho' I ask for him;
Tis but a peevish boy, yet he talks well;—
But what care I for words! yet words do well,
When he that speaks them pleases those that hear;
It is a pretty youth; not very pretty;
But sure he's proud, and yet his pride becomes him;
He'll make a proper man; the best thing in him
Is his complexion; and faster than his tongue
Did make offence, his eye did heal it up:
He is not very tall, yet for his years he's tall;
His leg is but so so, and yet'tis well;
There was a pretty redness in his lip,
A little riper, and more lusty red
Than that mix'd in his cheek; 'twas just the difference
Betwixt the constant red and mingled damask.
There be some women, Silvius, had they mark'd him
In parcels as I did, would have gone near
To fall in love with him: but for my part
I love him not, nor hate him not; and yet
I have more cause to hate him than to love him;
For what had he to do to chide at me?

THE TAMING OF THE SHREW

THE TAMING OF THE SHREW is almost the only one of Shakespeare's comedies that has a regular plot, and downright moral. It is full of bustle, animation, and rapidity of action. It shows admirably how self-will is only to be got the better of by stronger will, and how one degree of ridiculous perversity is only to be driven out by another still greater. Petruchio is a madman in his senses; a very honest fellow, who hardly speaks a word of truth, and succeeds in all his tricks and impostures. He acts his assumed character to the life, with the most fantastical extravagance, with complete presence of mind, with untired animal spirits, and without a particle of ill humour from beginning to end.—The situation of poor Katherine, worn out by his incessant persecutions, becomes at last almost as pitiable as it is ludicrous, and it is difficult to say which to admire most, the unaccountableness of his actions, or the unalterableness of his resolutions. It is a character which most husbands ought to study, unless perhaps the very audacity of Petruchio's attempt might alarm them more than his success would encourage them. What a sound must the following speech carry to some married ears!

> Think you a little din can daunt my ears?
> Have I not in my time heard lions roar?
> Have I not heard the sea, puff'd up with winds,
> Rage like an angry boar, chafed with sweat?
> Have I not heard great ordnance in the field?
> And heav'n's artillery thunder in the skies?
> Have I not in a pitched battle heard
> Loud larums, neighing steeds, and trumpets clang?
> And do you tell me of a woman's tongue,
> That gives not half so great a blow to hear,
> As will a chestnut in a farmer's fire?

Not all Petruchio's rhetoric would persuade more than 'some dozen followers' to be of this heretical way of thinking. He unfolds his scheme for the Taming of the Shrew, on a principle of contradiction, thus:

> I'll woo her with some spirit when she comes.
> Say that she rail, why then I'll tell her plain
> She sings as sweetly as a nightingale;
> Say that she frown, I'll say she looks as clear
> As morning roses newly wash'd with dew;
> Say she be mute, and will not speak a word,
> Then I'll commend her volubility,
> And say she uttereth piercing eloquence:
> If she do bid me pack, I'll give her thanks,
> As tho' she bid me stay by her a week;
> If she deny to wed, I'll crave the day,
> When I shall ask the banns, and when be married.

He accordingly gains her consent to the match, by telling her father that he has got it; disappoints her by not returning at the time he has promised to wed her, and when he returns, creates no small consternation by the oddity of his dress and equipage. This however is nothing to the astonishment excited by his madbrained behaviour at the marriage. Here is the account of it by an eye-witness:

Gremio. Tut, she's a lamb, a dove, a fool to him;
   I'll tell you. Sir Lucentio; when the priest
   Should ask if Katherine should be his wife?
   Ay, by gogs woons, quoth he; and swore so loud,
   That, all amaz'd, the priest let fall the book;
   And as he stooped again to take it up,
   This mad-brain'd bridegroom took him such a cuff,
   That down fell priest and book, and book and priest.
   Now take them up, quoth he, if any list.

Tronio. What said the wench when he rose up again?

Gremio. Trembled and shook; for why, he stamp'd and swore,
   As if the vicar meant to cozen him.
   But after many ceremonies done,
   He calls for wine; a health, quoth he; as if
   He'd been aboard carousing with his mates
   After a storm; quaft off the muscadel,
   And threw the sops all in the sexton's face;
   Having no other cause but that his beard
   Grew thin and hungerly, and seem'd to ask
   His sops as he was drinking. This done, he took
   The bride about the neck, and kiss'd her lips
   With such a clamorous smack, that at their parting
   All the church echoed; and I seeing this,
   Came thence for very shame; and after me,
   I know, the rout is coming;—
   Such a mad marriage never was before.

The most striking and at the same time laughable feature in the character of Petruchio throughout, is the studied approximation to the intractable character of real madness, his apparent insensibility to all external considerations, and utter indifference to everything but the wild and extravagant freaks of his own self- will. There is no contending with a person on whom nothing makes any impression but his own purposes, and who is bent on his own whims just in proportion as they seem to want common-sense. With him a thing's being plain and reasonable is a reason against it. The airs he gives himself are infinite, and his caprices as sudden as they are groundless. The whole of his treatment of his wife at home is in the same spirit of ironical attention and inverted gallantry. Everything flies before his will, like a conjurer's wand, and he only metamorphoses his wife's temper by metamorphosing her senses and all the objects she sees, at a word's speaking. Such are his insisting that it is the moon and not the sun which they see, &c. This extravagance reaches its most pleasant and poetical height in the scene where, on their return to her father's, they meet old Vincentio, whom Petruchio immediately addresses as a young lady:

> Petruchio. Good morrow, gentle mistress, where away?
>   Tell me, sweet Kate, and tell me truly too,
>   Hast thou beheld a fresher gentlewoman?
>   Such war of white and red within her cheeks;
>   What stars do spangle heaven with such beauty,
>   As those two eyes become that heav'nly face?
>   Fair lovely maid, once more good day to thee:
>   Sweet Kate, embrace her for her beauty's sake.

> Hortensio. He'll make the man mad to make a woman of him.

> Katherine. Young budding virgin, fair and fresh and sweet,
>   Whither away, or where is thy abode?
>   Happy the parents of so fair a child;
>   Happier the man whom favourable stars
>   Allot thee for his lovely bed-fellow.

> Petruchio. Why, how now, Kate, I hope thou art not mad:
>   This is a man, old, wrinkled, faded, wither'd,
>   And not a maiden, as thou say'st he is.

> Katherine. Pardon, old father, my mistaken eyes
>   That have been so bedazed with the sun
>   That everything I look on seemeth green.
>   Now I perceive thou art a reverend father.

The whole is carried on with equal spirit, as if the poet's comic Muse had wings of fire. It is strange how one man could be so many things; but so it is. The concluding scene, in which trial is made of the obedience of the new-married wives (so triumphantly for Petruchio), is a very happy one.—In some parts of this play there is a little too much about music-masters and masters of philosophy. They were things of greater rarity in those days than they are now. Nothing, however, can be better than the advice which Tranio gives his master for the prosecution of his studies:

> The mathematics, and the metaphysics,
> Fall to them as you find your stomach serves you:
> No profit grows, where is no pleasure ta'en:
> In brief, sir, study what you most affect.

We have heard the Honey-Moon called 'an elegant Katherine and Petruchio'. We suspect we do not understand this word ELEGANT in the sense that many people do. But in our sense of the word, we should call Lucentio's description of his mistress elegant:

Tranio. I saw her coral lips to move,
And with her breath she did perfume the air:
Sacred and sweet was all I saw in her.

When Biondello tells the same Lucentio for his encouragement, 'I knew a wench married in an afternoon as she went to the garden for parsley to stuff a rabbit, and so may you, sir'—there is nothing elegant in this, and yet we hardly know which of the two passages is the best.

THE TAMING OF THE SHREW is a play within a play. It is supposed to be a play acted for the benefit of Sly the tinker, who is made to believe himself a lord, when he wakes after a drunken brawl. The character of Sly and the remarks with which he accompanies the play are as good as the play itself. His answer when he is asked how he likes it, 'Indifferent well; 'tis a good piece of work, would 'twere done,' is in good keeping, as if he were thinking of his Saturday night's job. Sly does not change his tastes with his new situation, but in the midst of splendour and luxury still calls out lustily and repeatedly 'for a pot o' the smallest ale'. He is very slow in giving up his personal identity in his sudden advancement. 'I am Christophero Sly, call not me honour nor lordship. I ne'er drank sack in my life: and if you give me any conserves, give me conserves of beef; ne'er ask me what raiment I'll wear, for I have no more doublets than backs, no more stockings than legs, nor no more shoes than feet, nay, sometimes more feet than shoes, or such shoes as my toes look through the over-leather.—What, would you make me mad? Am not I Christophero Sly, old Sly's son of Burtonheath, by birth a pedlar, by education a cardmaker, by transmutation a bear-herd, and now by present profession a tinker? Ask Marian Hacket, the fat alewife of Wincot, if she know me not; if she say I am not fourteen- pence on the score for sheer ale, score me up for the lying'st knave in Christendom.'

This is honest. 'The Slies are no rogues', as he says of himself. We have a great predilection for this representative of the family; and what makes us like him the better is, that we take him to be of kin (not many degrees removed) to Sancho Panza.

MEASURE FOR MEASURE

This is a play as full of genius as it is of wisdom. Yet there is an original sin in the nature of the subject, which prevents us from taking a cordial interest in it. The height of moral argument' which the author has maintained in the intervals of passion or blended with the more powerful impulses of nature, is hardly surpassed in any of his plays. But there is in general a want of passion; the affections are at a stand; our sympathies are repulsed and defeated in all directions. The only passion which influences the story is that of Angelo; and yet he seems to have a much greater passion for hypocrisy than for his mistress. Neither are we greatly enamoured of Isabella's rigid chastity, though she could not act otherwise than she did. We do not feel the same confidence in the virtue that is sublimely good' at another's expense, as if it had been out to some less disinterested trial. As to the Duke, who makes a very imposing and mysterious stage-character, he is more absorbed in his own plots and gravity than anxious for the welfare of the state; more tenacious of his own character than attentive to the feelings and apprehensions of others. Claudio is the only person who feels naturally; and yet he is placed in circumstances of distress which almost preclude the wish for his deliverance. Mariana is also in love with Angelo, whom we hate. In this respect, there may be said to be a general system of cross-purposes between the feelings of the different characters and the sympathy of the reader or the audience. This principle of repugnance seems to have reached its height in the character of Master Barnardine, who not only sets at defiance the opinions of others, but has even thrown off all self-regard,—'one that apprehends death no more dreadfully but as a drunken sleep; careless, reckless, and fearless of what's past, present, and to come.' He is a fine antithesis to the morality and the hypocrisy of the other characters of the play. Barnardine is Caliban transported from Prospero's wizard island to the forests of Bohemia or the prisons of Vienna. He is the creature of bad habits as Caliban is of gross instincts. He has, however, a strong notion of the natural fitness of things, according to his own sensations—'He has been drinking hard all night, and he will not be hanged that day'—and Shakespeare has let him off at last. We do not understand why the philosophical German critic, Schlegel, should be so severe on those pleasant persons, Lucio, Pompey, and Master Froth, as to call them 'wretches'. They appear all mighty comfortable in their occupations, and determined to pursue them, 'as the flesh and fortune should serve'. A very good exposure of the want of self-knowledge and contempt for others, which is so common in the world, is put into the mouth of Abhorson, the jailer, when the Provost proposes to associate Pompey with him in his office—'A bawd, sir? Fie upon him, he will discredit our mystery.' And the same answer would serve in nine instances out of ten to the same kind of remark, 'Go to, sir, you weigh equally; a feather will turn the scale.' Shakespeare was in one sense the least moral of all writers; for morality (commonly so called) is made up of antipathies; and his talent consisted in sympathy with human nature, in all its shapes, degrees, depressions, and elevations. The object of the pedantic moralist is to find out the bad in everything: his was to show that 'there is some soul of goodness in things evil'. Even Master Barnardine is not left to the mercy of what others think of him; but when he comes in, speaks for himself, and pleads his own cause, as well as if counsel had been assigned him. In one sense, Shakespeare was no moralist at all: in another, he was the greatest of all moralists. He was a moralist in the same sense in which nature is one. He taught what he had learnt from her. He showed the greatest knowledge of humanity with the greatest fellow-feeling for it.

One of the most dramatic passages in the present play is the interview between Claudio and his sister, when she comes to inform him of the conditions on which Angelo will spare his life.

Claudio. Let me know the point.

Isabella.—O, I do fear thee, Claudio; and I quake,
  Lest thou a feverous life should'st entertain,
  And six or seven winters more respect
  Than a perpetual honour. Dar'st thou die?
  The sense of death is most in apprehension;
  And the poor beetle, that we tread upon,
  In corporal sufferance finds a pang as great
  As when a giant dies.

Claudio. Why give you me this shame?
  Think you I can a resolution fetch
  From flowery tenderness; if I must die,
  I will encounter darkness as a bride, And hug it in mine arms.

Isabella. There spake my brother! there my father's grave
  Did utter forth a voice! Yes, thou must die:
  Thou art too noble to conserve a life
  In base appliances. This outward-sainted deputy—
  Whose settled visage and deliberate word
  Nips youth i' the head, and follies doth emmew
  As faulcon doth the fowl—is yet a devil.

Claudio. The princely Angelo?

Isabella. Oh,'tis the cunning livery of hell,
  The damned'st body to invest and cover
  In princely guards! Dost thou think, Claudio,
  If I would yield him my virginity,
  Thou might'st be freed?

Claudio. Oh, heavens! it cannot be.

Isabella. Yes, he would give it thee, for this rank offence,
  So to offend him still: this night's the time
  That I should do what I abhor to name,
  Or else thou dy'st to-morrow.

Claudio. Thou shalt not do't.

Isabella. Oh, were it but my life,
  I'd throw it down for your deliverance
  As frankly as a pin.

176

Claudio. Thanks, dear Isabel.

Isabella. Be ready, Claudio, for your death to-morrow.

Claudio. Yes.—Has he affections in him,
  That thus can make him bite the law by the nose?
  When he would force it, sure it is no sin;
  Or of the deadly seven it is the least.

Isabella. Which is the least?

Claudio. If it were damnable, he, being so wise,
  Why would he for the momentary trick
  Be perdurably fin'd? Oh, Isabel!

Isabella. What says my brother?

Claudio. Death is a fearful thing.

Isabella. And shamed life a hateful.

Claudio. Aye, but to die, and go we know not where;
  To lie in cold obstruction, and to rot;
  This sensible warm motion to become
  A kneaded clod; and the delighted spirit
  To bathe in fiery floods, or to reside
  In thrilling regions of thick-ribbed ice:
  To be imprison'd in the viewless winds,
  And blown with restless violence round about
  The pendant world; or to be worse than worst
  Of those, that lawless and incertain thoughts
  Imagine howling!—'tis too horrible!
  The weariest and most loathed worldly life,
  That age, ache, penury, and imprisonment
  Can lay on nature, is a paradise
  To what we fear of death.

Isabella. Alas! alas!

Claudio. Sweet sister, let me live:
  What sin you do to save a brother's life,
  Nature dispenses with the deed so far,
  That it becomes a virtue.

What adds to the dramatic beauty of this scene and the effect of Claudio's passionate attachment to life is, that it immediately follows the Duke's lecture to him, on the character of the Friar, recommending an absolute indifference to it.

—Reason thus with life,—
If I do lose thee, I do lose a thing,
That none but fools would keep; a breath thou art,
Servile to all the skyey influences
That do this habitation, where thou keep'st,
Hourly afflict: merely, thou art death's fool;
For him thou labour'st by thy flight to shun,
And yet run'st toward him still: thou art not noble;
For all the accommodations, that thou bear'st,
Are nurs'd by baseness: thou art by no means valiant;
For thou dost fear the soft and tender fork
Of a poor worm: thy best of rest is sleep,
And that thou oft provok'st; yet grossly fear'st
Thy death, which is no more. Thou art not thyself;
For thou exist'st on many a thousand grains!;
That issue out of dust: happy thou art not;
For what thou hast not, still thou striv'st to get;
And what thou hast, forget'st; thou art not certain;
For thy complexion shifts to strange effects,
After the moon; if thou art rich, thou art poor;
For, like an ass, whose back with ingots bows,
Thou bear'st thy heavy riches but a journey,
And death unloads thee: friend thou hast none;
For thy own bowels, which do call thee sire,
The mere effusion of thy proper loins,
Do curse the gout, serpigo, and the rheum,
For ending thee no sooner: thou hast nor youth, nor age;
But, as it were, an after-dinner's sleep,
Dreaming on both: for all thy blessed youth
Becomes as aged, and doth beg the alms
Of palsied eld; and when thou art old, and rich,
Thou hast neither heat, affection, limb, nor beauty,
To make thy riches pleasant. What's yet in this,
That bears the name of life? Yet in this life
Lie hid more thousand deaths; yet death we fear,
That makes these odds all even.

MERRY WIVES OF WINDSOR

The MERRY WIVES OF WINDSOR is no doubt a very amusing play, with a great deal of humour, character, and nature in it: but we should have liked it much better, if any one else had been the hero of it, instead of Falstaff. We could have been contented if Shakespeare had not been 'commanded to show the knight in love'. Wits and philosophers, for the most part, do not shine in that character; and Sir John himself by no means comes off with flying colours. Many people complain of the degradation and insults to which Don Quixote is so frequently exposed in his various adventures. But what are the unconscious indignities which he suffers, compared with the sensible mortifications which Falstaff is made to bring upon himself? What are the blows and buffetings which the Don receives from the staves of the Yanguesian carriers or from Sancho Panza's more hard-hearted hands, compared with the contamination of the buck-basket, the disguise of the fat woman of Brentford, and the horns of Herne the hunter, which are discovered on Sir John's head? In reading the play, we indeed wish him well through all these discomfitures, but it would have been as well if he had not got into them. Falstaff in the MERRY WIVES OF WINDSOR is not the man he was in the two parts of HENRY IV. His wit and eloquence have left him. Instead of making a butt of others, he is made a butt of by them. Neither is there a single particle of love in him to excuse his follies: he is merely a designing, bare-faced knave, and an unsuccessful one.

The scene with Ford as Master Brook, and that with Simple, Slender's man, who comes to ask after the Wise Woman, are almost the only ones in which his old intellectual ascendancy appears. He is like a person recalled to the stage to perform an unaccustomed and ungracious part; and in which we perceive only 'some faint sparks of those flashes of merriment, that were wont to set the hearers in a roar'. But the single scene with Doll Tearsheet, or Mrs. Quickly's account of his desiring 'to eat some of housewife Keach's prawns', and telling her 'to be no more so familiarity with such people', is worth the whole of the MERRY WIVES OF WINDSOR put together. Ford's jealousy, which is the mainspring of the comic incidents, is certainly very well managed. Page, on the contrary, appears to be somewhat uxorious in his disposition; and we have pretty plain indications of the effect of the characters of the husbands on the different degrees of fidelity in their wives. Mrs. Quickly makes a very lively go-between, both between Falstaff and his Dulcineas, and Anne Page and her lovers, and seems in the latter case so intent on her own interest as totally to overlook the intentions of her employers. Her master, Doctor Caius, the Frenchman, and her fellow servant Jack Rugby, are very completely described. This last- mentioned person is rather quaintly commended by Mrs. Quickly as 'an honest, willing, kind fellow, as ever servant shall come in house withal, and I warrant you, no tell-tale, nor no breed-bate; his worst fault is, that he is given to prayer; he is something peevish that way; but nobody but has his fault.' The Welsh Parson, Sir Hugh Evans (a title which in those days was given to the clergy) is an excellent character in all respects. He is as respectable as he is laughable. He has 'very good discretions, and very odd humours'. The duel-scene with Caius gives him an opportunity to show his 'cholers and his tremblings of mind', his valour and his melancholy, in an irresistible manner. In the dialogue, which at his mother's request he holds with his pupil, William Page, to show his progress in learning, it is hard to say whether the simplicity of the master or the scholar is the greatest. Nym, Bardolph, and Pistol, are but the shadows of what they were; and Justice Shallow himself has little of his consequence left. But his cousin, Slender, makes up for the deficiency. He is a very potent piece of imbecility. In him the pretensions of the worthy Gloucestershire family are well kept up, and immortalized. He and his friend Sackerson and his book of songs and his love of Anne Page and his having nothing to say to her can never be forgotten. It is the only first-rate character in the play, but it is in that class. Shakespeare is the only writer who was as great in describing weakness as strength.

THE COMEDY OF ERRORS

This comedy is taken very much from the Menaechmi of Plautus, and is not an improvement on it. Shakespeare appears to have bestowed no great pains on it, and there are but a few passages which bear the decided stamp of his genius. He seems to have relied on his author, and on the interest arising out of the intricacy of the plot. The curiosity excited is certainly very considerable, though not of the most pleasing kind. We are teased as with a riddle, which notwithstanding we try to solve. In reading the play, from the sameness of the names of the two Antipholises and the two Dromios, as well from their being constantly taken for each other by those who see them, it is difficult, without a painful effort of attention, to keep the characters distinct in the mind. And again, on the stage, either the complete similarity of their persons and dress must produce the same perplexity whenever they first enter, or the identity of appearance which the story supposes will be destroyed. We still, however, having a clue to the difficulty, can tell which is which, merely from the practical contradictions which arise, as soon as the different parties begin to speak; and we are indemnified for the perplexity and blunders into which we are thrown by seeing others thrown into greater and almost inextricable ones.— This play (among other considerations) leads us not to feel much regret that Shakespeare was not what is called a classical scholar. We do not think his forte would ever have lain in imitating or improving on what others invented, so much as in inventing for himself, and perfecting what he invented,—not perhaps by the omission of faults, but by the addition of the highest excellences. His own genius was strong enough to bear him up, and he soared longest and best on unborrowed plumes.—The only passage of a very Shakespearian cast in this comedy is the one in which the Abbess, with admirable characteristic artifice, makes Adriana confess her own misconduct in driving her husband mad.

Abbess. How long hath this possession held the man?

  Adriana. This week he hath been heavy, sour, sad,
    And much, much different from the man he was;
    But, till this afternoon, his passion
    Ne'er brake into extremity of rage.

  Abbess. Hath he not lost much wealth by wreck at sea?
    Bury'd some dear friend? Hath not else his eye
    Stray'd his affection in unlawful love?
    A sin prevailing much in youthful men,
    Who give their eyes the liberty of gazing.
    Which of these sorrows is he subject to?

  Adriana. To none of these, except it be the last:
    Namely, some love, that drew him oft from home.

Abbess. You should for that have reprehended him.

Adriana. Why, so I did.

Abbess. But not rough enough.

Adriana. As roughly as my modesty would let me.

Abbess. Haply, in private.

Adriana. And in assemblies too.

Abbess. Aye, but not enough.

   Adriana. It was the copy of our conference:
    In bed, he slept not for my urging it;
    At board, he fed not for my urging it;
    Alone it was the subject of my theme;
    In company, I often glanc'd at it;
    Still did I tell him it was vile and bad.

   Abbess. And therefore came it that the man was mad:
    The venom'd clamours of a jealous woman
    Poison more deadly than a mad dog's tooth.
    It seems, his sleeps were hinder'd by thy railing:
    And therefore comes it that his head is light.
    Thou say'st his meat was sauc'd with thy upbraidings:
    Unquiet meals make ill digestions,
    Therefore the raging fire of fever bred;
    And what's a fever but a fit of madness?
    Thou say'st his sports were hinder'd by thy brawls;
    Sweet recreation barr'd, what doth ensue,
    But moody and dull melancholy,
    Kinsman to grim and comfortless despair;
    And, at her heels, a huge infectious troop
    Of pale distemperatures, and foes to life?
    In food, in sport, and life-preserving rest
    To be disturb'd, would mad or man or beast;
    The consequence is then, thy jealous fits
    Have scar'd thy husband from the use of wits.

   Luciana. She never reprehended him but mildly,
    When he demeaned himself rough, rude, and wildly.—
    Why bear you these rebukes, and answer not?

Adriana. She did betray me to my own reproof.

Pinch the conjurer is also an excrescence not to be found in
Plautus. He is indeed a very formidable anachronism.

   They brought one Pinch, a hungry lean-fac'd villain,
   A meer anatomy, a mountebank,
   A thread-bare juggler and a fortune-teller,

A needy, hollow-ey'd, sharp-looking wretch,
A living dead man.

This is exactly like some of the Puritanical portraits to be met with in Hogarth.

DOUBTFUL PLAYS OF SHAKESPEARE

We shall give for the satisfaction of the reader what the celebrated German critic, Schlegel, says on this subject, and then add a very few remarks of our own.

'All the editors, with the exception of Capell, are unanimous in rejecting TITUS ANDRONICUS as unworthy of Shakespeare, though they always allow it to be printed with the other pieces, as the scapegoat, as it were, of their abusive criticism. The correct method in such an investigation is first to examine into the external grounds, evidences, &c., and to weigh their worth; and then to adduce the internal reasons derived from the quality of the work. The critics of Shakespeare follow a course directly the reverse of this; they set out with a preconceived opinion against a piece, and seek, in justification of this opinion, to render the historical grounds suspicious, and to set them aside. TITUS ANDRONICUS is to be found in the first folio edition of Shakespeare's works, which it was known was conducted by Heminge and Condell, for many years his friends and fellow-managers of the same theatre. Is it possible to persuade ourselves that they would not have known if a piece in their repertory did or did not actually belong to Shakespeare? And are we to lay to the charge of these honourable men a designed fraud in this single case, when we know that they did not show themselves so very desirous of scraping everything together which went by the name of Shakespeare, but, as it appears, merely gave those plays of which they had manuscripts in hand? Yet the following circumstance is still stronger: George Meres, a contemporary and admirer of Shakespeare, mentions TITUS ANDRONICUS in an enumeration of his works, in the year 1598. Meres was personally acquainted with the poet, and so very intimately, that the latter read over to him his Sonnets before they were printed. I cannot conceive that all the critical scepticism in the world would be sufficient to get over such a testimony.

This tragedy, it is true, is framed according to a false idea of the tragic, which by an accumulation of cruelties and enormities degenerates into the horrible, and yet leaves no deep impression behind: the story of Tereus and Philomela is heightened and overcharged under other names, and mixed up with the repast of Atreus and Thyestes, and many other incidents. In detail there is no want of beautiful lines, bold images, nay, even features which betray the peculiar conception of Shakespeare. Among these we may reckon the joy of the treacherous Moor at the blackness and ugliness of his child begot in adultery; and in the compassion of Titus Andronicus, grown childish through grief, for a fly which had been struck dead, and his rage afterwards when he imagines he discovers in it his black enemy; we recognize the future poet of LEAR. Are the critics afraid that Shakespeare's fame would be injured, were it established that in his early youth he ushered into the world a feeble and immature work? Was Rome the less the conqueror of the world because Remus could leap over its first walls? Let any one place himself in Shakespeare's situation at the commencement of his career. He found only a few indifferent models, and yet these met with the most favourable reception, because men are never difficult to please in the novelty of an art before their taste has become fastidious from choice and abundance. Must not this situation have had its influence on him before he learned to make higher demands on himself, and by digging deeper in his own mind, discovered the richest veins of a noble metal? It is even highly probable that he must have made several failures before getting into the right path. Genius is in a certain sense infallible, and has nothing to learn; but art is to be learned, and must be acquired by practice and experience. In Shakespeare's acknowledged works we find hardly any traces of his apprenticeship, and yet an apprenticeship he certainly had. This every artist must have, and especially in a period where he has not before him the example of a school already formed. I consider it as extremely probable, that Shakespeare began to write for the theatre at a much earlier period than the one which is generally stated, namely, not till after the year 1590. It appears that, as early as the year 1584, when only twenty years of age, he had left his paternal home and repaired to London. Can we imagine that such an active head would remain idle for six whole years without making any attempt to emerge by his talents from an uncongenial situation? That in the dedication of the poem of Venus and Adonis he calls it "the first heir of his invention", proves nothing against the supposition. It was the first which he printed; he might have composed it at an earlier period; perhaps, also, he did not include theatrical labours, as they then possessed but little literary dignity. The earlier Shakespeare began to compose for the theatre, the less are we enabled to consider the immaturity and imperfection of a work as a proof of its spuriousness in opposition to historical evidence, if we only find in it prominent features of his mind. Several of the works rejected as spurious may still have been produced in the period betwixt TITUS ANDRONICUS and the earliest of the acknowledged pieces.

'At last, Steevens published seven pieces ascribed to Shakespeare in two supplementary volumes. It is to be remarked, that they all appeared in print in Shakespeare's lifetime, with his name prefixed at full length. They are the following:

'1. LOCRINE. The proofs of the genuineness of this piece are not altogether unambiguous; the grounds for doubt, on the other hand, are entitled to attention. However, this question is immediately connected with that respecting TITUS ANDRONICUS, and must be at the same time resolved in the affirmative or negative.

'2. PERICLES, PRINCE OF TYRE. This piece was acknowledged by Dryden, but as a youthful work of Shakespeare. It is most undoubtedly his, and it has been admitted into several of the late editions. The supposed imperfections originate in the circumstance, that Shakespeare here handled a childish and extravagant romance of the old poet Gower, and was unwilling to drag the subject out of its proper sphere. Hence he even introduces Gower himself, and makes him deliver a prologue entirely in his antiquated language and versification. This power of assuming so foreign a manner is at least no proof of helplessness.

'3. THE LONDON PRODIGAL. If we are not mistaken, Lessing pronounced this piece to be Shakespeare's, and wished to bring it on the German stage.

'4. THE PURITAN; OR, THE WIDOW OF WATLING STREET. One of my literary friends, intimately acquainted with Shakespeare, was of opinion that the poet must have wished to write a play for once in the style of Ben Jonson, and that in this way we must account for the difference between the present piece and his usual manner. To follow out this idea, however, would lead to a very nice critical investigation.

'5. THOMAS, LORD CROMWELL.

'6. SIR JOHN OLDCASTLE—FIRST PART.

'7. A YORKSHIRE TRAGEDY.

'The three last pieces are not only unquestionably Shakespeare's, but in my opinion they deserve to be classed among his best and maturest works. Steevens admits at last, in some degree, that they are Shakespeare's, as well as the others, excepting LOCRINE, but he speaks of all of them with great contempt, as quite worthless productions. This condemnatory sentence is not, however, in the slightest degree convincing, nor is it supported by critical acumen. I should like to see how such a critic would, of his own natural suggestion, have decided on Shakespeare's acknowledged masterpieces, and what he would have thought of praising in them, had the public opinion imposed on him the duty of admiration. THOMAS, LORD CROMWELL, and SIR JOHN OLDCASTLE, are biographical dramas, and models in this species: the first is linked, from its subject, to HENRY THE EIGHTH, and the second to HENRY THE FIFTH. The second part of OLDCASTLE is wanting; I know not whether a copy of the old edition has been discovered in England, or whether it is lost. THE YORKSHIRE TRAGEDY is a tragedy in one act, a dramatized tale of murder: the tragical effect is overpowering, and it is extremely important to see how poetically Shakespeare could handle such a subject.

'There have been still farther ascribed to him: 1st. THE MERRY DEVIL OF EDMONTON, a comedy in one act, printed in Dodsley's old plays. This has certainly some appearances in its favour. It contains a merry landlord, who bears a great similarity to the one in the MERRY WIVES OF WINDSOR. However, at all events, though an ingenious, it is but a hasty sketch. 2nd. THE ACCUSATION OF PARIS. 3rd. THE BIRTH OF MERLIN. 4th. EDWARD THE THIRD. 5th. THE FAIR EMMA. 6th. MUCEDORUS. 7th. ARDEN OF FEVERSHAM. I have never seen any of these, and cannot therefore say anything respecting them. From the passages cited, I am led to conjecture that the subject of MUCEDORUS is the popular story of Valentine and Orson; a beautiful subject which Lope de Vega has also taken for a play. ARDEN OF FEVERSHAM is said to be a tragedy on the story of a man, from whom the poet was descended by the mother's side. If the quality of the piece is not too directly at variance with this claim, the circumstance would afford an additional probability in its favour. For such motives were not foreign to Shakespeare: he treated Henry the Seventh, who bestowed lands on his forefathers for services performed by them, with a visible partiality.

'Whoever takes from Shakespeare a play early ascribed to him, and confessedly belonging to his time, is unquestionably bound to answer, with some degree of probability, this question: who has then written it? Shakespeare's competitors in the dramatic walk are pretty well known, and if those of them who have even acquired a considerable name, a Lilly, a Marlow, a Heywood, are still so very far below him, we can hardly imagine that the author of a work, which rises so high beyond theirs, would have remained unknown'— LECTURES ON DRAMATIC LITERATURE, vol. ii, page 252.

We agree to the truth of this last observation, but not to the justice of its application to some of the plays here mentioned. It is true that Shakespeare's best works are very superior to those of Marlow, or Heywood, but it is not true that the best of the doubtful plays above enumerated are superior or even equal to the best of theirs. THE YORKSHIRE TRAGEDY, which Schlegel speaks of as an undoubted production of our author's, is much more in the manner of Heywood than of Shakespeare. The effect is indeed overpowering, but the mode of producing it is by no means poetical. The praise which Schlegel gives to THOMAS, LORD CROMWELL, and to SIR JOHN OLDCASTLE, is altogether exaggerated. They are very indifferent compositions, which have not the slightest pretensions to rank with HENRY V or HENRY VIII. We suspect that the German critic was not very well acquainted with the dramatic contemporaries of Shakespeare, or aware of their general merits; and that he accordingly mistakes a resemblance in style and manner for an equal degree of excellence. Shakespeare differed from the other writers of his age not in the mode of treating his subjects, but in the grace and power which he displayed in them. The reason assigned by a literary friend of Schlegel's for supposing THE PURITAN; OR, THE WIDOW OF WATLING STREET, to be Shakespeare's, viz. that it is in the style of Ben Jonson, that is to say, in a style just the reverse of his own, is not very satisfactory to a plain English understanding. LOCRINE, and THE LONDON PRODIGAL, if they were Shakespeare's at all, must have been among the sins of his youth. ARDEN OF FEVERSHAM contains several striking passages, but the passion which they express is rather that of a sanguine tem-perament than of a lofty imagination; and in this respect they approximate more nearly to the style of other writers of the time than to Shakespeare's. TITUS ANDRONICUS is certainly as unlike Shakespeare's usual style as it is possible. It is an accumulation of vulgar physical horrors, in which the power exercised by the poet bears no proportion to the repugnance excited by the subject. The character of Aaron the Moor is the only thing which shows any originality of conception; and the scene in which he expresses his joy 'at the blackness and ugliness of his child begot in adultery', the only one worthy of Shakespeare. Even this is worthy of him only in the display of power, for it gives no pleasure. Shakespeare managed these things differently. Nor do we think it a sufficient answer to say that this was an embryo or crude production of the author. In its kind it is full grown, and its features decided and overcharged. It is not like a first imperfect essay, but shows a confirmed habit, a systematic preference of violent effect to everything else. There are occasional detached images of great beauty and delicacy, but these were not beyond the powers of other writers then living. The circumstance which inclines us to reject the external evidence in favour of this play being Shakespeare's is, that the grammatical construction is constantly false and mixed up with vulgar abbreviations, a fault that never occurs in any of his genuine plays. A similar defect, and the halting measure of the verse are the chief objections to PERICLES OF TYRE, if we except the far-fetched and complicated absurdity of the story. The movement of the thoughts and passions has something in it not unlike Shakespeare, and several of the descriptions are either the original hints of passages which Shakespeare has engrafted on his other plays, or are imitations of them by some contemporary poet. The most memorable idea in it is in Marina's speech, where she compares the world to 'a lasting storm, hurrying her from her friends'.

POEMS AND SONNETS

Our idolatry of Shakespeare (not to say our admiration) ceases with his plays. In his other productions he was a mere author, though not a common author. It was only by representing others, that he became himself. He could go out of himself, and express the soul of Cleopatra; but in his own person, he appeared to be always waiting for the prompter's cue. In expressing the thoughts of others, he seemed inspired; in expressing his own, he was a mechanic. The licence of an assumed character was necessary to restore his genius to the privileges of nature, and to give him courage to break through the tyranny of fashion, the trammels of custom. In his plays, he was 'as broad and casing as the general air'; in his poems, on the contrary, he appears to be 'cooped, and cabined in' by all the technicalities of art, by all the petty intricacies of thought and language, which poetry had learned from the controversial jargon of the schools, where words had been made a substitute for things. There was, if we mistake not, something of modesty, and a painful sense of personal propriety at the bottom of this. Shakespeare's imagination, by identifying itself with the strongest characters in the most trying circumstances, grappled at once with nature, and trampled the littleness of art under his feet: the rapid changes of situation, the wide range of the universe, gave him life and spirit, and afforded full scope to his genius; but returned into his closet again, and having assumed the badge of his profession, he could only labour in his vocation, and conform himself to existing models. The thoughts, the passions, the words which the poet's pen, 'glancing from heaven to earth, from earth to heaven', lent to others, shook off the fetters of pedantry and affectation; while his own thoughts and feelings, standing by themselves, were seized upon as lawful prey, and tortured to death according to the established rules and practice of the day. In a word, we do not like Shakespeare's poems, because we like his plays: the one, in all their excellences, are just the reverse of the other. It has been the fashion of late to cry up our author's poems, as equal to his plays: this is the desperate cant of modern criticism. We would ask, was there the slightest comparison between Shakespeare, and either Chaucer or Spenser, as mere poets? Not any.- -The two poems of VENUS AND ADONIS and of TARQUIN AND LUCRECE appear to us like a couple of ice-houses. They are about as hard, as glittering, and as cold. The author seems all the time to be thinking of his verses, and not of his subject,—not of what his characters would feel, but of what he shall say; and as it must happen in all such cases, he always puts into their mouths those things which they would be the last to think of, and which it shows the greatest ingenuity in him to find out. The whole is laboured, up-hill work. The poet is perpetually singling out the difficulties of the art to make an exhibition of his strength and skill in wrestling with them. He is making perpetual trials of them as if his mastery over them were doubted. The images, which are often striking, are generally applied to things which they are the least like: so that they do not blend with the poem, but seem stuck upon it, like splendid patchwork, or remain quite distinct from it, like detached substances, painted and varnished over. A beautiful thought is sure to be lost in an endless commentary upon it. The speakers are like persons who have both leisure and inclination to make riddles on their own situation, and to twist and turn every object or incident into acrostics and anagrams. Everything is spun out into allegory; and a digression is always preferred to the main story. Sentiment is built up upon plays of words; the hero or heroine feels, not from the impulse of passion, but from the force of dialectics. There is besides, a strange attempt to substitute the language of painting for that of poetry, to make us SEE their feelings in the faces of the persons; and again, consistently with this, in the description of the picture in

TARQUIN AND LUCRECE, those circumstances are chiefly insisted on, which it would be impossible to convey except by words. The invocation to Opportunity in the TARQUIN AND LUCRECE is full of thoughts and images, but at the same time it is overloaded by them. The concluding stanza expresses all our objections to this kind of poetry:

> Oh! idle words, servants to shallow fools;
> Unprofitable sounds, weak arbitrators;
> Busy yourselves in skill-contending schools;
> Debate when leisure serves with dull debaters;
> To trembling clients be their mediators:
> For me I force not argument a straw,
> Since that my case is past all help of law.

The description of the horse in VENUS AND ADONIS has been particularly admired, and not without reason:

> Round-hoof'd, short-jointed, fetlocks shag and long,
> Broad breast, full eyes, small head, and nostril wide,
> High crest, short ears, straight legs, and passing strong,
> Thin mane, thick tail, broad buttock, tender hide:
>   Look, what a horse should have he did not lack,
>   Save a proud rider on so proud a back.

Now this inventory of perfections shows great knowledge of the horse; and is good matter-of-fact poetry. Let the reader but compare it with a speech in the MIDSUMMER NIGHT'S DREAM where Theseus describes his hounds—

> And their heads are hung
> With ears that sweep away the morning dew—

and he will perceive at once what we mean by the difference between Shakespeare's own poetry, and that of his plays. We prefer the PASSIONATE PILGRIM very much to the LOVER'S COMPLAINT. It has been doubted whether the latter poem is Shakespeare's.

Of the Sonnets we do not well know what to say. The subject of them seems to be somewhat equivocal; but many of them are highly beautiful in themselves, and interesting as they relate to the state of the personal feelings of the author. The following are some of the most striking:

CONSTANCY

> Let those who are in favour with their stars
>   Of public honour and proud titles boast,
>   Whilst I, whom fortune of such triumph bars,
>   Unlook'd for joy in that I honour most.
>   Great princes' favourites their fair leaves spread,
>   But as the marigold in the sun's eye;
>   And in themselves their pride lies buried,

For at a frown they in their glory die.
The painful warrior famous'd for fight,
After a thousand victories once foil'd,
Is from the book of honour razed quite,
And all the rest forgot for which he toil'd:
    Then happy I, that love and am belov'd,
    Where I may not remove, nor be removed.

LOVE'S CONSOLATION

When in disgrace with fortune and men's eyes,
    I all alone beweep my outcast state,
    And trouble deaf heaven with my bootless cries,
    And look upon myself, and curse my fate,
Wishing me like to one more rich in hope,
    Featur'd like him, like him with friends possess'd,
    Desiring this man's art, and that man's scope,
    With what I most enjoy contented least;
Yet in these thoughts myself almost despising,
    Haply I think on thee,—and then my state
    (Like to the lark at break of day arising
    From sullen earth) sings hymns at heaven's gate;
    For thy sweet love remember'd, such wealth brings
    That then I scorn to change my state with kings.

NOVELTY

My love is strengthen'd, though more weak in seeming;
    I love not less, though less the show appear:
    That love is merchandiz'd, whose rich esteeming
    The owner's tongue doth publish every where.
Our love was new, and then but in the spring,
    When I was wont to greet it with my lays;
    As Philomel in summer's front doth sing,
    And stops his pipe in growth of riper days:
Not that the summer is less pleasant now
    Than when her mournful hymns did hush the night,
    But that wild music burthens every bough,
    And sweets grown common lose their dear delight.
    Therefore, like her, I sometime hold my tongue,
    Because I would not dull you with my song.

LIFE'S DECAY

That time of year thou mayst in me behold
    When yellow leaves, or none, or few, do hang
    Upon those boughs which shake against the cold,

190

Bare ruin'd choirs, where late the sweet birds sang.
In me thou see'st the twilight of such day
As after sunset fadeth in the west;
Which by and by black night doth take away,
Death's second self, that seals up all in rest.
In me thou see'st the glowing of such fire,
That on the ashes of his youth doth lie,
As the death-bed whereon it must expire
Consum'd with that which it was nourish'd by.
 This thou perceiv'st, which makes thy love more strong,
 To love that well which thou must leave ere long.

In all these, as well as in many others, there is a mild tone of sentiment, deep, mellow, and sustained, very different from the crudeness of his earlier poems.

Made in the USA
Lexington, KY
14 March 2013

21476653R00105